D0712986

HARRY TRUMAN
AND THE
STRUGGLE FOR
RACIAL JUSTICE

BOOKS BY ROBERT SHOGAN

Prelude to Catastrophe: FDR's Jews and the Menace of Nazism

No Sense of Decency: The Army–McCarthy Hearings

Backlash: The Killing of the New Deal

The Battle of Blair Mountain: The Story of America's Largest Labor Uprising

War Without End: Cultural Conflict and the Struggle for America's Political Future

Bad News: Where the Press Goes Wrong in the Making of the President

The Double-Edged Sword: How Character Makes and Ruins Presidents from Washington to Clinton

Fate of the Union: America's Rocky Road to Political Stalemate

Hard Bargain: How FDR Twisted Churchill's Arm, Evaded the Law, and Changed the Role of the American Presidency

Riddle of Power: Presidential Leadership from Truman to Bush

None of the Above: Why Presidents Fail and What Can Be Done About It

Promises to Keep: Carter's First 100 Days

A Question of Judgment: The Fortas Case and the Struggle for the Supreme Court

The Detroit Race Riot: A Study in Violence (with Tom Craig)

HARRY TRUMAN
AND THE
STRUGGLE FOR
RACIAL JUSTICE

Robert Shogan

UNIVERSITY PRESS OF KANSAS

© 2013 by the University Press of Kansas
All rights reserved

Published by the University Press of Kansas (Lawrence, Kansas 66045),
which was organized by the Kansas Board of Regents and is
operated and funded by Emporia State University, Fort Hays State University,
Kansas State University, Pittsburg State University, the University of Kansas,
and Wichita State University

Library of Congress Cataloging-in-Publication Data

Shogan, Robert.
Harry Truman and the struggle for racial justice / Robert Shogan.
page cm
Includes bibliographical references and index.
ISBN 978-0-7006-1911-5 (alk. paper)
1. Truman, Harry S., 1884–1972. 2. African Americans—Civil rights—History—
20th century. 3. United States—Politics and government—1945–1953. 4. United States—
Race relations. I. Title.
E813.S54 2013
973.918092—dc23
2013014064

British Library Cataloguing-in-Publication Data is available.

Printed in the United States of America

10 9 8 7 6 5 4 3 2 1

The paper used in this publication is recycled and contains 30 percent
postconsumer waste. It is acid free and meets the minimum
requirements of the American National Standard for Permanence of
Paper for Printed Library Materials Z39.48–1992.

For Ellen Shrewsbury Shogan
In Loving Memory
And for our daughters
Cynthia and Amelia

CONTENTS

Illustrations follow page 98.

AUTHOR'S NOTE

When I first saw Harry Truman in the flesh, nearly a decade had passed since the end of his presidency, and more than that since he had waged his improbable 1948 campaign. But the man who strode into the news room of the *Miami News* seemed just as forceful as when he took the stage at that long-ago convention in Philadelphia and promised to win the election "and make those Republicans like it."

Now it was 1960, another presidential year, and Truman, once again campaigning against the GOP, had taken time to visit South Florida's only Democratic newspaper. He paused at the desk where I was working as telegraph editor, an already antiquated term that meant dealing with the wire service copy that covered national and world news. He glared at me in mock resentment: "So you're the fellow who blue pencils all my speeches," he growled.

I confessed my sins, invited him to sit down at my desk, gave him a wire service story—reporting a speech by Harry Truman—along with a blue pencil, and urged him to edit to his heart's content. He grinned, scribbled for a minute, and withdrew, leaving behind a tic-tac-toe box on the margin of the wire copy.

Later, when it was question time, he proved he had lost none of his old form. Someone asked him to size up Richard Nixon, then well on his way to the Republican presidential nomination. Truman demurred. "There is a lady present," he said.

"Can't you clean it up?" he was asked.

"No," Truman said. "Every time anything is said about him now it just means another headline for him. It gives him a chance to get out on the front page."

That brief encounter with Truman served as a start in helping me to better understand his performance as president and his place in history. In the years to come, I read more about Truman and often compared him with those who succeeded him in the White House, often to his advantage. I came to recognize those traits that had been underappreciated during most of his time in office by other politicians in both parties, and by many of his fellow citizens. His mind had a sharp partisan edge, grounded in populist ideology. His natural aggressiveness took on depth and breadth from his championship of the underdog. Most important of all, he was a man who had come to terms with himself; this gave him the strength and the courage to face obstacles and odds that others thought would overwhelm him.

Years later, in a conversation with Joseph Biden, then an aspirant for the presidency and later Barack Obama's vice president, Truman's name came up. The political leaders most likely to succeed, Biden said, "are those at peace with themselves. They're the leaders least likely to let their own insecurities impact on the well-being of the nation. It's the difference between a Harry Truman and a Richard Nixon." A judgment from a partisan, but not necessarily a partisan judgment. Consider the number of leading Republicans, from Gerald Ford to John McCain and even Sarah Palin, who have tried to rub off a bit of Truman's reputation for plain speaking and steadfastness on themselves.

A half century ago when I encountered Truman in Miami, most Americans probably thought of his mobilizing America for the cold war as the outstanding accomplishment of his tenure in the Oval Office. I myself as a political reporter was most intrigued by his 1948 election campaign. But as time passed and the civil rights revolution gained force, I came to believe that his jump-starting that movement represented his most significant achievement and that his self-assurance and self-knowledge helped make that possible.

To be sure, when the drive for racial justice gained steam, Truman's sense of propriety was offended by the tactics of the demonstrators. Characteristically, he made his irritation known. When a trusted friend reminded him that his criticism contravened the record he had compiled in the nation's highest office, Truman held his fire. Whether he acknowledged it or not, history makes clear that it was his own actions that had paved the way for the tumultuous drive for equality. That is the story this book tries to do justice to.

I owe an initial debt to Ivan Dee, my former publisher and still my friend, for suggesting that I do a book on Truman. It would have been impossible to write without the resources and support of the Johns Hopkins University library staff, particularly Sharon Morris, Zena Mason, and Feraz Ashraf of the Washington center library. Also invaluable was the assistance of Lorna Grenadier, a retired Justice Department official, who proved to be a tireless and resourceful researcher.

Chevy Chase, Maryland

HARRY TRUMAN
AND THE
STRUGGLE FOR
RACIAL JUSTICE

1

★ ★ ★ ★ ★

THE PRESIDENT'S DILEMMA

The last thing Harry Truman needed was another problem. It was December 1946 and Truman's first two years in the White House were drawing to an end—and, many believed, for all practical purposes, so was his presidency. Not since Herbert Hoover's futile stewardship in the depths of the Great Depression had any president stood as low in the regard of his fellow citizens as the nation's thirty-third chief executive.

The evidence of this dismal state of affairs was abundant, most significantly on Capitol Hill. There the Republican Party, only a minority presence since Hoover's downfall, had suddenly established overwhelming control. That takeover had been accomplished in the November 1946 congressional elections when voters, fed up with Truman's handling of the myriad economic disruptions that had followed World War II, had taken revenge on Truman's Democrats.

But now the president had to confront a challenge that in significance and complexity transcended anything else on the domestic horizon. This was race—the conflict between the growing demands of black Americans for economic and political equity and the fears and anxieties of the white majority. "An American Dilemma," the Swedish scholar Gunnar Myrdal had called the contradiction between the democratic creed and the suppression of black citizens. Now it was Truman's dilemma.

The conundrum was as old as the country. But the long-festering resentment of blacks had been dramatically escalated by the war. It was not hard to see why. The fundamental rationale for the war as a crusade

1

against racism and injustice abroad created a glaring contradiction with the inequities imposed on black Americans, particularly in the South, in nearly every aspect of their lives. More tangible were the broader horizons the war opened for blacks, as their mobility elevated their economic and political circumstances. For blacks, the war generated a new zeitgeist, dark with discontent, bright with hope, and red-hot with anger. "This war is crucial for the future of the Negro and the Negro problem is crucial in the war," Gunnar Myrdal wrote in 1944. "There is bound to be a redefinition of the Negro's status in America as a result of this war."

All this would have made it hard for any chief executive to win the trust of his black fellow citizens. For Missourian Truman, the task was made that much harder because of his birth into a family of slaveholders and Confederate sympathizers. The resentment aroused by this heritage was made apparent when the announcement of Truman's selection as vice president in 1944 led to charges of betrayal from blacks against the leaders of the party that had become their new political home.

If blacks were suspicious of Truman, he had also yet to win the confidence of many whites. In the nation's capital, fairly or not, many of his fellow Democrats blamed their debacle in the midterm elections on Truman's inept stewardship. Indeed, with the Republican-controlled Congress in a position to stifle any of Truman's initiatives, a senator in Truman's own party, Arkansas's J. William Fulbright, proposed that Truman resign after first appointing a Republican secretary of state. Then, according to current laws of succession, with the vice presidency vacant, the nation's designated chief diplomat would move up to become chief executive. That would avoid a partisan stalemate between the branches of government, Fulbright, a former law professor and Rhodes scholar, explained. Truman did not have to think very long before rejecting that idea, while privately referring to its author as "Senator Halfbright."

In his first public statement after the election, Truman adopted a more dignified tone. He pledged to be guided by "a simple formula: to do in all cases without regard to political considerations what seems to me to be for the welfare of all our people." But that high-minded stance did not alter the judgment many had made on him. The president's words, *Time* commented caustically, "were like a wistful echo: this was in effect what Harry Truman had said when he first undertook the office that had proved too much for him." The *New York Times'* Cabell Philips was even blunter, describing the prevailing attitude of Democrats toward Truman as "simple despair and futility." Though they liked the man, "most seem to think that he has done the best he could, but that his best simply was not good enough."

Such harsh judgments in part probably reflected the fact that no one in Washington had intended Harry Truman to be president of the United States in the first place—least of all Truman himself. Indeed, he had not much wanted even to be vice president. But extraordinary circumstances overshadowed his preferences. The major reason was that the incumbent president, Franklin D. Roosevelt, probably the most successful American politician of the modern era, was regarded by party leaders who had seen him at close hand as perilously near to meeting his maker. This gave Roosevelt's choice of a running mate as he sought a fourth term in 1944 far-reaching significance.

The easiest answer might have seemed to be to stick with the incumbent vice president, Henry A. Wallace of Iowa, who had made himself in his four years in office the hero of the party's liberals. But that ideological bent, along with Wallace's chilly personality, stirred irritation and anxiety among most party leaders, not to mention the reports of peculiar letters written years before to a White Russian mystic that almost forced him off the ticket in 1940.

The ultimate choice of Wallace's successor would be Roosevelt's. But the Skipper, as intimates referred to him, characteristically delayed his decision, meanwhile boosting the hopes of various aspirants for the office. When he finally made up his mind to pick a Missouri senator to whom he had always been a distant figure, Truman was among the last to know, and the most surprised. There was nothing for Truman to do but accept his fate. Just as he had loyally supported the president during his ten years in the Senate, Truman dutifully pitched in during the fall campaign, stumping around the country, while the ailing Roosevelt mostly stayed on the sidelines. That formula was enough to win a fourth term for FDR and to elevate his running mate into the vice presidency. Five months later, FDR was dead and Truman was president.

Not surprisingly, Truman was overwhelmed at first, so much so that he asked White House reporters to pray for him. But Harry Truman, at age sixty-two, had been in politics for nearly all his adult life. He had been a poll watcher and precinct captain on the winning side and also for losing causes. He had been town postmaster and had quit in disgust because the pay was not worth the trouble. Serving as county road supervisor, he found that the position arguably carried more prestige than dogcatcher—but not by much. The voters made him a county district judge, then threw him out after one term. Back he came two years later to the same bench, but this time as presiding judge.

Eight years later, the voters of his state had sent him to Washington as a U.S. senator. Yet after six years of diligent service, he was held in such low regard that leaders in his own party, including FDR himself, assumed his forthcoming political demise without much lament. Truman stunned them all by winning a second term, during which he so distinguished himself that the same party leaders who had written him off now wrote his name onto the national ticket as FDR's understudy. These years had seen crises and challenges beyond counting. Truman had always met the moment, one way or another, although not always gracefully or successfully. But whatever the problem was, he had put it behind him and moved on.

Succeeding to the presidency in the middle of a global conflict of course presented him with a task that surpassed anything he had previously faced. At first, as he oversaw the final days of victory over Adolf Hitler's Third Reich and ordered the dropping of the atomic bombs that crushed the Japanese empire, his modesty and matter-of-fact manner struck just the right note. Americans, trying to recover from the passing of the captain who had seemed in his person to embody the office of chief executive, seemed willing to give the benefit of the doubt to a new leader who appeared vigorous, decisive, and, after the first frisson of self-doubt, sure of purpose. He was, many people concluded, a decidedly ordinary man, but some found a virtue in that. "His regard for the common run of people, including himself, is probably greater than that of many who speak in their name," observed the *Nation*. His approval rating soared close to 90 percent in the polls.

But anxiety over postwar problems soon ended that political honeymoon. The abundance of jobs during the war had not erased the bitter memories of the Depression. For many Americans, the joy over peace and victory was mixed with fear of a return to the grim days when it appeared the economic bottom had fallen out. There seemed to be sound reason for this anxiety. At war's end in 1945, the civilian labor force had reached a record level of more than 53 million. Some 12 million more Americans were still under arms, with the vast majority of them anticipating a swift return to civilian life. No wonder government planners foresaw eight million unemployed, while labor experts predicted the figure would be even higher—up to 18 million. But the fears of depression, like the early reports of Mark Twain's death, turned out to be greatly exaggerated. In Truman's entire first term, unemployment never exceeded 4 percent, the level that economists came to consider full employment.

Thanks to the GI bill, the last great beneficence of the New Deal, tens of thousands of ex-GIs headed for college campuses instead of factory gates. Just as important, pent-up wartime demand kept cash registers jingling and assembly lines rolling, when manufacturers could find the materials for production.

And therein lay the rub, or part of it. The scarcity of goods fed what turned out to be the true economic demon of the early postwar era—not depression but inflation. The shortages of materials and products was made even more frustrating by the hard cash that Americans had accumulated during the war when new autos, appliances, and other consumer goods were nonexistent. That naturally drove up prices. Added pressure came from wages, which had been tightly suppressed during the war while, as union members knew only too well, management salaries had soared. All across the board, big unions demanded what amounted to on average a 30 percent raise. Management, still in most cases having to contend with government ceilings on prices, resisted. The inevitable result, which Truman tried desperately to forestall, was a wave of strikes that disrupted the return to market of the goods consumers wanted, soured the public mood, and made Truman seem over his head in the Oval Office.

In fact, as Truman's months in the Oval Office piled up, so did the criticism. "To err is Truman," a stinger attributed to Republican senator Robert Taft's wife, Martha, was repeated time and again among the political set in Washington, and elsewhere too. As the initial glow that had bathed his presidency faded, it became clear that in addition to the economic and foreign policy difficulties Truman faced, there was a problem he could do little about. Many Americans could not forgive him for not being FDR.

The contrast started with physical appearance. Roosevelt's leonine head and chiseled features, together with his patrician manner, epitomized elegance and grace. Truman's square-cut Midwestern face, thick-lensed glasses, and nondescript bearing brought to mind a shopkeeper, which it was remembered he had been, and a failed one at that. For Truman, oratory was probably the most devastating point of comparison. FDR's mellifluous tones and meticulous timing had helped rouse a nation to overcome the Depression and defeat the Axis powers. Truman's thin, rasping monotone tended to set his auditors to drowsing off.

Meanwhile, in his efforts to ease mounting discontent on all sides, Truman found himself yielding to pressure. In October 1945, he eased controls on wages, going on the radio to support substantially higher wages through collective bargaining but warning against inflation. Unions must be reasonable in their demands, Truman urged.

Good luck on that. Pushing for fatter paychecks, unions struck the auto and steel industries. Both walkouts were ultimately settled, but only after hikes in wages and prices that damaged Truman's efforts to stabilize the economy, not to mention his prestige.

Difficulties extended beyond industry to farming. Fearful of a postwar agriculture surplus that would devastate farmers much as they had suffered in 1929, FDR's advisers had adjusted production controls to limit output. They succeeded too well. By the spring of 1945, meat, sugar, and other commodities had vanished from grocery stores. Black markets in these goods flourished, adding to the nation's dissatisfaction with its president. No wonder, as Truman addressed Washington journalists and their prominent guests at the annual Gridiron Dinner, he declared, "Sherman was wrong. I'm telling you I find peace is hell."

His most urgent problem was the mustering out of the vast military forces the nation had called to the colors. As the clamor "to bring the boys home" grew louder, Truman announced that more than two million soldiers would be back with their families by Christmas. But there was a potential downside to these homecomings. Truman himself told a press conference that the process really amounted to "disintegration" of the nation's military. Truman's concern went beyond the boost in unemployment that the influx of veterans into the job market might produce. His worries had far more to do with the palpable rise in tensions in relations with the country's wartime ally, the Soviet Union. In response to this danger, Truman proposed a program for universal military training that would require all men from eighteen to twenty to take a year of military training. But Congress was more preoccupied with getting World War II soldiers back to civilian life, and Truman's plan died in the hearing rooms of Capitol Hill.

The new year of 1946 brought no relief of the headaches for the president and his fellow Americans. Overseas, increased Soviet intransigence in dealing with the contours of postwar Europe heightened edginess about the danger of communist subversion within the United States. At home, the seemingly unending labor trouble boiled over with a nationwide railway strike. Truman seized the railroads, and in a melodramatic speech to a joint session of Congress, he asked for power to draft the workers. The strike collapsed and no one was drafted. But Congress was still so indignant at unions that it passed the toughest antilabor bill enacted since the Democrats came to power in 1932—so tough that Truman vetoed it. Congress passed it over his veto. Liberals declared that with his overwrought appearance on Capitol Hill, Truman had killed his chances of being elected in 1948, and David Dubinsky, the powerful president of the Garment Workers Union, called for a labor-based third party.

As the 1946 elections approached, it seemed as if Truman's circumstances could hardly have been worse. Ever since he had been sworn in as president and had begun to think about his own reelection prospects, Truman had realized that the key to his chances was to hold together the great coalition that FDR had molded during his course of the presidency. It was an unlikely combination: Southern whites, small farmers, urban minorities, and the burgeoning labor movement whose growth Roosevelt had helped foster. The needs of the Depression and the unifying patriotic spirit during the war and his own dexterity had enabled Roosevelt to maintain support from these disparate groups. But war's end and the economic disarray stemming from conversion to peace created new pressures that generated conflict rather than harmony. Now that the Depression had been banished, the South's natural conservatism reasserted itself. Dixie's leaders turned against the New Deal economic reforms and the enlarged role for government that came with those policies.

Elsewhere in the country, Truman's response to the epidemic of strikes made liberals question his adherence to the pro-labor principles that had been a cornerstone of FDR's programs and his electoral success. Even more important to many liberals was what they regarded as Truman's overly harsh response to the Soviet Union. In February 1947, he proclaimed what came to be called the Truman Doctrine, pledging U.S. support for Greece and Turkey and other nations threatened by communism. The hard edge of that stance was broadened somewhat a few months later, when Secretary of State George C. Marshall proposed a cooperative international effort to help European economies recover from the ravages of World War II. Still, liberals worried that U.S. commitment to help abroad could turn the cold war that had broken out between the United States and the Soviet Union hot.

As their discontent intensified, liberals increasingly turned to Henry Agard Wallace, FDR's former vice president, as their chief spokesman. Though privately resentful when FDR jettisoned him in 1944, Wallace publicly took that setback with good grace, and Roosevelt named him secretary of commerce at the start of his fourth term. The appointment placated Wallace's disappointed supporters and provided a forum that he could use to promote his beliefs, particularly on relations with the Soviet Union.

Given Wallace's stature on the left and the divergence of his views from Truman's foreign policy, an explosion was bound to happen. It finally took place during the preliminaries to the 1946 congressional elections, when Truman unaccountably approved an advance copy of a Wallace campaign speech that directly clashed with the tough line just laid down by Secretary of State James Byrnes. With world capitals in an uproar, Truman demanded Wallace's resignation in a letter so intemperate that when Wallace complied, he offered to return the letter, a courtesy Truman accepted. "He was so nice about it I almost backed out," Truman wrote home, describing Wallace as "the most peculiar fellow I'd ever met," a sentiment that may well have been mutual.

Many anticipated that Wallace's departure would lead to his running for president on an independent ticket. Meanwhile, his ouster not only strained Truman's relations with Democratic liberals over foreign policy, but also rubbed salt into another, even more sensitive political sore spot. This was the uneasy relationship of border-state–bred Harry Truman with millions of increasingly frustrated black Americans. Just as comparisons with FDR inevitably hurt Truman, so did the contrast with Wallace, particularly among blacks. In May 1946, a few months before Wallace's ouster from the cabinet, a poll by the *Negro Digest* showed that 91 percent of black voters favored Wallace for the Democratic presidential nomination in 1948. But Wallace aside, Truman—or, for that matter, any American president—was headed for trouble on race. The cynicism of black Americans had inevitably mounted over the years as a result of a system infused with hypocrisy and designed to shut them out.

Duplicity began with the birth of the nation and the drafting of the Constitution. Nearly half the convention delegates were slave owners, so it was no wonder that they demanded and won a provision granting them what they wanted, the so-called three-fifths compromise. Even though Southern states denied slaves any rights, they were allowed to count them toward their representation in Congress on the basis of each slave equaling three-fifths of a free white citizen. The slaves were not even mentioned as such but were instead referred to in the language of the nation's founding charter only as "other persons."

Things did not improve for a long while. Lincoln and emancipation seemed to toll the bell of liberty. But that sound was soon muffled as Northerners made a fateful bargain with the South in the 1877 Wormley Hotel agreement. In return for the Southern electoral votes that allowed Republican nominee Rutherford B. Hayes to edge out Democratic standard-bearer Samuel Tilden and gain the White House, Republicans agreed to withdraw federal troops from the Old Confederacy. With that, the early promise of post–Civil War Reconstruction collapsed, and Jim Crow took over. This left a nation in which blacks could at most lay claim to second-class citizenship, and in parts of the South, not even that.

The ignominious status of black Americans in post–Civil War America was illustrated when Theodore Roosevelt broke precedent by inviting Booker T. Washington, a sometime adviser, for dinner. Even given Washington's well-known dedication to accommodation with whites, that gesture was too much for many Americans. The cries of outrage assured that Roosevelt never asked Washington back. And Roosevelt's Republican successors in the Oval Office abjured even such token displays.

As for the first Democrat to follow Theodore Roosevelt into the White House, Virginia-born and Georgia-bred Woodrow Wilson was not content to merely ignore blacks. Instead, he gave them the back of his hand, providing blacks even more reason to resent his party than they already did. Running for president in 1912, Wilson's glowing rhetoric about the New Freedom won the trust of some blacks, including the eminent scholar William E. Burghardt Du Bois, and gained him more Negro votes than any previous Democratic candidate. But if some blacks hoped that Wilson might lift the yoke of Jim Crow, they were sorely disappointed. Instead, the new president adhered to the values of his native Dixie. He allowed his Southern cabinet chiefs to segregate their departments. They rid the civil service of hundreds of blacks appointed by Republican presidents and set up a Jim Crow system that offended the dignity of government employees in Washington and elsewhere.

"Public segregation of civil servants, necessarily involving personal insult and humiliation, has for the first time in history been made the policy of the United States government," complained Du Bois, whose outrage was all the deeper because he himself had been deluded into voting for Wilson. In 1914, a delegation of black leaders headed by William Monroe Trotter, editor of the *Boston Guardian*, met with Wilson at the White House to protest the change in policies. When Trotter asserted that continuing the new policy would lead blacks to vote against the president, Wilson, as he privately admitted later, lost his temper and ordered him out. The episode raised a hullabaloo in the black press, and some white ministers publicly offered their support for Trotter. But nothing changed. Wilson explained that the racial separation was for the benefit of blacks, to save them from conflict with whites.

Fed up with Wilson and his Democrats, blacks found new reason for hope in Republican Warren Harding, who, in accepting the nomination of his party, stated his belief that "Negro citizens of America should be guaranteed the full enjoyment of all their rights." Vague as this rhetoric was, it was enough after Harding's election for some black leaders to press their case at the White House for better treatment on a variety of issues. But even before Harding's fatal illness ended his presidency, it was clear to blacks that he had little to offer them besides hazy promises. Once again, Du Bois inveighed against the nation's political leadership. "May God write us down as asses," he declared in the spring of 1922, "if ever again we are found putting our trust in either the Republican or the Democratic Parties."

No wonder, then, that blacks viewed Franklin D. Roosevelt, the first Democrat in the White House since Wilson, with skepticism from the start. And indeed for most of his presidency, FDR gave only grudging support to civil rights. That was a cause he mainly left to the first lady, Eleanor Roosevelt, whose heart was on the side of blacks, but who could back her sentiments up with nothing but the moral authority of her position.

Nevertheless, in 1936, for the first time in history, a majority of black American voters supported a Democrat, Franklin Roosevelt. They did so not because of any action on his part to promote racial justice, but rather because of the economic reforms of the New Deal. These measures brought at least a glimmer of hope to blacks, who were devastated even more than most other Americans by the Depression. Still, black leaders were impatient with the pace of economic relief. Matters came to a head in Roosevelt's third term as the United States geared up for World War II and the economy began to revive, but blacks were still left out in the cold. A. Philip Randolph, president of the Brotherhood of Sleeping Car Porters and the most influential civil rights leader of his day, was moved to action. In 1941, he announced plans for a protest march on Washington by 50,000 people. Eager to avoid what would have been a national embarrassment, Roosevelt for once defied the will of the Southern barons who still dominated his party on Capitol Hill. He got Randolph to call off his march by establishing the Fair Employment Practices Committee to eliminate racial discrimination in war plants. However, in the next few years, Congress whittled away at the committee until little was left of it by the time Truman moved into the presidency. The estrangement of black Americans remained for Truman to face.

For much of their postslavery history, blacks had depended on sympathetic whites to make their case. They still counted heavily on such allies, but they increasingly began to speak for themselves. They relied most often on organizations whose growth the dynamics of wartime America had fostered, principally the National Association for Colored People but also the Urban League. "Negro militancy and implacable determination to wipe out segregation grew more proportionately during the years 1940 to 1945 than during any other periods of the Negro's history in America," asserted Walter White, head of the NAACP.

In this yeasty environment, black leaders increasingly found purpose and direction in the arguments made contemporaneously by Du Bois, one of the founders of the NAACP, and in the previous century by Frederick Douglass, the first great black intellectual leader, rather than in the limited strategy advocated by Booker T. Washington. The latter, as Du Bois pointed out in a seminal treatise on the outlook for black Americans, wanted blacks to set aside, at least for the present, political power, civil rights, and higher education for their young people. Instead, Washington urged them to concentrate on industrial education, boosting their incomes and conciliating the South. For his part, Du Bois believed exactly the opposite—that blacks needed to demand the vote, civic equality, and the education of their youth according to ability.

Washington's message to blacks was to urge the building of a separate community, setting aside social integration. At the Atlanta Exposition of 1895, he famously told a white audience, "In all things that are purely social we can be as separate as the fingers, yet one as the hand in all things essential to mutual progress." Washington did not intend for this segregation to be permanent. He assumed that once the education of blacks led to their improvement they could mingle easily with the other fingers on the hand.

But in the wake of World War II, and after three-quarters of a century had passed since the abolition of slavery, blacks were fed up with waiting. Indeed Du Bois, in his frustration, left the NAACP in the 1930s and sought to promote African American nationalism as opposed to integration, then returned to the NAACP leadership during the war. Meanwhile, Du Bois and other impatient black leaders harked back to the arguing point Frederick Douglass had set forth years before. "Find out what any people will quietly submit to," Douglass had said. "And you have found the exact measure of injustice and wrong which will be imposed upon them."

While among some Americans the increasing black militancy had met with support or at least sympathetic understanding, such was not the case among most Southerners, who responded with intransigence. Even before the end of the war, Virginus Dabney, editor of the *Richmond Times Dispatch* and considered a relative moderate on race among white Southerners, sounded the alarm in the liberal *Atlantic Monthly*. "A small group of Negro agitators and another small group of white rabble rousers are pushing this country closer and closer to an interracial explosion which may make the race riots of the First World War and its aftermath seem mild by comparison," he warned. It was revealing of Dabney's thinking that among the Negro leaders he singled out as extremist were such mainstream figures as A. Philip Randolph and Roy Wilkins, a leader of the NAACP.

Dabney, who himself seemed to typify the Southern attitudes he cautioned about, proved prescient. Starting in the early months of the postwar era, unyielding Southern whites, spearheaded by the Ku Klux Klan, met black militancy with violence—though what was perceived as militancy often turned out to be nothing more than riding a public bus or trying to vote. Making the violence particularly abhorrent not only to blacks but to many whites outside the South was a number of attacks directed against black war veterans. A particularly horrific example took place in Batesburgh, South Carolina, on February 13, 1946, when Isaac Woodward, newly discharged and still in his Army uniform, was hauled off a bus after a verbal tiff with the driver, and assaulted and blinded by the local chief of police.

Black leaders and their white allies were up in arms. To demonstrate concern, in August 1946, Truman's attorney general, Texan Tom Clark, announced he would seek enactment of a long-demanded federal antilynching law in the next Congress. But no one knew what, if anything, would come of that. Besides, blacks and their allies wanted action from the president himself.

"Speak! Speak! Mr. President" and "Where is Democracy?" These were the slogans on the banners carried by fifty women from the NAACP as they picketed the White House. In response, on September 19, 1948, Truman agreed to meet with the National Emergency Committee against Mob Violence, a group of civil rights advocates including union leaders and clergy, led by Walter White. The fifty-two-year-old head of the NAACP was the obvious choice to head such a delegation. No black leader, with the possible exception of Randolph, matched his stature among both blacks and whites; further, Randolph was more militant, while White's strength, and his appeal to Truman in this circumstance, was as a conciliator. In White's case, even more than for most people, chromosomes shaped his destiny. Only five-thirty-seconds of his ancestry was black. "I am a Negro," he wrote in his autobiography. "My skin is white, my eyes are blue, my hair is blond. The traits of my race are nowhere visible upon me." The son of college-educated parents, he attended Atlanta University and soon joined the NAACP. His ability to pass as white helped him in investigating lynchings and race riots in the South, though he was careful to identify himself as black in dealing with the black community. In 1931, White succeeded James Weldon Johnson as the head of the NAACP and during the next decade became probably the principal advocate for the struggle against America's racist rules and traditions. In his new role, White's appearance continued to help him because many whites seemed more comfortable with a black who looked like them. However, he had to walk a tightrope, making sure that whatever advantages he gained from his skin color did not result in the loss of trust of the people he tried to lead.

Having been to the White House on similar errands to meet with every president since Coolidge, White was skeptical that this meeting would be any more productive than those in the past. Nevertheless, he dutifully laid out the narrative of racial violence that had terrorized blacks all over the South that year. Truman surely must have been informed of some of these incidents, but the cumulative impact of the awful chronicle recited by White seemed to shock him and stir his emotions. "My God. I had no idea it was as terrible as that," he told the group. "We've got to do something!" That spontaneous utterance, with its implied promise of action, hung over the meeting after it had adjourned. "We've got to do something," the president had said. Everyone present, and many others not in that room, agreed. But what?

Liberals in his party urged Truman to act against discrimination and racism deeply embedded in the South, but also evident nearly everywhere else in the country. Their case was moral and also political. Democrats needed black votes in the big cities to hold on to the White House in 1948. Six weeks after Truman had declared the need to do something, his party's landslide defeat in the congressional elections raised the political stakes and risks for whatever he did. Truman knew that whatever gains he made with black Americans would carry a price among whites, particularly in the South. Yet he also knew that political calculus would not provide a definitive answer for a troubled president.

More than politics, whatever decision he reached would reflect his view of his office and his country—and of the long and troubled relationships of black and white Americans. And that understanding had been shaped by where he had come from and how he had gotten to where he was.

2

★ ★ ★ ★ ★

FACING THE CENTURY

From 1861 to 1865, the American Civil War claimed the lives of more than 700,000 Union and Confederate soldiers. Even today, it ranks as the deadliest conflict in the nation's history. Yet along the Kansas–Missouri border, where Harry Truman was born and came of age, the killing and the maiming started earlier. In this region, thanks to the Kansas–Nebraska bill of 1854, pro-slavery and free soil forces had been at each other's throats more than six years before the first cannonballs rained down on Fort Sumter.

The Kansas–Nebraska bill climaxed the series of compromises starting with the three-fifths rule for voting representation in the Constitution, which reflected the Republic's unwillingness to deal directly with race—the fundamental question that would haunt its existence for nearly a century. But the three-fifths rule turned out to be only a temporary solution, as became clear when the United States acquired from Napoleon the Louisiana Territory stretching from the Mississippi to the Rockies, out of which thirteen states were eventually carved. In 1820, under the Missouri Compromise, one of these states, Missouri , was admitted to the Union as a slave state and Maine as a free state, maintaining the delicate balance among the twenty-four states, with twelve slave states and twelve free.

That line was obliterated by the Kansas–Nebraska Act, which established popular sovereignty, or local choice, as the determining factor for Kansas and Nebraska. This ill-conceived measure led to the event the nation's leaders had desperately tried to avoid: civil war. Supporters of slavery, many from neighboring Missouri, and their opponents poured into Bloody Kansas, determined to control the state for their side, a struggle marked by unremitting violence. John Brown, the most fanatical of the abolitionists, struck at the slavery partisans, and they struck back. A vengeful raid at Brown's camp at Osawatomie, Kansas, killed five of Brown's men, including one of his sons. Kansas ultimately was admitted as a free state.

As for Missouri, with its admission to the Union as a slave state in 1821, slave owners from Kentucky, Tennessee, and elsewhere in the South arrived in strength. Many were big planters; others were small farmers who raised corn, hogs, and cattle. But over the next decades, they were outnumbered by migrants from the East and by German and Irish immigrants. These newcomers opposed slavery, which in most parts of the state the nature of the land made an unprofitable proposition anyway. The proportion of slaves in Missouri's population shrank from nearly 20 percent in 1830 to less than 10 percent in 1860.

Meanwhile Missouri was the ignition point for an historic legal battle that roiled tensions over slavery everywhere and hardened the lines between abolitionists and defenders of slavery, the Dred Scott case. In 1847, Scott, a Missouri slave, sued to gain his freedom on the grounds that the fact that his previous residence was a free state ended his bondage under Missouri law. But after convoluted litigation, the U.S. Supreme Court ruled against him in a decision that would ultimately bring down the utmost obloquy upon the court and hasten the onset of the Civil War.

Just weeks before the South formally seceded, Missouri voters elected a statewide convention that rejected the Confederate cause by a vote of 89 to 1. The vote meant little to the state's secessionists, who battled Union forces for political and military control. Even after the Union Army drove the rebel forces out, the bloodshed continued, with guerrilla fighters taking up the cause of the South.

One of the most horrific episodes was the 1863 onslaught of Quantrill's raiders on Lawrence, Kansas, a stronghold of pro-union redlegs. Leading the raid was William Quantrill, who, though officially a captain in the Confederate Army, took orders from no one as he went his violent way. Quantrill burned a good part of the town and killed more than 150 men and boys. The murders stunned people across the country—and indeed in much of the world—and forced the Richmond government to officially repudiate Quantrill and cut off aid.

But his raiders continued to rampage through the region, and the Truman family and many of their neighbors regarded them as heroes. Their hearts belonged to Dixie and its way of life, founded on the institution of slavery. All four of Truman's grandparents, Anderson and Nancy

Truman and Sol and Harriet Louisa Young, parents of Truman's mother, Martha, were natives of Kentucky and slave owners; the Trumans received slaves as a wedding gift. And both couples brought their slaves with them when they moved to Missouri in the 1840s. Sol Young owned some two dozen slaves on his 5,000-acre spread in Missouri.

A man of more modest means, Anderson Truman and his wife, Mary Jane, owned only 200 acres and five slaves. "They were slave holders, not great slave holders," as their granddaughter, Ethel Noland, pointed out. "They never bought one, never sold one." In fact, Grandfather Anderson had no slaves at all when he was courting Mary Jane Holmes, a circumstance that cast a cloud over their romance. To Nancy Tyler Holmes, Mary Jane's mother, who lived in the Jackson County, Missouri, town of Westport, not owning slaves bore a social stigma. For that reason, the couple did not ask her consent before getting married in Anderson Truman's home in Shelby County in Kentucky in 1846. They had first met in Shelby County before the Holmes family had moved to Missouri. It was left to Andy, as he was known, to go to Westport to seek his new mother-in-law's forgiveness. This was promptly granted, along with a gift of five slaves to the newlyweds, who set up housekeeping on a farm just outside Westport. When war came, Anderson Truman, "a quiet, gentle man," moved his family across the Missouri to Platte County, out of harm's way, and signed a loyalty oath to the Union. Even so, the threat of pillaging was always there. Warned of a redleg assault, the Trumans once spent a cold autumn night cowering in a cornfield to avoid the attack, which fortunately never came.

For the young couple, the slaves turned out to be a mixed blessing— or so Ethel Noland was given to understand. "It was quite a heavy burden for my grandfather to support his family of a wife and five children and five grown slave women," she said. As for his wife, although the slaves did most of the housework, looking after their food, clothing, and other needs demanded much of her time. Adding to the responsibility were the children born to the slave women from marriages with slaves owned by neighbors. Family members thought Mary Jane was actually relieved when the war ended and Anderson Truman hauled the five women, their children, and a wagonload of food to their new home in Leavenworth, Kansas, their chosen destination. Soon after, he moved his own family back to Jackson County and resumed what had been an uneventful life.

Sol Young, like Anderson Truman, signed a loyalty oath, but that did not save his land from an assault by barn-burning, hog-killing redlegs, who stole the family silver for good measure. That memory stayed with Truman's mother, Martha, so that many years later, when her son returned from a business trip to Kansas City, she asked if he had seen any of the family silver. Martha's hatred was further inflamed when she and the rest of her family were forced to spend months in a federal stockade under a Union Army crackdown on Confederate sympathizers.

For the matriarch of the Young clan, Harriet Louisa Young, the war seemed never to have ended. Half a century after Appomattox, when her grandson, Harry, joined the National Guard and made the mistake of appearing before her in his dress blues, she told him, "Harry, this is the first time since 1863 that a blue uniform has been in this house. Don't bring it here again." He didn't. Truman's mother, Martha, was just as bitter. When she visited her son in the White House and he teasingly offered to put her up in the Lincoln bedroom, she replied, according to her son, "I'll sleep on the floor first."

One of Truman's uncles by marriage, an unsavory character named James J. Chiles, nicknamed Jim Crow after a popular dance of the day, rode with Quantrill's raiders. Another uncle, Will Young, was a regular in the Confederate Army. Yet as became apparent, Truman's roots in Independence provided him far more than the bitter memories of the Civil War, which had been over for nearly two full decades when he was born in 1884.

Those twenty years had been relatively peaceful except for the political turmoil as Republicans and Democrats struggled for power. Republicans had held the upper hand in the aftermath of the Civil War. Then Democrats took over for a while, bolstered by resentment of the so-called Radical Republicans. In the following years, dissension over such issues as regulation of big business, particularly the railroads, and state and county financial policies prevented Missouri's Democrats from establishing the sort of hegemony for their party that prevailed in the Deep South. Then too, a relatively modest percentage of blacks in the population helped keep race from becoming as dominant and divisive an issue as it was in the heart of Dixie.

Meanwhile, during these years, young Harry gained a strong sense of national pride as he came to recognize that his state of Missouri, whatever its links to the Old South, was far more significant for his country's future as the connecting point for the Santa Fe and Oregon trails. Starting with the California Gold Rush, his Missouri became celebrated as the gateway to the West for thousands of mid-nineteenth-century pioneers. Just as his family often reminisced about their Confederate heritage, they also passed on frontier lore drawn from the adventures of his ancestors. His great-grandfather, whose own father was a comrade of Daniel Boone, was reputed to have been the first white child born in Kentucky. His wife still bore the scar left by an Indian scalp wound. But the legend of his grandfather, Solomon Young, topped them all. As a Conestoga wagon master, he drove huge herds of cattle across the plains to Sacramento, leaving in the spring and not returning until the following year. Not shy about exploiting this background, particularly as he waged his underdog campaign for the presidency in 1948, Truman cited so many places that Grandfather Solomon had stopped on his journey that reporters wondered how he had ever made it to California.

Important as his family's history was, other factors would be at least as significant in shaping Truman's future and his outlook on the world, particularly his tendency to identify with the underdog. He had "flat eyeballs," a rare condition called hypermetropia, and was probably close to being legally blind without wearing glasses—"blind as a mole," in his own words. This condition was not discovered until he was five years old, when, on the Fourth of July, Martha Truman noticed that her son seemed to react more to the blast of the fireworks than to the display. She rushed him to a Kansas City optometrist, who prescribed a pair of extra-strength eyeglasses.

The wire-rimmed spectacles opened the outside world to young Harry, allowing him to see things he had never been able to see before. But the glasses—a great curiosity at that time and place—also affected the way the outside world, particularly his peers, looked at him. "Of course they called me four eyes," Truman later told Merle Miller. "That's hard on a boy. It makes him lonely and gives him an inferiority complex." And he referred to his handicap as a "deformity."

A more enduring problem was that Truman, following the orders of his eye doctor and his mother, ran away from quarrels with other boys and avoided most of the roughhouse games of childhood. "I was never popular," Truman acknowledged years later. "The popular boys were the ones who were good at games and had big tight fists," he remembered. "I was never like that. To tell the truth I was kind of a sissy."

He did what sissies often do. He read voraciously. By his own account, he consumed every volume in the library in his hometown, Independence. For his tenth birthday, his mother bought him four large illustrated volumes called *Great Men and Famous Women,* dealing with eminent politicians, cultural figures, and military leaders. It was to be worthy of his mother, he said later, that he studied great men, intending to emulate them someday.

But he had more purpose than that. "I wanted to know what caused the successes or failures of all the famous leaders of history," he wrote in his memoirs. "A leader is a man who has the ability to get other people to do what they won't want to do, and like it," he concluded. "There's always a lot of talk about how we have to fear the man on horseback," he would say later. "But it isn't the strong men who have caused us most of the trouble; it's the ones who were weak." He had in mind the string of ineffectual presidents, from William Henry Harrison to James Buchanan, who served in the years leading up to the Civil War. They seemed to believe that "if they just didn't rock the boat," America's differences over slavery would disappear. "That won't happen in a million years," Truman insisted.

The satisfaction Truman gained from reading and the devotion of his mother were all the more important because his path to maturity was otherwise a bumpy road. One problem was his relationship to his father, John Truman, the son of Anderson Truman, who made his living as a livestock trader. A notably short man, about five feet four inches tall, John Truman was known for his occasional angry outbursts. Once, during a lawsuit, when an opposing lawyer accused him of lying in his testimony, he jumped from the witness stand and chased the offending attorney into the street, even though his intended adversary stood over six feet. Eager to win his father's respect, young Truman tried to give him his wages from his first job as a teenage drugstore clerk. But John Truman told his son to keep his money for himself.

Just as Martha Truman favored her firstborn son, her husband leaned toward Harry's younger brother, John Vivian. He was no student, nor did he have any interest in music, unlike his older brother, who did very well at his piano lessons and dreamed of a career as a concert pianist. Vivian, by contrast, loved the outdoors and the hurly-burly of life, inclinations that matched the personality and preferences of his father.

Truman did share at least one interest with his father, and that was politics, though the boy seemed more caught up than his parent with the populism that was contagious among hard-pressed Midwestern farmers of the period. Still, it was John Truman who took his son to the 1900 Democratic Convention in Kansas City when Harry had just turned sixteen. There he came face to face with the politics of the brand-new twentieth century in the person of William Jennings Bryan. Despite his defeat in 1896, Bryan as the Democratic standard-bearer would be nominated to run a second time against incumbent Republican president William McKinley. At the 1900 convention, Harry's father sat in a box seat as the guest of one of the city's most prominent citizens, a leading banker, William T. Kemper. Harry, thanks to Kemper, a member of the Democratic National Committee, had a job as page. "As a page I was a dud," as Truman remembered many years later. But the impact of the convention on the young man was enduring. It helped shape Truman's political philosophy. Bryan had given populism its voice, and he would become Harry Truman's first political hero.

Since Bryan had no opposition for the nomination, the gathering turned into a coronation. As the convention opened, a flag-draped statue of Bryan was hauled to the platform. When Bryan himself finally appeared in the flesh, Truman was at first disappointed. "From where I was watching he didn't look more than a foot high," he recalled. But then Bryan began to speak. He had no microphone, but his sonorous voice boomed through the huge new hall. "I could hear every word he said," Truman remembered. "I will never forget it." That seemed to be literally true. "I used to drive a hundred miles to hear that old man speak; I didn't care what the subject was," he said later.

Though the 1900 convention was Truman's first, his memory of presidential elections went back even further to 1892, when he was a boy of eight and the Democrats nominated Grover Cleveland of New York. In that partisan family, Truman wore a cap that said, "Cleveland and Stevenson," the latter name referring to Adlai Stevenson, whose grandson would become the Democratic standard-bearer in 1952 and 1956. Cleveland defeated Republican Benjamin Harrison, and his election brought great joy to the Truman household. John Truman climbed up onto the roof of their house and decorated the highest point with red, white, and blue bunting, then rode on horseback in a victory parade.

The joy over Cleveland's triumph did not last long. Following the Wall Street panic of 1893, hard times beset the nation—and Cleveland's presidency. Cleveland's response reflected his conservative thinking on economics. More worried about inflation than unemployment, he fought to maintain the gold standard against demands for free coinage of silver, angering the farmers and populists of the West. Led by Jacob Coxey, Western workers staged a mass protest march on Washington, posing no serious threat to the government but dramatizing discontent with Cleveland's leadership. Truman later blamed Cleveland's performance on his ties to the major corporations he had represented as a Wall Street lawyer. "He was more interested in the big money people than he was in the common people, and he accomplished very, very little," he said. "Some men are greedier than others and they get to thinking they are the power rather than the instrument of power."

Bryan's assaults against the vested interests were much more to Truman's taste. The Great Commoner helped to transform the Democratic Party from a nebulous conglomeration of Southern politicians and big-city bosses into an alliance of underdogs with a powerful theme: the responsibility of government to control the excesses of the marketplace for the benefits of its citizens. In the process, Bryan would both reflect and reinforce Truman's own beliefs.

"Old Bill Bryan was a great one, one of the greatest," Truman came to believe, citing the enduring reforms he had championed, among them the direct election of U.S. senators, the federal income tax, and women's suffrage. "If it hadn't been for Bill Bryan there wouldn't be any liberal outfit at all in the country today," Truman contended.

Born in Illinois the year before the Civil War began and raised and trained in that state as a lawyer, Bryan was still in his twenties when he headed west, where wise men claimed the nation's destiny was being forged, settling in Nebraska. There, amid the ferment and discontent of the times, he soon found his calling in the world of politics. No intellectual powerhouse, he had a flair for simplifying complex ideas and for infusing his rhetoric with emotional fervor.

The opportunity for which his life seemed destined came at the 1896 Democratic convention, when he was chosen to be the final speaker in the debate on the money plank to the platform, the decisive issue for the delegates. Likening the cause of free silver to nothing less than the struggle for independence in 1776 and denouncing the Republicans for their commitment to the gold standard, Bryan enraptured the delegates. Then came his peroration: "We will answer their demand for a gold standard by saying to them, 'You shall not press down upon the brow of labor this crown of thorns,'" adding, "You shall not crucify mankind on a cross of gold," stretching his arms straight out from his sides, as if reenacting Calvary.

After a moment of stunned silence, the convention erupted in a demonstration that would set Bryan, then only thirty-six years old, on the road to three presidential nominations, each of which would end in defeat. But while he was at it, he did enliven the nature of campaigning for both parties. Until Bryan came on the scene, presidential candidates had conducted relatively sedate campaigns, as if it were somehow vulgar or unseemly to blatantly seek votes. Bryan, as he demonstrated in 1896, had no such compunctions, barnstorming the land with a vigor not seen before. It would not be matched again until half a century later, when another Democratic standard-bearer, Harry Truman, made his coast-to-coast whistle-stop tour. When Bryan's opponents charged him with lack of decorum, the same complaint that would be made against Truman, Bryan responded, "I would rather have it said that I lack dignity than that I lack backbone to meet the enemies of the government who work against its welfare on Wall Street."

For all his zest for electoral combat, Bryan's real passion was for the moral and cultural issues that, to his mind, were more fundamentally important than the competition of the marketplace. He was the first great cultural warrior of American politics, crusading against evolution and for Prohibition. For many Americans, their most vivid memory of the Commoner was at age sixty-four as the zealous defender of creationism against the sinister doctrine of evolution at the Scopes trial in 1924.

Truman passed that episode off as a symptom of old age. "What he said then shouldn't be held against him because of the things he said and stood for when he was at the height of his powers," he said later.

The pursuit of his beliefs sometimes led Bryan into sharp twists and turns. An ardent supporter of independence for Cuba, he put aside his pacifist beliefs with the outbreak of the war with Spain, joined the Nebraska national guard, and was elected a colonel. But he was bitterly opposed to the annexation of the Philippines that followed the American victory. In 1900, running again against McKinley, who had overseen the seizure of the former Spanish colony, Bryan warned Americans that "no nation can long endure half republic and half empire." Yet while decrying the oppressive impact of imperialism on the Filipinos, Bryan failed to see the connection to the injustices inflicted on black Americans right at home in the South. Indeed, in the Southern states, where the populist movement flourished, many of its spokesmen also helped promote the rise of segregation. As a Midwesterner, Bryan escaped the fervor of Southern-style racism. He did, for example, condemn lynching. But he had little to say about the denial of the vote to blacks all through Dixie, which he rationalized as "merely suffrage qualifications."

At any rate such abstractions meant little to voters. Times were generally good, and McKinley's "full dinner pail" slogan promised that they would stay that way. With many times more money to support his candidacy than his Democratic challenger, McKinley won by a bigger margin than in 1896. Remarkably, despite that defeat, Bryan managed to get the Democratic nomination once more in 1908—and lose again, this time to William Howard Taft.

"He was just too far ahead of time," was the explanation Truman offered for the dim showing of his hero. "And the people in the East, the big money people were against him and did everything they could to defeat him." Even after that debacle, Bryan retained enough of a following to dictate the party's 1912 platform and pave the way for the nomination of Woodrow Wilson. This was much to the delight of the twenty-eight-year-old Truman, who saw Wilson as the logical inheritor of Bryan's liberalism. "The Democratic Party was split every which way," Truman recalled. "And Bryan held it together behind Wilson." John Truman, by contrast, had backed the early leader, Missouri's favorite son, House of Representatives Speaker Champ Clark.

The success of Truman's political favorites contrasted with his own personal circumstances, which resulted from his father's financial difficulties. John Truman had managed to make a decent living from his livestock trading, and he earned extra money by managing his in-laws' farm in Grandview, a small town just south of Kansas City. He was doing well enough that in 1900, when Harry was six, he moved his family from Grandview into the up-and-coming town of Independence so Harry could get a better education. Truman bought a sizable house in a middle-class neighborhood, and he hired a black couple to help Martha Truman with the housework. The couple often brought their children along to play with the Truman youngsters.

Things went well for most of the next decade as John Truman improved his financial standing by investing in the grain market. However, lacking the financial resources and contacts of the bigger speculators, John started losing heavily in the summer of 1901, just after Harry graduated from high school. To recover his losses, he did what small gamblers invariably do: he doubled down, risking more and more until he had lost nearly everything he owned. That included about $40,000 in cash and stock, even 160 acres of prime land in the Blue Ridge left to Martha Truman by her father. John Truman sold the fine home he had bought only six years before in Independence and moved into a modest neighborhood in Kansas City. Lacking either capital or the confidence to continue speculating, he took a job as night watchman. "He got the notion that he could get rich," Harry said later. "Instead he lost everything at one fell swoop and went completely broke."

The financial debacle had a profound impact on Truman's young manhood. It destroyed whatever chance he had of going to college—two of his close friends, Charlie Ross and Elmer Twyman, enrolled at the University of Missouri. He had dreamed of attending West Point, where his education would have been free, and had taken special tutoring to prepare himself. But then the young man learned at a recruiting station that his eyesight would disqualify him.

Like his father, Harry Truman cherished the hope of sometime, in some business venture, striking it rich. He now realized how difficult and risky that prospect was. For a semester he attended a local business school, but he soon quit and found work as a timekeeper for a railway construction firm that paid $35 a month plus board. "It took all I received to help pay family expenses and keep my brother and sister in school," he recalled later. By the time he was nineteen, he was working for the National Bank of Commerce in Kansas City for $35 a month. He ultimately found other bank jobs that paid as much as $100 a month.

Meanwhile, John Truman had suffered another reverse. Weary of city life, he had rented a farm in the town of Clinton, about seventy miles away, where he diligently worked the land. But his bad luck would not go away. The spring floods ruined what had promised to be a fine corn crop. John had no recourse but to agree to the plea of Martha Truman's mother, Louise Young, to move in with her and manage her 600-acre farm in Grandview. Soon after that, in 1906, his son, Harry, who had been doing fairly well for himself as a bank clerk in Kansas City, decided he had no choice but accede to his father's request to join him and his brother, Vivian, in working the farm.

There ensued the dreariest period of his young manhood. Gone was the carefree life he had spent in Kansas City. For nine glum years, from 1905 to 1914, the farm took over his existence. John Truman was manager. He, his two sons, and hired hands did the gritty work of seeding and harvesting the crops and collecting the rent from the pastureland they leased to other farmers. Harry kept the books and handled the money. The farm bank account was kept in his name, to avoid attachment by his father's creditors. At the end of 1910, John Truman broke his leg in a barn accident. Three months later, a balky calf knocked Harry down and he fractured his leg.

With the exception of that year, the Trumans always had some income from their farming, though it never added up to a substantial profit. This was supposedly the golden age of American agriculture. But as Harry said years later, "We always owed the bank something—sometimes more, sometimes less—but we always owed the bank."

What made all this travail particularly difficult to bear was that the Trumans did not have clear ownership of the land they tilled. It was Grandma Young's property. They were sustained by the understandable belief that when the old lady passed on, they would inherit the property. Sure enough, in 1909, Grandma Young died and left the farm to the Trumans and a son, Harrison. But four of her other children challenged the will, charging that the old lady's faculties had been fading and that she had been manipulated.

The stakes were high. If the will prevailed, the Trumans' inheritance would be worth about $50,000; if not, their interest would be reduced to $15,000. The battle dragged on for four years, until Truman was able to reach an out-of-court settlement that provided that Martha would divide the farm with Harrison. She took out a mortgage on her share but seemed to be assured a measure of financial security.

Harry continued to do his share of work on the farm, but he made no secret of his dislike for the tedium. His principal interest during these years became the courtship of Bess Wallace, a high-spirited, attractive young woman, one year his junior, whom he had admired from afar since childhood. Harry's long-standing uneasiness around females his own age had stood in the way of his pursuit—and so had Bess's mother, Madge. The Wallaces were one of the leading families in Independence in terms of social and financial standing, and Madge Wallace left no doubt she did not consider Truman in the same league. Yet Bess remained unmarried at age twenty-five, and about then, in 1910, Harry's ardor overcame his shyness. He began to press his suit. By the next year, he had mustered the courage to propose to her by letter. She turned him down, but the two continued to see each other, a circumstance that Truman accepted with a grace that reflected the depth of his affection. "I am more than happy to be your good friend for that is more than I expected," he wrote her.

Around this time, in another letter to Bess Wallace, the thirty-year-old Truman gave voice, however facetiously, to his political ambition. Having just recently visited Montana to participate in a land lottery, he wrote to the object of his affections, "Who knows I may be his excellency the governor of Montana. How would you like to be Mrs. Governor?"

The land lottery came to nothing much, in contrast with Truman's political ambitions. As lighthearted as he sounded about the subject, he and his father had already taken steps along that path. In 1912, the year Harry rooted for Woodrow Wilson on the national scene, in his own back-yard, he had attended meetings of the Pendergast faction of the Democratic Party. They were known as the goats, in contrast to their rivals, the rabbits. That same year, along with his father, he had campaigned for goat candidate R. D. Mize in a run for eastern district judge. With Mize's victory, John Truman sought and gained appointment from the new judge as road supervisor, a post that provided minimal financial reward but, more important to John Truman, a measure of public recognition and authority. However, John Truman's public life ended tragically. Trying to lift a huge rock as part of his duties, he suffered an injury that contributed to his death a few months later at the age of sixty-three.

His son continued on, though with mixed results. With the Democrats in power in Washington, and with the backing of his local congressman, Harry Truman was appointed Grandview postmaster in December 1914, the month after John Truman's death. This turned out to be a dubious prize. Absorbed with his responsibilities on the farm, he quit after a few months and wound up owing the government 38 cents for a shortage in his accounts.

Judge Mize then named him to the road overseer job his father had held. But when Mize died soon after, his successor had Truman replaced. Resentful of his ouster, Truman ran for the Democratic township committee. He was so involved in various business enterprises that he had little time to campaign, and lost his bid.

Meanwhile, Harry's life had changed dramatically. Though Truman genuinely mourned the loss of his father, who had dominated him in so many ways while denying him the respect he sought, his demise left his son free to chart his own course. Unfortunately, the early results of this liberation were unsatisfying. Truman spent a good part of the next three years dabbling in a series of entrepreneurial ventures—land speculation, lead and zinc mining, oil exploration. His enthusiasm could not make up for his lack of capital and direct experience in any of the areas of business he was looking into, and little came of his efforts. Truman pressed on, counting on fortune to smile on him. "My ship is going to come in yet," he wrote Bess in 1913. Three years later, he had come to believe, as he wrote to Bess, that determining the outcome of any business venture is "one big guess, and the fellow who guesses right is the man of good judgment. I am going to keep guessing." After three years, Truman had run out of guesses and confidence. The best that can be said about that period is that he emerged with no lasting damage to his reputation. Now a bigger challenge awaited him, one that depended not so much on guesses as on courage and determination, and Truman proved more than up to the task.

With the United States' entry into the Great War, Truman once again demonstrated his allegiance to the federal Union his forebears had warred again when he reenlisted in his old national guard unit. After two three-year tours of duty, he had decided not to reenlist in 1911, though not because of his grandmother's objections to the uniform. He was simply too busy with his business pursuits and keeping up with the sundry organizations he had joined. But in June 1917, two months after President Wilson had gained a declaration of war against the Central Powers from Congress, he reenlisted in his old outfit, which soon became Battery F in the Second Missouri Field Artillery Regiment. Truman still had many friends in the unit from his earlier service. That turned out to be a plus because the guardsmen chose their own officers, and his friends helped elect him a first lieutenant. He left for training and overseas shipment amid the tears of his mother—and of the handsome young woman, Bess Wallace, whom he had admired since childhood. Indeed, at this point, she wanted to marry him, but Truman gallantly refused. "I don't think it would be right for me to ask you to tie yourself to a prospective cripple," he wrote, adding, "But I am crazy about you."

Truman, then thirty-three, was too old for the draft. He could have reasonably contended that he was serving his country by running his farm. He seems to have been motivated mainly by pure patriotism and a romantic sense of idealism, which he shared with many Americans as the nation followed Wilson into a crusade to make "the world safe for Democracy." "I felt I was Galahad after the grail," he wrote years later. "I rather felt we owed France something for Lafayette." These better instincts were well rewarded. Truman had a splendid war. Though he eventually saw plenty of action, his first success had little to do with the valor he hoped to demonstrate.

At Camp Doniphan in Oklahoma, where his regiment trained for overseas deployment, he was assigned to establish a canteen, which would provide the sundry items that soldiers would buy from the Post Exchange. Truman was shrewd enough to take on as his assistant an old friend, Eddie Jacobson, who had the advantage of having clerked in a Kansas City clothing store. The canteens were set up like a private enterprise, with each man in the regiment ordered to put up $2 to give it initial capital.

"I have a Jew in charge of the canteen by the name of Jacobson and he is a crackerjack," Truman wrote Bess. With Jacobson's retail savvy and Truman's entrepreneurial instincts, the canteen not only gave the regiment the items it needed, it returned a profit, paying its shareholders a dividend—this while every other canteen on the post went bust. Given the commonly accepted ethnic stereotypes of the day, it was no surprise that some of his comrades began to call him Trumanheimer. If a slur was intended, Truman laughed it off.

He could afford to. His retailing triumph had impressed his superiors. So did his diligence and energy at the more soldierly tasks assigned to him. Indeed, his efficiency reports were so glowing that the regimental commander, Colonel Karl Klemm, sent one back with the comment, "No man can be that good." Such skepticism did not keep Lieutenant Truman from being promoted to captain. Equally important, he was one of a handful of officers selected to ship out to France in advance of the division for special training, which they would then pass on to the main body of troops.

Truman completed the special training in time to rejoin his regiment in June, where the newly commissioned captain was given the dubious reward of command of his regiment's Battery D. His new outfit was made up mostly of roughneck Irish Catholics who gloried in their justly earned reputation for insubordination. Inwardly fearful that he would flop in his new post, Truman nevertheless laid down the law at his first muster. "I didn't come over here to get along with you," he said. "You've got to get along with me." Those who could not, he warned: "I'll bust you right back now." That bluster seemed to have impressed the unruly members of his command. Truman backed up his words by bearing down on his troops in training. His unit ultimately won the praise of regimental higher-ups.

Now in the late summer of 1918, Truman, in his first combat assignment, learned that his men were not yet quite ready for battle. When they first came under fire in the rugged hills of the Vosges, with their muddy, twisting roads, the battery panicked. "All except five or six scattered like partridges," Truman recalled. "Finally I got them back together without losing any men, although we had six horses killed."

Traumatic as it was, the episode seemed to provide the seasoning the unit needed. The battery stood its ground in its next challenge, the American Expeditionary Force's climactic drive of the war in the Meuse Argonne, which helped break the back of German resistance. When the guns fell silent in November, Truman and his unit could count themselves fortunate: only one of their number killed and two wounded. Truman had shown himself to be a courageous and efficient soldier. His official evaluation called him "resourceful and dependable."

Truman had played his part in what, as he would come to realize, was the seminal event of the twentieth century. He could be grateful for having survived in one piece, despite his fears of being a cripple. Moreover, he also had made friendships that would stand him in excellent stead in business and in the political career which awaited him. Just as important, he had gained confidence in himself.

"I love you as madly as a man can," he wrote Bess. For the future, he dreamed of owning a new Ford and touring the country with his bride. He added, "Maybe have a little politics." They would marry on June 28, 1919, in Independence's Trinity Episcopal Church.

There would, of course, be more than "a little politics." Before that became his full-time career, Truman once again indulged his zest for venture capitalism. In May 1919, only three weeks after being mustered out and a month before his marriage, Truman and his old Army sidekick, ex-sergeant Eddie Jacobson, opened their brand-new haberdashery business in the heart of downtown Kansas City. The two believed that they could duplicate their great success at the Camp Doniphan canteen. But their experience dealing with Army trainees in the sheltered environment of a military post was poor preparation for competing in the fast world of big-city retailing.

The firm of Truman & Jacobson appears to have been a losing proposition from the start, made worse by a severe farm depression. Truman blamed his debacle in part on tight money and the Republicans. "In 1921, after the Republicans took over Andrew Mellon was made Secretary of the Treasury. He immediately started a 'wringing out' process, which put farm prices down to an all-time low, raised interest rates and put labor in its place," he wrote later. This allegation reflects Truman's partisanship and populism more than economic history. It was the Federal Reserve Board, that, then as now, set interest rates, which declined as the economy slumped after the war. Federal economic policies were probably less to blame than the recession and Truman's outmoded approach to retailing. At any rate, there was no question about the outcome. The store closed in 1922, leaving the partners saddled with debt. Jacobson declared bankruptcy in 1925. Concerned about protecting his public reputation,

Truman forbore from taking that step, but it took him years to pay off the debt.

As the haberdashery doors closed, another door opened. In came Mike Pendergast, the father of another Truman Army comrade, Jim Pendergast, and more to the point the brother of Tom Pendergast, who was establishing himself as the leading Democrat in Kansas City, if not the whole state. His visitor had a proposal: would Truman be willing to run for district judge in Jackson County with the active backing of the Pendergast organization?

This proposition was not as one-sided as it might seem. Despite his early reverses in politics, Truman could give the Pendergasts a boost. Two generations of Trumans had lived in Jackson County, boasting a good reputation and wide friendships, which Harry himself had expanded. His natural gregariousness had led him to stay on close terms with his former national guard comrades even after he dropped out in 1911. As if to make up for his departure from the guard, Truman seemed bent on joining nearly everything else in sight—the Kansas City Athletic Club, the Grandview Commercial Club (which elected him as its president), the Grandview Orchestra, the Woodmen of the World, the Order of Masons. He founded and headed a new Masonic lodge in Grandview and won acceptance into the influential Scottish Rite. Whatever his motives, Truman certainly knew that links he established from these activities could only help him if he should choose to seek public office.

On top of all this, by virtue of his service in the Great War, Captain Truman enjoyed a bond with other members of an important new political interest group: war veterans. Many of them, like Truman, were finding that their return to civilian life had not gone as smoothly as they hoped, and they were eager for someone to represent them who understood their problems firsthand. Captain Truman was eager to show that he could shoulder that burden. It did not take him long to give Mike the answer he and his brother wanted.

Though he could not have fully realized it at the time, the direction of Truman's life was now set for the next half century. No one—not Truman and not the Pendergast brothers—could foresee how far this course would take him or how high he would reach. But to a considerable degree, the outlook and attitudes that would help to shape his destiny had already been colored by the first four bumpy decades of his life.

He had not totally escaped the racial animosities that were part of his heritage. In the letter to Bess Truman in which he first proposed marriage, the twenty-seven-year-old Truman set out his views on people of color, yellow as well as black, in no uncertain terms. "I think one man is just as good as another," he wrote to his future bride, "so long as he's honest and decent and not a nigger or a Chinaman." Truman noted that his uncle Will, the Confederate veteran, had a theory. "The Lord made a white man of dust and a nigger from mud then threw up what was left and it came down a Chinaman. He does hate Chinks and Japs," he said of Uncle Will, "and so do I. It is race prejudice I guess. But I am strongly of the opinion that Negroes ought to be in Africa, yellow men in Asia and white men in Europe and America."

It is hard to tell how much to make of this outburst, set forth in a rambling missive, sandwiched between a denunciation of European royal families and his view of a forthcoming job change by a mutual acquaintance. Truman's acknowledgment that his harsh judgments amounted to "race prejudice" suggests that he himself was somewhat abashed by his own opinions. His comments may have been an attempt at the bravado young men sometimes use to impress young women.

Truman often used slurs about blacks, and Jews too, out of habit and mental laziness. (Though after twice using the racial epithet for black Americans in the bigotry he spewed to Bess, he was careful to refer to "Negroes" in his next reference.) But there is no other evidence from Truman's early life to suggest his actually harboring such deep-seated contempt for other races as expressed in his letter to Bess. Nor is there indication that the rest of his family shared old soldier Will's feelings. This is not surprising because there were not enough blacks in Independence, or elsewhere in eastern Jackson County, to cause white folks to fret. The town was sedate and genteel, free from the discord of bustling up-to-date Kansas City. As for the Civil War, Martha Truman talked about the bloody conflict often with her oldest son, fostering his own interest in history. According to her granddaughter, Margaret, Harry's mother seemed to reserve most of her hostility not for blacks, but for the Union leadership, starting with Lincoln, and also the Yankee raiders who had slaughtered the pigs and cattle and swiped the family silver. She saw to it that her son had the chance to play with the children of Caroline Hunter, the black woman hired to help Martha Truman with the housework, with whom, by his own recollection, the boy had "a grand time." There were fewer such occasions in the future. Like most Americans of his time and from nearly everyplace in the country, Harry Truman grew into adulthood with little social contact with blacks or Asians, and little reason to think about them much one way or another.

Probably a much more important influence on his career than the residue of the Civil War was the populism that set the prairies ablaze, magnified by Bryan, its dynamic messenger. This was already evident in his skewed diagnosis of the failure of his haberdashery business and would become even more prominent as the years went by. Resentment of the powerful interests that dominated the nation's economy, and to a considerable degree the everyday lives of its citizens, was more than an abstraction. Truman had seen his father, struggling to improve the living he scratched out from the land, wiped out by the swings of the grain market. He himself had expended his energy and imagination in a variety of business enterprises, only to come away defeated and frustrated, climaxed by the collapse of his haberdashery business.

Personal circumstances fostered an affinity for underdogs. As a child, the thick lenses he wore to correct his poor vision made him an easy target for ridicule by his peers and led to his isolation. Years later, that same problem with his eyesight robbed him of a chance to attend West Point, while the collapse of his father's fortunes ruled out his attending college. Though he tried to put these youthful setbacks behind him, as an adult, he had to deal with his rejection by the family of the young woman he eventually married because he was deemed not to measure up in worldly goods.

The knocks and bruises Truman absorbed did not produce self-pity or bitterness. They did add an undertone of realism to his expectations from life while leaving undimmed his ambition and confidence. The most important political consequence was that he came to maturity with an understanding of the less fortunate, including those whose chief misfortune was the color of their skin. This compassion was bolstered by a feisty willingness to challenge the powers that be on behalf of the disadvantaged. In combination, these qualities would help carry him to a point in life higher than he or the Pendergasts had ever imagined.

3

THE BOSS'S APPRENTICE

In 1927, when blacks in Missouri's Jackson County had cause to complain about the mistreatment of patients at the home for the aged, they took their problem to the county's presiding judge, Harry S. Truman. Truman, in office less than a year, investigated and fired the chief physician. In the next year, Judge Truman helped push through a county bond issue to finance the construction of a new home for black delinquent girls and proposed naming the home for a black craftsman who had worked on the Santa Fe trail. These were not isolated acts by Truman. He was following the pattern set by the Pendergast organization, starting with the founder of the machine, Jim Pendergast. Big Jim won the praise of Kansas City blacks for his humane treatment of prisoners early in his political career while serving as county marshal. Later, during Truman's formative years in Missouri politics, the Pendergast machine and its allies in the state legislature fought against bills to undercut voting rights for blacks and to segregate streetcars.

When Harry Truman accepted Mike Pendergast's offer to run for office, he began a relationship that was to last for most of his political life and benefit him greatly. The most evident advantages he gained were the resources and experience of the fast-growing Pendergast organization. Another asset the machine provided, although less conspicuous, would prove over the long run to be perhaps the most valuable of all. This was the opportunity to work with, draw support from, and meet the needs of black voters and their leaders. This background, given the strength of the base the Pendergast organization assembled among black voters, would set him apart from other national politicians of his era in both parties. The relationship that resulted would contribute greatly to Truman's political future and to the black quest for racial justice.

The Pendergast backing for the interests of blacks, like similar efforts by city bosses around the country, was part of a broad drive to remake the torn and tattered Democratic Party. The urban machines had started late in the nineteenth century by recruiting the immigrants who came to the United States from abroad. That paved the way for later reaching out to the blacks who left their Southern birthplaces to live and strive in the big cities of the North and West, an effort in which Pendergast stood out among the Democracy's urban chieftains.

The need for the Democrats to overhaul themselves was clear on both the local and national levels. Of the sixteen presidential contests after the Civil War, from 1868 through 1928, Democratic candidates won only four times, twice each for Grover Cleveland and Woodrow Wilson. The partisan divide was defined vividly, if somewhat hyperbolically, by Senator George Hoar of Massachusetts, an eloquent nineteenth-century leader of the Grand Old Party. "The men who do the work of piety and charity in our churches, the men who administer our school system, the men who own and till their own farms, the men who perform skilled labor in the shops, the soldiers, the men who went to war and stayed all through, find their places in the Republican Party," Hoar contended, replying to a European inquirer. "While the old slave owner and slave driver, the saloon keeper, the ballot box stuffer, the Ku Klux Klan, the criminal class of the great cities, the men who cannot read or write find their congenial places in the Democratic Party."

Two great waves of migration offered the chance to escape from this perdition. First, however, the erstwhile Jeffersonian party of small landholders had to establish new strongholds in the mushrooming cities of the East and Midwest. There Democrats created relatively efficient organizations that flourished by serving the interests of the polyglot mass of newcomers from overseas. In contrast to the Republican Party, whose backbone was made up of white middle-class Protestants, the Democrats vigorously recruited Irish and Italian Catholics, then Jews.

The flood of new citizens from abroad slowed down in about 1914 because of the Great War and the legislative restrictions after the war, driven in part by the pervasive mistrust of the foreign born. Feeding the xenophobia, besides the economic hard times stemming from converting the economy to peacetime, was the great Red scare. Its leader, Attorney General A. Mitchell Palmer, describing the alleged subversives he had apprehended, resorted to phrenology: "Out of the sly and crafty eyes of many of them leap cupidity, cruelty, insanity and crime," he told Congress. Such rhetoric added steam to a fervid atmosphere, bolstering racism and fostering the revival of the Ku Klux Klan.

But the decreased flow to the cities from Europe was offset by another portentous population shift, the Great Migration of Southern blacks. This influx began gradually, keyed to the pace of the North's industrial growth. Between 1900 and 1910, the black population outside the South climbed to 450,000 from 335,000. By 1920, reflecting the employment boom generated by the Great War, the non-South black population increased by 70 percent to 785,000. The next ten years, the decade of the 1920s, despite the onset of the economic slowdown, saw another dramatic increase. At the start of this massive movement, less than 10 percent of black Americans lived outside the South. But by 1940, with the country emerging from the Great Depression and on the brink of World War II, nearly 40 percent of Americans of color, about five million people, lived outside the South.

With the attack on Pearl Harbor, the black tide gained new momentum. In industrial centers like Detroit, for example, the black population increased twentyfold. The newcomers left the South to escape the threat of lynching, pervasive discrimination, and wages barely above the starvation level. In the North, they sought housing fit to raise a family, wages sufficient to feed themselves and their children, and ultimately the right to cast their ballots and help choose their government. Thus was opportunity's door opened to the urban leaders of the Democratic Party.

Missouri, particularly St. Louis, but also the Pendergast's stronghold, Kansas City, was getting its share of the black migrants. Both cities had substantial black populations before the Great Migration began. In 1910, St. Louis ranked sixth in black population in cities outside the South, with more than 43,000; Kansas City, with nearly 24,000 blacks, ranked eighth among Northern cities; only six other cities in the North had a black population of more than 10,000.

Not surprisingly, both cities drew heavily from the new wave of black migrants. By 1920, Kansas City's black population would climb to more than 38,000, a jump of 25 percent, faster than the city's overall population growth and giving blacks 10 percent of the total population. Blacks poured into St. Louis at an even faster rate, with more than 25,000 arrivals, bringing the city's black population to nearly 70,000, a gain of nearly 60 percent, giving blacks there, as in Kansas City, about 10 percent of the total population. Neither city had as much of the polyglot immigrant populations that reached the nation's largest cities, such as Chicago and New York, and this gave blacks more prominence in the Missouri cities. The blacks came to Missouri's two big cities not only from the South but also from rural parts of the state. Nearly all of Missouri's 114 rural counties lost black population between 1910 and 1930.

The Pendergast machine was quick to seek black support using many of the same tactics developed in cultivating white immigrants decades earlier. The founder of the Pendergast dynasty, Jim Pendergast, himself the children of Irish immigrants, was close to penniless when, legend had it, in 1881 he rashly put his pittance on a long shot named Climax at the local track. Climax paid enough for Pendergast to invest in an inn and a saloon, which, with a gambler's sentimentality, he named Climax.

Jim Pendergast was then twenty-five years old, and so far as is known, he made no more bets on long shots. He did not have to. His inn and tavern did well enough. He was dubbed Big Jim for his heft—standing a couple of inches below six feet, he had massive shoulders and arms— and the power he wielded in his adopted city. He was one of many city politicians of the era to take advantage of the affinity between politics and saloons. "The saloon is the natural club and meeting-place for the ward heelers and leaders, and the bar-room politician is one of the most common and best recognized factors in local government," Theodore Roosevelt observed, drawing on his experience as New York's police commissioner. With Big Jim's knack for organizing and catering to his neighbors, particularly the low-income black, Irish, German, and native laborers who lived in his own West Bottoms neighborhood, home to the stockyards and the city's first train terminal, Pendergast became known as Kansas City's first boss. It was a term he disliked. "I've got friends," he said. "And that's all there is to this 'boss' business, friends."

This theme resounded with the folks in West Bottoms, particularly those in Kansas City's first ward, who elected him to the city council in 1891. While Alderman Pendergast fought to pave their streets and keep up public buildings, all of which not incidentally provided jobs in the community, they kept reelecting him—for eighteen years. In 1895, his vote against renewing the franchise for the local gas company won the headlined praise of the reform-minded *Kansas City Star*, which declared that he STOOD BY THE CITY AT A CRITICAL MOMENT. After his death in 1911, his former constituents raised money for a ten-foot bronze statue of him that saluted "his rugged character and splendid achievements" and devotion to "truth and courage."

But Jim Pendergast's machine had a longer life than its founder. Brother Tom, sixteen years Jim's junior, kept the apparatus in good order, with the aid of Michael Pendergast, who had recruited Harry Truman. Like his older brother, Tom's powerful and bulky frame seemed to fit the physical stereotype for a political boss, or a saloon keeper, too, for that matter. But they differed in manner and personality. Jim had exuded congeniality. His brother had a heavy, commanding voice and a hot temper. Brother Tom lived big, ate big, and drank too much, and he became addicted to gambling, which ultimately was his undoing. But he followed the tactics of his brother in reaching out for black support. Compared to the earlier newcomers from Europe, blacks offered some advantages from a political standpoint. They already enjoyed citizenship, even though most had a hard time claiming its full benefit. They did not have to learn a new language. They had special disadvantages too, notably feelings of inferiority growing from their legacy of slavery and racial bigotry.

Nevertheless, Tom Pendergast wooed them much as his brother had. For example, in 1922, he saw to it that the Democratic Party's city platform denounced the police for their heavy-handed enforcement of Prohibition, often directed against blacks, who seemed to resent the ban on liquor even more than most other Americans. But in the 1920s, as Tom Pendergast pursued such efforts and Harry Truman arrived on the Jackson County political landscape, both had to contend with the opposition of a new force in Missouri politics, and indeed across the country: the Ku Klux Klan.

The Klan was born in the post–Civil War South with the principal aim of undoing the political gains made by blacks during Reconstruction and reestablishing white supremacy. Once that was accomplished, the Klan, for all intents and purposes, disappeared. However, it was revived in 1915 at Stone Mountain, Georgia, by William Joseph Simmons, an itinerant preacher and garter salesman turned history teacher. In the decade that followed, the Invisible Empire began a dramatic resurgence, spurred by the nativism and paranoia of the times. In this incarnation, its appeal went well beyond the South to rural areas all over the country, as well as to new urban dwellers, whose values seemed threatened by the waves of immigrants and the rise of urban culture.

At its peak, the KKK counted some five million members. Their cause was broader than white supremacy. Now they targeted Catholics as threatening the Protestant faith in which nearly all Klansmen had been raised. "The real indictment against the Roman Catholic Church," said Imperial Wizard Hiram Evans, "is that it is actively alien, un-American and usually anti-American."

In this respect, Harry Truman's background was an asset to the Pendergasts. He was a Baptist and a prominent Mason, while the Pendergast organization was dominated by Irish Catholics. For all of that, Truman, like other Democratic politicians around the country, could not avoid having qualms about the power of the Klan. While in areas like Jackson County, where the power of the Catholic-run Pendergast machine led the Klan to focus on Catholics, the Klan continued to terrorize blacks whenever the chance arose. In Missouri's rural Pemiscot County, as Harry Truman was campaigning for district judge, the Klan was making its presence felt. Any of the 1,500 blacks interested in voting in the local elections had to consider pamphlets bearing the imprimatur of the KKK, which declared that the election was "For White Voters only. Nigger you are not wanted." This was particularly threatening to Missouri's Republican governor, Arthur Hyde, whose party could usually count on getting the support of most black voters. Hyde wrote to the U.S. justice department asking for federal protection for blacks in Missouri's rural areas, but no action followed.

Although the federal government would not act against the Klan, white politicians could not ignore its influence. Among those disturbed was an ambitious young Alabama lawyer named Hugo Black, who, like Harry Truman, had been an artillery officer in the Great War. Black practiced in Birmingham, which, with its native-born, white, and Protestant population, was a Klan stronghold. This was particularly worrisome for Black, a prosecutor and a criminal defense lawyer who had fought for the rights of Alabama blacks. But his most sensational case was his successful defense of a man accused of murdering a Catholic priest. Concluding that the verdict would alienate Catholic voters, Black decided to make the best of a bad situation. He joined the Klan in 1923, and during his 1926 campaign for the U.S. Senate, he made a strong case against Catholics. He ultimately quit the Klan, although his membership would always haunt him. Years later, after compiling a record on the Supreme Court as a champion of civil rights and civil liberties, Black would concede that joining the Klan was a mistake. But still, he claimed, "there was a political need to join."

In Missouri, Harry Truman had concerns similar to Black's about the Klan as he contemplated joining near the climax of his 1922 campaign for district judge. He was in a close fight for the Democratic nomination. True, he could count on the Pendergast machine's support, and his familiarity with the district and the backing of fellow war veterans provided advantages. However, the rural eastern district where Truman was running was one of the Pendergast machine's weak spots; indeed, this was a major reason why the Pendergasts had chosen him as their candidate there. Meanwhile, the Klan was flexing its muscles all around Jackson County. Its members staged a motorcade through Independence, congregated in an open field where they went through their ritual of cross burning, and claimed to have signed up nearly 1,000 new members. Two of Truman's three opponents in the primary contest had Klan backing. A former Army buddy, Edward G. Hinde, who had himself joined the Klan "to see what it was, to see what was going on," persuaded Truman to join, and Truman gave Hinde the $10 membership fee to pass on. But then a Klan organizer met with Truman and made it clear he would get no support in the election unless he promised not to give any jobs to Catholics if he won office. Truman thought of the mostly Catholic battery he had commanded in France and of the Catholic Pendergasts who were sponsoring his candidacy. He got his $10 back.

Truman was fortunate to escape that easily from an involvement that could have wrecked his career, and that did in fact vex him later on. On its face, Hinde's account of the episode, which Truman himself never discussed, seems either disingenuous or reflective of a remarkable naïveté about the Klan. The KKK made no secret of its aversion to Catholics in every walk of life, and certainly on the public payroll. For Truman not to realize the implications of this stand seems hard to understand or excuse.

Despite this misadventure, Truman won the nomination, though not by much. He came in ahead in the four-man race by fewer than 300 votes out of about 12,000 cast. His encounter with the Klan did not leave a favorable impression with that organization. On Election Day, in the sample ballot distributed by Klansmen outside Protestant churches, Truman was not one of the judicial candidates it endorsed. Next to his name, the ballot stated, "Church affiliation Protestant, endorsed by Tom and Joe," who it more fully identified as "two Roman Catholic Political bosses." The month before the election, 20,000 Klansmen assembled in the Kansas City convention hall to listen to denunciations of Catholics and pleas of support for Protestant candidates, of whom Truman was not one. Nevertheless, facing a novice Republican candidate, Truman won easily and was on his way to the courthouse.

For the next two years, Harry Truman had little time to worry about the Klan and its issues. He was too busy haggling with his two fellow judges over patronage and property taxes and pushing through road improvements. But the Klan, along with another cultural issue, Prohibition, was bringing the political pot to a boil across the nation. The mounting divisiveness over both concerns reached an explosive climax at the Democratic National Convention of 1924 at no less prominent a stage than New York's Madison Square Garden. One reason for the passions on display was the Eighteenth Amendment to the Constitution, passed just four years before, which paved the way for prohibition of all alcoholic beverages. At first, a bitter battle appeared inevitable between the wets and the drys over the stand the party's platform would take on this issue. But that was avoided by a compromise resolution, which did little more than call for enforcement of the Constitution and all its laws.

But for the Klan, there could be no compromise. What hardened the lines of battle was that the conflict had become linked to what was supposedly the convention's main business: the nomination of a presidential candidate. The two leading contenders were New York governor Al Smith (dubbed the Happy Warrior by Franklin Roosevelt), a Catholic and a bitter foe of the Klan, and William Gibbs McAdoo, Woodrow Wilson's son-in-law, his former treasury secretary, and the early front-runner. For his part, McAdoo tried to duck the issue, but many of his supporters from the South and West were strong for the Klan.

The Klan's foes, from the North and East, making up about half the delegates, had fought for a plank on the Democratic platform that would pledge the party to oppose any effort by the Klan to interfere with religious freedom. However, just about as many delegates from the South and the West, either because they themselves supported the Klan or feared angering those who did, were against putting in a single harsh word about the Klan. This group had their way in the first test of strength on the issue when the convention's platform committee adopted a plank that merely deplored efforts to limit constitutional liberties, but made no mention of the Klan. Meanwhile, as the struggle over the Klan headed to a confrontation on the floor of the full convention and neither Smith nor McAdoo could gain a clear lead in the contest for the presidential nomination, no fewer than sixty favorite sons vied for that prize. Among them was Missouri's own three-term senator and Pendergast ally, James Reed. He had a better idea than most of what to expect at the Garden, since in April his own state's Democratic convention had torn itself apart fighting over a proposed anti-Klan resolution.

Hoping to avoid such pandemonium in New York, party leaders selected the venerable William Jennings Bryan to soothe the delegates just before the crucial vote on the Klan platform plank. But the Commoner was more concerned with preserving the culture of the Protestant countryside than with the Klan, which he branded a "false issue." With this condescension, Bryan's mission of harmony imploded in a cascade of boos.

The momentous roll call followed, in which delegates would choose between the bland plank approved by the platform committee and an attack on the Klan proposed by its foes. Fearing the worst, convention managers had summoned 1,000 extra police to the Garden. New York's finest managed to avoid a full-scale riot. Even so, some delegates brawled in the aisles while spectators in the galleries howled. Finally, the tally was announced: 541 3/20 votes for the minority report attacking the Klan, and 542 3/20 against. The opponents of the Klan had lost their fight by a hairbreadth, a one-vote difference.

Yet deep schisms remained. The convention dragged on for sixteen days and took a record 103 ballots to settle on John W. Davis, far more accomplished and recognized as a Wall Street lawyer than as a national politician. The divisiveness of the convention, the tumult of which was carried for the first time on a nationwide radio hookup, ruined whatever chance Davis might have had of running successfully against incumbent Calvin Coolidge and the prosperity for which he claimed credit. In November, Davis did not carry a single state outside the Solid South.

The discontent all too publicly displayed at the Garden and overheard around the country reverberated across the Democratic echelons. Local party leaders struggled in vain to settle disputes, and grassroots workers lost heart, as did rank-and-file voters. One victim of this fallout was Harry Truman, who was seeking reelection as eastern district judge after one term. Truman had worked hard during his first term, relying on the habits of honesty and efficiency bred in him by his family. He also managed to find time to take night courses at the Kansas City School of Law. As eastern district judge, by concentrating on cutting the huge budget deficit he had inherited and maintaining the rural road system, he earned a reputation for competence and relative independence from the tentacles of the Pendergast machine. He even won the praise of the *Kansas City Star*, normally no admirer of Democrats.

Despite his semiautonomy, in 1924, Truman was caught up in the antagonism between Tom Pendergast and rival Democratic factions vying for influence not only in Jackson County but throughout the state. Truman won the nomination, but anti-Pendergast forces in his own party turned their backs on his candidacy. Another negative voice was the NAACP, which took out an ad in the *Kansas City Call* to declare that Truman's answers to a questionnaire the organization had submitted to him were unsatisfactory. Though the ad did not explain, one issue on the questionnaire had to do with the KKK, and the NAACP may have been troubled by Truman's dalliance with that organization.

The NAACP stance could not have hurt Truman seriously because few blacks lived in the Jackson County district he represented. But the Klan was a different story. Members rang church bells all through the district to make sure Klan supporters got to the polls. By some accounts, Joe Shannon, leader of the so-called anti-Pendergast rabbit faction in the Jackson County Democracy, secretly worked with the Klan to defeat Truman.

On Election Day, Truman lost by less than 1,000 votes out of 22,000 cast. In his district, he ran 1,800 votes behind the party's gubernatorial candidate, Arthur Nelson, who had the Klan's backing but nevertheless lost his governor's race. If Truman had had the 1,800 votes that presumably came with Klan backing, he probably would have won a second term as district judge. On the other hand, the Klan backing apparently hurt Nelson elsewhere in the state, particularly in the black strongholds of Kansas City and St. Louis, where the GOP ran well above its previous levels in wards with large black populations.

There is probably no good time for a politician to lose an election, but November 1924 was a particularly unpropitious period for Harry Truman. He was burdened with debt, including the demands of his haberdashery business creditors. His family responsibilities now included a new daughter, Margaret, born in February 1924, whose arrival for this doting father turned out to be one of the brightest spots of his life.

Truman had no doubt that he would return to politics. Meanwhile, to make ends meet, he made a modest income—about $5,000 a year—from selling memberships in the Kansas City auto club. "Harry would never stay idle," recalled a former wartime buddy, Ted Marks. "If one thing did not work out he'd get into something else." Truman also used his out-of-office interval to finish a second year at Kansas City School of Law, but, short of time and money, he quit in 1925.

Early in 1926 came his big break. Tom Pendergast offered him the nomination for presiding judge, providing far more prestige and influence than the district judgeship he had won in 1922. This new post gave Truman enough authority over the other two judges to get most things done the way he wanted. By this time, Pendergast had outmaneuvered his rabbit rivals, and his authority among Jackson County Democrats was supreme.

With no opposition in the Democratic primary, Truman won easily in November, along with the rest of Pendergast's slate. In the next eight years, during two terms as leader of the Jackson County court, Truman's populist instincts were overshadowed by the commitment to efficient management of the public's affairs. It was a sort of Midwest version of New England's Yankee Protestant work ethic, which he had demonstrated four years earlier as an eastern district judge.

Truman used patronage skillfully to dominate the county court during his eight years as a presiding judge. He also made a point to stress bipartisanship in designing county projects and competitive bidding in awarding contracts. To convince Republicans and independents to support bond issues for new roads, he argued they could be more economical than rebuilding the old dirt thoroughfares. Moreover, he worked closely with the Kansas City Public Service Institute, a nonpartisan advocate of the managerial approach to local government, promoting road improvements, zoning regulation, and fairer tax assessments in a more or less politically neutral style.

Truman's adherence to such standards helped shield him from most of the less savory machinations practiced by the Pendergast machine. In his memoirs, Truman told of being summoned to Pendergast's office in 1928 to meet with some friends of Pendergast who were eager to get the contract for a substantial road building contract. "I told them I expected to let the contracts to the lowest bidder as I had promised the taxpayers I would do," Truman recalled. Whereupon Pendergast supposedly turned to the contractors and remarked: "Didn't I tell you boys he's the contrariest cuss in Missouri?" When the contractors had gone, Pendergast told Truman, "You carry out the agreement you made with the people of Jackson county." Truman added, "I never heard anything from him again."

That was the story Truman told for public consumption on numerous occasions. Privately, however, he provided a variant account, in the so-called Pickwick Papers. These were memoranda he wrote to himself, and kept to himself, on the stationery of Kansas City's Pickwick Hotel, a nondescript hostelry where he occasionally stayed when his schedule obliged him to spend the night in the city. According to one memo in Truman's handwriting, Pendergast was furious and called Truman a sucker who was passing up a chance to get rich. "Harry," he said, "your honor isn't worth a pinch of warm snuff." But Truman stuck to his guns in the face of Pendergast's scorn.

Despite such encounters, Truman never disparaged Tom Pendergast, even in his private memos. The big boss was "a real man," Truman wrote, someone who kept his word, though "he gives in very seldom and usually on a sure thing." As for Pendergast, no doubt he would have preferred that road contracts go to his friends and allies, like those he had assembled to meet Truman. But he could afford to indulge Truman on this point since in addition to helping preserve Truman's reputation, Pendergast's own concrete company, which dominated the local road building market, would get fat on these projects, never mind who got the contract.

Still, as his jottings in the Pickwick Papers made clear, during the time of his judgeship, Truman was plagued by self-doubt. In these notes, he confessed to putting "a lot of no account sons of bitches" on the county payroll and to winking at some dubious expenditures. "Am I an administrator or not?" he asked himself. "Or am I just a crook?" One answer from an influential and disinterested observer in Jackson County was provided by the anti-Pendergast *Kansas City Star*. In endorsing Truman's U.S. Senate candidacy in 1934, the paper asserted that he was "a capable and honest public official" and "a man of unimpeachable character and integrity." The backing of the *Star* reflected Truman's ability as presiding judge to walk the tightrope between the strictures of his conscience and the needs of his constituents on one hand and the pressures of the Pendergast organization on the other.

Another challenge for Truman's political skills and those of other

Missouri Democrats was to gain support of the state's black voters despite their traditional loyalty to the GOP. In 1926, the year Harry Truman ran for presiding judge of Jackson County, Missouri Democrats, mindful that the furor over the Klan had made blacks more sensitive and sophisticated about civil rights issues, broadened their state party platform. For the first time, the document included a promise to improve school conditions for blacks as well as for whites. Another argument the Democrats offered echoed the claim often made by Missouri blacks themselves: that Republican strength in the state depended heavily on black votes. The state's Democrats bluntly asked blacks to consider what benefit they got from the GOP's exploitation.

Meanwhile, at the local level, Kansas City Democrats saw to it that blacks got a share of patronage and also pushed for improvements in schools and municipal hospitals used by blacks. By 1926, by one reckoning, Democratic administrations in Kansas City and Jackson County had appointed hundreds of blacks to positions throughout city and county government. They had also built homes for elderly blacks and for wayward black youths. The 1926 elections brought evidence that these efforts were beginning to pay off. In St. Louis, for the first time, a black entered a Democratic congressional primary, and though defeated by a prominent businessman, he got more than 30 percent of the vote.

Many blacks in the North, particularly those who had lived there longer, retained their allegiance to the Republicans. But Democrats were able to make significant inroads among newcomers, aided by the apparent disinterest of Republican leaders, most of whom seemed to take black support for granted. This was particularly true in the Pendergast machine's Kansas City and elsewhere in Missouri. That was the complaint of C. A. Franklin, editor of the *Kansas City Call,* the city's leading black newspaper. A staunch Republican who would a few years later become a supporter and friend of Democrat Harry Truman, Franklin warned Republican governor Arthur Hyde that blacks must receive "good treatment" and be made the focus of voter registration drives if they were to be kept in the Republican fold. Other black Republicans echoed this view. Blacks "can no longer be hoodwinked into the acceptance of a five dollar bill upon election day, a ground hog dinner or an opossum supper as a reward for our efforts to advance the Republican clause," a black Republican asserted publicly at a 1924 Lincoln Day dinner.

Indifference and consequently impatience—that was the pattern for GOP relations with black Americans across the country in those days, following the example of the first postwar Republican president, Warren G. Harding. The quintessential middle-class man of the twentieth-century Midwest, Harding believed in getting along by going along, without making a fuss or muss. A small-town newspaper publisher, he was a trustee of the Trinity Baptist Church, a member of the board of directors of almost every enterprise of consequence in Marion, Ohio, and a leader of fraternal organizations and charitable causes. He harbored no ill feeling toward anyone and instead sought to make friends on all sides. So pliant was he that his own father was said to have remarked that "it's a good thing Warren wasn't a woman or he would be pregnant all the time." Harding surely wished black Americans well, not woe, as he might have put it. But one of the last things in the world he had in mind was to use the majesty and power of the federal government to disrupt the racial order that had prevailed since the Civil War.

The fact that black political leaders had been drawn to Harding's candidacy, failing to recognize the improbability of his championing any unpopular cause, was a measure of their desperation and embitterment. Harding was perfectly willing to string black leaders along. He met with some, notably James Weldon Johnson—lawyer, poet, and diplomat, the first person of color to actually run the NAACP—and Robert Moton, the head of Tuskegee Institute. After hearing their complaints about the Klan and lynching and their pleas for an interracial commission, he called on Congress to eradicate "the stain of barbaric lynching" from the nation. Even Du Bois was impressed, calling it "the strongest statement ever made by a president in a message to Congress."

But Harding never mentioned the subject again in public.

A federal ban on lynching, for which Harding had called, authored by Republican representative Leonidas Dyer of Missouri, passed the House of Representatives. But it was filibustered to death in the Senate while Harding ignored pleas from black leaders for him to put his prestige behind the bill, which, if nothing else, would have helped call public attention to the issue.

Harding's successor, Calvin Coolidge, did nothing to improve black relations with the GOP, nor did Herbert Hoover, who followed Coolidge. Black visitors to the White House were rare during the Republican era. Hoover would on occasion admit groups of some distinction, such as the famed Fisk University Jubilee Singers, but he refused the normal courtesy of posing for a photograph with them. Harder to take for blacks was Hoover's nomination of Judge John J. Parker of North Carolina for the Supreme Court. Despite protests because of racist statements Parker had made while running for governor, Hoover stuck to guns, and Parker was defeated 41 to 39. The controversy reverberated in Missouri, where the state's Republican senator supported Parker while his Democratic colleague voted with the majority to defeat the nomination. By the time the presidencies of Harding and his two Republican successors ended, an

NAACP study concluded that rather than abolishing segregation in the federal bureaucracy, as blacks had hoped, Republicans had maintained it, and in some instances had extended its grip.

The consequent disillusionment of black leaders with the GOP was typified by the attitude of publisher C. A. Franklin, who had seemed to perfectly fit the GOP mold when he came to Kansas City from Denver in 1913 and launched the *Call*. An admirer of Booker T. Washington, Franklin believed that civil rights for blacks would grow out of economic success, which required devotion to the Protestant work ethic. He did not hesitate to chastise his own race for the difficulties they faced. If black labor was not in demand, he contended, this was because "it is not responsible."

However, over the years, Franklin's affection for the GOP began to chill in response to Democratic efforts to appeal to blacks, and also to what he viewed as Republican efforts to exploit the racist feelings stirred by the Klan. In the 1920s, Franklin saw evidence of this at the 1928 GOP convention, which happened to be held in his home base of Kansas City, when the Republican Party announced that for the first time it would segregate housing for black and white delegates. When Republican leaders ignored black protests and gave what Franklin regarded as only cursory treatment to racial issues in their national platform, the *Call* headlined its indignation: "LILY WHITISM NOW OFFICIAL REPUBLICANISM." By contrast, the *Call* had kind words for Democratic judge Truman, acknowledging his efficiency and honesty on county road development. Coming in for particular praise was Truman's support for the home for the aged and a home for delinquent girls. Accompanying a 1928 *Call* article on the home for the aged, headlined "Jackson County Shows Its Great Heart of Love," was a prominent photo of the presiding judge. According to Missouri law and custom, both institutions were segregated, but this did not diminish Franklin's appreciation of Truman's efforts on their behalf, which he further demonstrated in a 1930 editorial endorsing Truman's reelection as presiding judge under the headline "County Cares for the Sick."

The home for girls was a new institution, a brainchild of Truman's, who had proposed a bond issue in 1928 to finance its construction. The bond issue passed, but staffing the home was delayed by a dispute with a Democratic leader in Truman's old eastern district, who wanted to control the hiring. In 1930, buoyed by his own clean-government reputation and Tom Pendergast's blessing, Truman won reelection as presiding judge by an overwhelming margin. That victory ended the dispute over staffing, and the home opened in 1931. Moreover, despite efforts to cut funding to both the home for the aged and the home for girls as hard times set in, Truman managed to avoid deep slashes in their budgets.

Democratic prospects for taking advantage of rift between blacks and Republicans seemed heightened by the Democratic nominee in 1928, Al Smith. That Smith himself, as the first major-party Catholic nominee for the White House, was the target of vicious religious prejudice gave his candidacy the potential for striking a symbolic blow against racial prejudice. There were reasons beyond symbolism for Smith to seek black support. Not only because of his religion but also because of his opposition to Prohibition, Smith was anathema in the South, where, as *Time* noted, he was regarded as a "knave of Rum and Romanism wearing the stripes of Tammany." This made him more dependent than other Democrats on the urban North, thus increasing the incentive for wooing black voters.

Hoping to exploit this opportunity, Smith persuaded Walter White, then a rising star in the NAACP, to help him win over blacks after promising White he was serious about the effort. White and James Weldon Johnson drafted a statement for Smith appealing directly to blacks, but it was rejected on the advice of Arkansas senator Joe Robinson, Smith's running mate, and his Southern colleagues, who feared alienating the South. Fed up, White quit the Smith campaign and went back to the NAACP.

Given the depth of Smith's difficulties in the South, if he had been less dominated by prejudice Robinson might well have considered risking the displeasure of some Southern whites on race because he had little to lose. Besides his religion, Smith was bedeviled by charges that he had a weakness for hard liquor, which supposedly accounted for his opposition to Prohibition. Robinson's desperation about these charges, along with the religious bigotry, was reflected by his response in a campaign speech in Dallas. "The statement has been made that he is a drunkard," said Robinson, pausing for effect. Then he shouted at the top of his voice: "THERE'S NOT ONE WORD OF TRUTH IN IT!" All that exercise demonstrated, besides the strength of Robinson's vocal chords, was the near impossibility of effectively refuting such gossip.

Despite Robinson's veto, Democrats still tried harder than before to get black votes. A Smith for President Colored League helped pull in more blacks—about 27 percent of the black vote in Chicago, up from 10 percent in 1924, for example—but nowhere near a majority anywhere.

The 1932 election seemed to offer Democrats an even better opportunity. Despite the onset of the Great Depression and Hoover's failure to reach out to blacks any more than had his predecessors in the White House, the Republican nominee ran far ahead of Roosevelt among blacks in many cities and in some did better than he had in 1928. Many blacks, considering Roosevelt's strong ties to the South and his choice of Texan congressman and Jim Crow stalwart John Nance Garner as his running mate, agreed with a colleague of Walter White's, who called FDR "the weakest possible candidate." One analyst concluded that in that bleak year, Hoover and his party blacks broke with the GOP in smaller numbers than any other traditional Republican cohort.

A notable exception to this pattern was Tom Pendergast's Kansas City, where Hoover carried only two of the forty black precincts, and the city's two Negro wards gave FDR more than 75 percent of their vote. That compared favorably with St. Louis, where Hoover still got a majority of the black vote, though smaller than in 1928. The Democratic success was a reflection of Pendergast's assiduous efforts to serve blacks as he served white constituents—efforts in which Truman and other Democrats participated.

Every Christmas, the Pendergast organization fed thousands of the poor and unemployed, many of them blacks. In 1920, when the construction of a new hospital that would provide care for blacks stalled, blacks blamed the city manager and appealed to Pendergast. Boss Tom saw to it that the hospital was finished. When a black man was lynched in Maryville, Missouri, in 1931, Democrats condemned the killing and introduced an antilynching bill that the Republican governor vetoed. These responses probably meant more to blacks than they would have to whites because blacks were accustomed to being ignored by most politicians. Blacks shrugged off criticism that Tom Pendergast ruled like a despot. "It is not how much power T. J. Pendergast has," C. A. Franklin editorialized, "but what he does with it that concerns people."

Meanwhile, in the wake of his substantial reelection victory in 1930, Truman, looking up at the next rung in the ladder, set his mind and heart on the governorship. It was a one-term job that had generally been a dead end, but it was the first available opportunity as 1932 approached. It was not to be. Pendergast wanted someone else, a Kansas City lawyer named Francis Wilson, who, by winning the Democratic primary, made Pendergast the top Democrat not just in Kansas City but in all of Missouri. Even Wilson's death three weeks before the election did not open the door for Truman. Pendergast picked Judge Guy B. Park, a close friend of Wilson's, who in 1932 won an election that probably no Democrat could have lost.

It was not until May 1934 that Pendergast settled Truman's future by making him his choice for the U.S. Senate seat. In his last Pickwick Papers memorandum, Truman wrote that if God willed his election, he would pray for the wisdom to do the job. But in addition to the help of Providence, he needed the resources that Pendergast provided, as well as his own relentless energy, to win the Democratic primary, in which his chief opponent was a six-term congressman from St. Louis, Jacob Mulligan.

In the primary vote, the Pendergast Kansas City machine bested its rival operation in St. Louis. Truman, despite broken ribs suffered in an auto accident the day he launched his campaign, and with the help of

Pendergast's handpicked Democratic governor, won the outstate vote. Kicking off his campaign for the general election, Truman announced his total allegiance to FDR, and he fired a populist blast at his Republican foe, whom he branded "a rugged individualist, imbued with the cruelties of jungle strife."

The outcome, with the New Deal offering salvation to a stricken land, was never in doubt. Truman carried 60 percent of the vote. Joining in the near landslide were the state's black voters. They were pleased not only with Truman's eight-year performance as presiding county judge, but also with his efforts to help blacks find jobs in his brief stint as state director of reemployment, a post the New Deal had given him. "If ever a man deserved public confidence on the basis of the record made in the public's service that man is Harry S. Truman," wrote Franklin in the *Call*. Black voters evidently agreed because Truman got nearly 90 percent of their vote.

In his prestigious new job in the nation's capital, Truman would have to deal with a flood of problems far removed from Jackson County. But he would not forget the *Call's* words or those votes.

4

★ ★ ★ ★ ★

BACK FROM THE DEAD

As Truman started his third year in the Senate, Franklin Roosevelt, battling for the life of the New Deal, submitted to Congress his plan to restructure the Supreme Court. Seemingly at the height of his powers, the newly reelected president was confident of success. Loyalist Truman gave the measure all-out support. However, FDR's bold assault on the court turned into the first serious mistake of his presidency as members of the U.S. Senate steadily turned against it. In the end, FDR's dream of packing the court found enemies in both parties and every section of the nation. No one fought the bill more intensely than a group of Southern senators who regarded the Democratic Party as the political fortress of the segregated South.

North Carolina's Josiah Bailey, one of the New Deal's fiercest Senate foes, was quick to make up his mind. "Roosevelt is determined to get the Negro vote, and I do not have to tell you what *this* means," Bailey wrote to a friend in the wake of the unveiling of the court plan in February 1937, barely a fortnight after Roosevelt had been sworn in for his second term. Bailey soon found allies among other influential Southern senators, notably Georgia's Walter George, Virginia's Harry Byrd, South Carolina's Ellison "Cotton Ed" Smith, and Virginia's Carter Glass. The Virginian called the plan an attempt to "rape the Supreme Court." What these Dixie lawmakers feared was that the president would use his expanded appointive power under his plan to pick justices who would overturn segregation and thus win more black votes for the New Deal. More objective legislators might argue that they were way off base. Desegregating the South was nowhere on Roosevelt's cluttered agenda. Yet the fixation of the Southern foes of the court with race held an important lesson for Harry Truman.

For the Southerners who sought to preserve the racial order in the South, race was the prism through which they looked at nearly every national issue. This was a force Truman would have to confront throughout his career in Washington. Moreover, the anxiety of the Southerners amounted to more than just paranoia. For they fully appreciated that as entrenched as the racist codes that governed their region seemed, they were part of a fragile structure that could not long withstand a tide of economic and social change.

Southern resistance even to minuscule change was illustrated by the reaction encountered by future New Dealer Aubrey Williams, when, as a social activist during the Hoover administration, he had visited the South. Williams, who later served on the advisory panel to FDR's National Youth Administration, urged Southern planters to distribute seeds to their black field hands so they could supplement their meager food supply. "They did not want their 'niggers' planting gardens," Williams recalled, because they feared it might make them a tad less dependent on the feudal structure that governed the relations between the planters and their field hands. Now Southerners worried that the changes the New Deal was bringing about far transcended the sowing of vegetable seeds.

During his first term, FDR had done little to threaten the barriers of racism behind which Southern Democrats had entrenched themselves. "When Roosevelt came in 1933 there were more things to worry about than what happened to civil rights," Tom Corcoran, who with Ben Cohen drafted the most important early New Deal economic reforms, told an interviewer. Given the ethos of most politicians and of the American public, it would have been unusual if Roosevelt had paid more attention to "Negroes," the prevailing term in use at the time. Ignoring the vast influx of blacks to the North, the president, along with most Americans, thought of the "Negro problem," to the extent that they thought about it at all, as a Southern problem. And besides, in the midst of the Depression, when Americans in every part of the country, black and white, struggled to get by, it made no political sense to single out the difficulties of blacks. What this reasoning did not take into account, to the despair and frustration of black people, was that for more than half a century, blacks had suffered under a special burden of oppression and injustice that even in good times had left them at a terrible disadvantage. Black leaders well understood this disinterest in racial problems by FDR and nearly all his team. But they also realized that their constituents were in desperate need of help from the programs the New Deal was launching, and that many

New Dealers wanted them to share in this largesse. So for these blacks, among them Walter White, head of the NAACP, and their supporters, the priority became getting blacks a piece of the economic action, with racial issues taking second place. "We had no racial doctrine," said Will Alexander, an early New Deal official, whose origins in Morrisville, Missouri, were similar to Truman's roots. The one rule that was followed was that "we were not to discriminate in the distribution of the benefits." So far as Jim Crow was concerned, "We accepted the pattern," admitted Alexander.

But some liberals and black leaders believed that the way to alter that pattern was through votes. In 1936, a group of independent liberals and blacks seeking to gather political support sent out speakers and canvassers to the ghettos and rural slums and distributed, among other literature, a pamphlet titled "Has the Roosevelt New Deal Helped the Colored Citizen?" Election Day made the answer clear. In black precincts around the country, Roosevelt, who won 60 percent of the popular vote nationwide, piled up majorities of 70 to 80 percent among blacks. But what was good news to New Dealers and their black allies had a very different and ominous reading to Democrats below the Mason–Dixon Line, like Josiah Bailey. In those numbers, Southern Democrats thought they saw the handwriting on the political wall.

Senator Bailey, for one, did not restrict his fears to private correspondence. In the course of denouncing the court plan in a speech in Chapel Hill, he accused FDR's interior secretary, Harold Ickes, of trying to break down segregation in the South. Thrust onto the defensive, Ickes wrote to Bailey to assure him that he had misstated Ickes's position. "While I have always been interested in seeing that the Negro has a fair deal," Ickes recorded in his diary, "I have never dissipated my strength against the particularly stone wall of segregation. After all we can't force people on each other who do not like each other." Ickes's comments suggest that in their fears of how Roosevelt might use a stacked Supreme Court to battle racism, Bailey and Glass were far ahead of their time, and far ahead of Roosevelt, and in this case, of Ickes too.

To be sure, FDR appointed enough blacks to federal agency jobs so that many of them met informally, calling themselves the Black Cabinet, to ponder ways to influence government policy. They had no authority to act; their biggest impact stemmed from the individual efforts of their leader and "mother confessor," Mary McLeod Bethune. One of seventeen children of a sharecropper, who had worked her way through two years of Chicago's Moody Bible Institute, she was not cowed by authority. "We have been eating the feet and the head of the chicken long enough," she told FDR at a White House meeting. "The time has come when we want some white meat." The president, by Bethune's account, was moved to tears but not to action. Of more practical consequence was the alliance Bethune managed to establish with Eleanor Roosevelt, whom she persuaded to address national conferences on the problems of blacks, and of young blacks in particular.

Throughout his presidency, Roosevelt would frustrate blacks pushing for civil rights, refusing even to offer more than pro forma backing for a federal law against lynching. Politics aside, Roosevelt had no cultural or ideological connection with the black drive for equality. He had no personal friends among blacks. The blacks he knew best were Graham Jackson, an accordionist who played for him at Warm Springs, and Irvin and Elizabeth McDuffie, who served as his valet and maid. Irvin McDuffie never talked race with his boss, but his wife told Roosevelt that she was going to serve as his "SASOCPA, self-appointed secretary on colored people's affairs." Indeed, her lobbying apparently helped persuade the president to pardon a black fifty-one-year-old former soldier imprisoned at Leavenworth Penitentiary after the 1919 Houston race riot, part of the racial violence that erupted around the country after World War I. Because of his many visits to Warm Springs, Georgia, where he had established a center for treatment of polio, Roosevelt regarded the Peach State as a second home. He easily adjusted to the segregation governing Southern life. Indeed, the Warm Springs center did not admit black polio victims.

Though first lady Eleanor Roosevelt was far more sympathetic to the cause of racial justice, she was hobbled by the reluctance of most New Dealers to challenge the intransigence of the South. When she was invited to attend an NAACP protest rally against lynching, she stayed away from the event after FDR's secretary, Missy LeHand, scribbled the warning advice: "President says this is dynamite."

Even if FDR took no short-term action to help blacks, Southerners like Senator Bailey still feared that the long-term impact of his programs would bring more and more blacks into Democratic ranks as their economic mobility increased and their status improved. Therefore, they did what they could to obstruct him, often finding common cause with many Republicans. Their resistance mounted despite Roosevelt's remarkable political successes that followed his defeat of Herbert Hoover in 1932, and that spilled over into succeeding elections. When Harry Truman took his seat in the U.S. Senate in January 1935, he was one of thirteen new Democrats in that chamber, nine of whom had replaced Republican incumbents. This gain, along with the addition of ten seats in the House of Representatives, shattered a seventy-year precedent. Not since the Civil War had a party won the presidency, as the Democrats had done in 1932 led by FDR, and added to their numbers in Congress in the following election. Just as remarkable were the returns from the 1936 vote. When Truman came back to the Senate at the opening of the Seventy-fourth Congress in 1937, he was part of an immense personal triumph by Roosevelt. The thirty-second president had won office by a bigger popular and electoral vote margin than any of his modern predecessors. Moreover, his success extended beyond his own individual triumphs, endowing his party with almost an embarrassment of riches. Adding to their already substantial majorities in both branches of the previous Congress, the Democrats gained twelve seats in the House of Representatives, giving them three-quarters of that body in the Seventy-fifth Congress, along with seven seats in the Senate. This gave the president's party almost 80 percent control of that chamber. When Roosevelt himself returned to Washington promptly on the day after the election, tens of thousands of supporters, many job holders in the burgeoning New Deal bureaucracies and others simply admiring citizens, lined the streets, cheering wildly as the smiling president waved at them from his open car. The scene reminded the veteran Washington journalists Joseph Alsop and Turner Catledge of imperial Rome. "One wondered," they wrote, "why the vanquished Republican candidate, accompanied by a selection of Du Ponts and newspaper editors, did not follow the presidential cortege in chains."

Yet as Roosevelt fully realized from his years in national politics, the New Deal, which he had fathered and to which Senator Harry Truman had pledged allegiance, faced mounting trouble. A number of reasons accounted for this dour expectation, but the most fundamental causes could be traced back to the founding of the Republic. The men who gathered in Philadelphia in the sweltering summer of 1787 to remake the ramshackle Articles of Confederation into a durable structure were vexed not only by the heat but by substantive dilemmas. Though wary of government, they felt obliged to strengthen the existing feeble regime. Committed to the principle of popular sovereignty, they nevertheless mistrusted human nature and doubted the wisdom of the populace. Fearful of monarchy and dictatorship, they also dreaded the tyranny of the majority.

Confronted with this array of perils, James Madison, the chief architect of the Constitution, created a design that would convert the human frailty that worried him and his colleagues into a self-generated restraint on power. Short, slim, and introverted, Madison was an unlikely figure to dominate a gathering of dynamic and powerful personalities. But the little Virginian more than compensated for his shortcomings with disciplined rhetoric and meticulous reasoning. To curb the will of the majority, Madison gave the Congress and the president separate constituencies and armed each with power to check and balance the other. One house of Congress could reject legislation approved by the other house; even if both passed a bill, the president could veto it. Madison and his cohorts also created the Supreme Court, whose justices ultimately assumed for themselves the power to checkmate either or both of the other branches. The inevitable clash of personal rivalries produced by this design, Madison believed, would make these restrictions work. "Ambition must be made to counter-act ambition," he wrote. "The interest of the man must be connected with the Constitutional rights of the place." That was indeed the way things worked out—a lesson learned by Madison himself when he was in the White House, and by every succeeding president, including FDR. Meanwhile, the powers of government and the demands placed upon it expanded beyond anything imagined by Madison and his colleagues. But their eighteenth-century legacy lingered in the strictures of the Constitution, warping the political system that Franklin Roosevelt had to contend with.

While the Great Depression led to the aggrandizement of federal power during Roosevelt's first years in the White House, his awareness of the structural limitations on his authority restrained his governance. As a result of his reluctance to commit himself ideologically, his programs lacked coherence; he relied on instinct more than intellect, and he liked to play off ideas and advisers against each other. Roosevelt could not have been greatly surprised when in 1935 he struck out at the much-abused system of public utility holding companies and ran into a hailstorm of opposition, even within his own party. These included a score or more of relatively moderate Democratic senators who had not previously opposed the New Deal, among them Harry Truman's Missouri colleague, Senator Bennett Clark. Truman took the opposite side and fought vigorously for the White House proposal, though he had been in the Senate barely three months. His stand was all the more striking because it pitted him not only against Clark, but also against utility interests allied with Tom Pendergast. "Some measure of protection must be given the investing public against the blue sky operators and the unscrupulous promoters who have used the holding companies as a means to rob the small investor," he declared. FDR wheedled the House and Senate into a face-saving compromise. But his conservative opposition had learned they could resist the New Deal and survive to fight another day.

One battle Roosevelt chose to avoid was over civil rights. This was so despite pressure from his allies and from blacks. In FDR's first two years, civil rights had not even appeared on his legislative horizon because of the urgency of the nation's economic problems and Roosevelt's lack of interest in the issue. But in January 1935, as the Seventy-fourth Congress opened with freshman senator Harry Truman in attendance, Democratic senator Robert Wagner of New York introduced an antilynching bill. "Cotton Ed" Smith immediately launched a defense of lynching as needed "to protect the fair womanhood of the South from beasts."

Liberal lawmakers pleaded with Roosevelt to intervene, and so did Walter White, for whom Eleanor Roosevelt wangled an interview with her husband at the White House. White ran into a stone wall. Telling White what he already knew, Roosevelt pointed out that Southerners by reason of seniority chaired or had key roles on most Senate and House committees. "If I come out for the anti-lynching bill now they will block every bill I ask Congress to pass to keep America from collapsing," he claimed. "I can't afford to take that risk." Roosevelt's explanation may have overstated that case. But White was in no position to quibble with the president, so with FDR on the sidelines, Southerners succeeded in filibustering the lynching bill to death.

When Wagner introduced a new version of his antilynching bill in January 1937, the increased Democratic majorities in the Congress gave supporters reason to hope. But they knew they would face a filibuster, and to break that barricade, they would need help from the president. Lynchings continued to be a horror and disgrace to the nation and to the South, where most of them took place. Since FDR had taken office, no fewer than eighty-three blacks had been put to death without any semblance of legality. Indeed, things had gotten so bad that according to a Gallup poll, antilynching action was supported by most Americans, including 65 percent of Southerners. Moreover, Wagner's new bill was designed to give minimum offense to Southern sensibilities. Instead of making lynching a federal crime, the bill stipulated that if local officials had not brought a prosecution within thirty days of a lynching, the federal justice department could bring charges against them. Still, that was not enough to mollify the stalwarts of the South. South Carolina senator James Byrnes branded it "a bill to destroy the Democratic Party." Georgia's Richard Russell proclaimed that Wagner's bill was designed "to lynch the last remaining evidence of State's rights and sovereignty."

The bill passed the House easily in April 1937. In the Senate, the legislation moved to the top of the legislative calendar for 1938. Senator Truman was prepared to vote for the bill when the roll was called, though according to journalist Samuel Lubell, Truman told a fellow senator, "You know I'm against this bill, but if it comes to a vote, I'll have to be for it," adding that "the Negro vote in Kansas City and St. Louis is too important." Then Truman supposedly added sheepishly, "Maybe the thing for me to do is to be playing poker this afternoon." This widely repeated story, which Truman critics point to as evidence of Truman's duplicity and cynicism, was based on a Lubell interview with an anonymous source identified only as a "leader of the Southern opposition," a description that could apply to any number of lawmakers. It appeared for the first time in Lubell's book, *The Future of American Politics*, published in 1951, thirteen years after the purported conversation took place. It is probably true that Truman had conflicting feelings about civil rights issues, but it is hard to understand why he would whine about such feelings in such detail to other lawmakers who probably already understood his situation. At any rate, the circumstances raise the question of why Lubell waited so long to publish such a telling anecdote. The vagueness of the sourcing and the remarkable word-for-word recall of long-ago remarks raise the possibility that this story, with its ring of apocrypha, was embellished and recounted to Lubell years after the events of 1938 by a Southern leader eager to try to discredit Harry Truman, who by this time as president had become a champion of the civil rights cause. At any rate, the story builds toward an anticlimax. When Wagner's bill got to the floor, it was met with a sustained filibuster by Southern senators. With FDR unwilling to intervene, Wagner withdrew the bill, so Truman never cast the vote against it that he had apologized for in advance. Presumably Roosevelt, if he had been challenged, would have rationalized his inaction on the same basis he had provided to Walter White three years earlier, that he could not afford to risk offending the Southern leaders on Capitol Hill.

FDR's cautious stance on civil rights, which he had explained to White in 1935, contrasted sharply with his frontal assault on the Supreme Court, one of the boldest gambles in the history of the presidency. Roosevelt may well have felt he had no choice. On May 27, 1935, a date that became known to New Dealers as Black Monday, the court handed down a series of decisions that confirmed the administration's darkest suspicions and fears about the "Nine Old Men" who made up the tribunal. The most severe blow overturned the National Industrial Recovery Act, the foundation of the New Deal. Roosevelt was outraged but also fearful. The broad thrust of the ruling was such that the president and his aides felt, as one of them, Jerome Frank, put it, "that it was going to be impossible for him to carry out his program." But the court was not through yet. In 1936, it dealt another blow to the New Deal's underpinning, overturning, among other statutes, the law establishing the Agricultural Adjustment Administration, the principal agency created to deal with the farm depression, probably the hardest-hit sector in all the economy. The president mulled over possibilities to hit back but kept his own counsel, avoiding any discussion of the court's impact in his 1936 campaign for reelection.

In the wake of the election, mindful that the court would soon be deciding cases crucial to the New Deal's future, including testing the validity of the Social Security Act and the Wagner Labor Relations Act, he began to plan his response. Confiding only in Attorney General Homer

Cummings, who was unlikely to disapprove of whatever FDR wanted to do, he devised a scheme that would have done credit to the antic cartoonist Rube Goldberg. It would allow FDR to increase the size of the court by naming a new justice for each incumbent who had reached the age of seventy, up to a total of six. Indeed, there were already six at that age. The most ingenious aspect of the plan, or so FDR and Cummings believed, was that it relied on the argument not that the court was too conservative in its views, but that it was undermanned and needed the additional younger members to catch up with its work.

This rationale turned out to contribute to the demise of the proposal when Chief Justice Charles Evans Hughes told the Senate that the court was "fully abreast of its work." Adding new justices, Hughes contended, would only make the court's decision making more cumbersome. Then, that spring, the Court pulled the rug from under its liberal critics by upholding the constitutionality of the minimum wage act, the Wagner Act, and then Social Security. To some, it seemed that the justices' more liberal tone reflected political convenience, leading one New Dealer to quip, "A switch in time saves nine."

Missouri senator Truman, though some believe he had misgivings about the plan, kept them to himself. His public support for the president's proposal never wavered, even when a Gallup poll showed Missourians in opposition 52 percent to 48 percent, and the senior senator from his state, Bennett Clark, had announced his opposition. Unfazed, Truman explained his lonely stance to his constituents. "The Constitution doesn't need an amendment at all," he wrote them. "It merely needs a liberal interpretation." In an ill-conceived attempt to argue that the court plan was not as unpopular as it might seem, Truman suggested that most ordinary folks did back the president because the mail he got in support of FDR was most often scribbled on cheap paper. Comments of opponents, on the other hand, were usually typewritten on good-quality stationery. That logic offered an irresistible target to some wag on the *Kansas City Times* editorial board, who wrote, "Down with the economic royalists who use typewriters is Senator Truman's slogan."

But Truman's steadfast support, along with that of a hard core of New Deal loyalists, was not nearly enough to buck the rising tide against FDR's plan. Roosevelt ultimately had to accept a humiliating compromise. In later years, Roosevelt's supporters would claim that though he had lost the battle over his plan in the Senate, he had won the war over the Supreme Court. They pointed out that the high tribunal, now largely staffed with FDR's own appointees, gave the green light to almost every reform he proposed that Congress passed. But as history would show, FDR's chancy thrust at the court had helped to catalyze a formidable combination of conservative lawmakers of both parties, who were now convinced that they could stop liberals in their tracks. This daunting legacy would shadow the future of FDR's court fight ally when Harry Truman found himself in the Oval Office.

In return for Truman's loyalty on the Supreme Court matter and a host of other New Deal priorities, FDR treated the junior senator from Missouri much like a poor relation—or, as Truman put it himself to White House press secretary Steve Early, "an office boy." When it came to patronage, the White House almost invariably favored Bennett Clark, who had been less directly tied to the unsavory Pendergast. Clark also had numerous social and political contacts stemming from his father's prominent career on Capitol Hill. Truman was in no position to put on such airs, even if he had chosen to.

Unlike most of his colleagues, he had no family money to draw on, and was forced to subsist on his $10,000 salary, which had to cover the expense of his household in the capital as well as his home in Independence. To buy furniture and rent a piano, he had to borrow money. Years later, speaking to a banking group, he thanked the Washington institution that had "been willing to float a little slow paper for me." In addition to providing for himself, Bess, and their daughter, Margaret, Truman also helped to support his mother and had to worry about the mortgage on the family farm. Behind on the payments, in a lapse of discretion, he arranged a loan from the Jackson County school fund for $35,000, about one-third more than the farm's value. This amounted to a violation of state law, as the *Kansas City Star* pointed out. Ultimately, the county foreclosed the mortgage. This stress, combined with the pressure of the Senate, took its toll. Truman was sensible enough to get himself admitted to the military hospital at Hot Springs, Arkansas, three times from 1937 to 1943, complaining of nausea, headaches, and general debilitation. Truman welcomed the medical attention. "Excellent treatment by everyone," he wrote on the Army medical report. "Remarkable rest and very pleasant environment." He wrote to Bess Truman, "The staff here really know their business. I've about made up my mind to do it once a year."

As trying as the legislative and financial pressures were, he probably found them easier to bear than the odium stemming from his Pendergast link. Truman himself rejected the idea that there was anything wrong with Pendergast. "He was a boss, an American political boss," he told an interviewer. "You've got to have leadership in politics and a boss is only a leader." Nevertheless, others saw things differently. From the beginning of his Senate career, he was "under a cloud," said Victor Messall, who became his top Senate staffer and served through his first term. Indeed, Messall turned down Truman's offer of a job the first time it was made.

"Here was a guy—a punk sent up by gangsters," he later recalled. "I told myself I'd lose my reputation if I worked for him." Messall changed his mind after his second meeting with Truman. So did many other senators who at first shunned him. By his fifth year in the Senate, Truman had become one of the most popular members of the so-called world's most exclusive club, reflecting his own outgoing style and lack of pretension. His friendships cut across party and ideological lines: Among his chums were ardent New Dealers like New York's Robert Wagner, labor-baiting Democrats like Vice President Garner, and Republican leaders like Charles McNary of Oregon.

Truman's congenial persona with his Senate colleagues contrasted with the harsh edge of his populist rhetoric when he found a suitable target. His labors on a Senate investigation of railroad financing gave him all the ammunition he needed. He fired his first volley in June 1937 when he recalled that the legendary outlaw Jesse James had to rise before sunrise and risk his life to make off with a mere $3,000 from the Rock Island Railroad. Truman noted that modern holding companies had made off with $70 million from the same line. "Senators can see," he added, "what pikers Mr. James and his crowd were compared to some real artists."

He unleashed another Bryanite barrage a few months later, targeting Wall Street law firms and their influence on the nation's economy in a speech that surely would have delighted the Great Commoner himself. "It probably will catalogue me as a radical," he warned Bess in advance. "But it will be what I think." He took out after the high-priced, high-powered law firms of New York and Chicago, whose conniving he claimed had ruined the railroads at great profit to themselves, reeling off their names and the fat fees they had received. "Do you see how it pays to know all about these things from the inside?" he asked. "How these gentlemen, the highest of the high hats in the legal profession, resort to tricks that would make an ambulance chaser in a coroner's court blush with shame?"

The speech thrust Truman to stage center of the national political theater. The *New York Times* reported the assaults against the railways by Truman and others on page one, and Truman's name was in the headlines: "Truman attacks reorganization lawyers." Labor leaders and liberal reformers sat up and took notice. A few months later, when the railroads petitioned the Interstate Commerce Commission to approve a 15 percent cut in the wages paid its workers, Truman lambasted the proposal. The railroads had been plundered by Wall Street operatives, he charged, while rail workers were highly efficient. The ICC rejected the wage cut, and Truman had made an important ally in rail labor.

Just as he seemed to be hitting his stride in the Senate, three years before he would have to run for reelection, Truman faced serious trouble in a politician's most vulnerable spot: his own backyard. The U.S. attorney for Kansas City, Maurice Milligan, was probing into the excesses of the Pendergast machine, prosecuting Boss Tom's operatives for vote fraud and racketeering, and making it plain that Pendergast himself was his ultimate target. Just as he had been in his early career, Pendergast had continued as a major force in Truman's life in the Senate. Truman made no bones about their closeness, and he gave a photo of the boss a prominent place on his Senate office wall. If he knew that Pendergast liked to tell Kansas City visitors that Truman was his "office boy" in the nation's capital, Truman did not seem to let that bother him.

He and Pendergast appeared to operate as a sort of limited partnership. Pendergast did not ordinarily involve himself in substantive issues on which the senator had to vote. Mostly what the boss wanted from his "office boy" was occasional intervention with the Washington bureaucracy to help out Pendergast friends with business interests at stake. When these friends benefited, they would generally express their gratitude to Pendergast, often in material terms. Pendergast could rationalize such dealings as also benefiting the state of Missouri or Jackson County. There is no evidence that Truman himself was rewarded for such activities, which were common in Washington, except to stay in Pendergast's good graces. For a long time Pendergast was satisfied with such "honest graft," as defined by Tammany Hall's fabled George Washington Plunkett. But then he found himself forced to reach out for more.

The problem was that Pendergast had to support his powerful addiction, not to liquor or drugs, but to big-time gambling, specifically horse racing. He not only bet on horses, he also bred thoroughbreds, one of which he raced in the Kentucky Derby. This upscale hobby was well within Pendergast's means. What he could not afford were his growing debts to bookmakers with whom he wagered often and not wisely. Constant losses in six figures drove him to outright criminal excesses, such as theft and bribery, including payoffs from underworld kingpins, many of whom seemed to have found an oasis in Jackson County and its environs. These were risks he had not taken before, and the consequent anxiety had forced him into a hospital in 1933, from which he emerged fifty pounds lighter.

It was far easier for Boss Tom to lose weight than to shake his chief pursuer, Milligan, who hounded Pendergast like a latter-day Inspector Javert. Milligan, whose brother, Tuck, had been one of Truman's opponents in the 1934 Democratic primary, had been a long-term foe of Pendergast and all his works. The prosecutor's term expired early in 1938, but Roosevelt and Bennett Clark wanted him reappointed to demonstrate their anticorruption credentials. Truman, at FDR's personal request, chose not to invoke senatorial privilege to block his reappointment. Instead, on February 15, 1938, he made a bitter speech on the Senate floor that demonstrated one of his persistent strengths, personal loyalty, but also illustrated an occasional weakness, poor judgment. "I say to the Senate," Truman averred, "that a Jackson County Democrat has as much chance of a fair trial in the Federal District Court of Western Missouri as a Jew would have in a Hitler Court or a Trotsky follower before Stalin."

Truman had a point; Milligan and his cohorts were engaged in a vendetta against Pendergast and all his works. But Boss Tom had given them the fat in which to fry him. As for Truman, his outburst allowed him the satisfaction of knowing he had not let his friend down. But this tirade did more harm to himself than good for his benefactor in Jackson County. Truman brought down on his head the scorn of the nation's press. "Tom Pendergast may have lost the cemetery vote, but he can't lose Harry Truman," gibed the *New York Times*. Milligan's nomination was confirmed, with Truman casting the only Senate vote against him.

Meanwhile, the vise was closing on the Boss. Missouri's new Democratic governor, Lloyd Stark, who, like Truman, had been a Pendergast protégé, had joined the posse.

Prodded by Stark and Milligan, in April 1939, federal agencies found enough evidence to indict Pendergast for income tax evasion, notably for failure to declare $315,000 in bribes from fire insurance companies. Pendergast pleaded guilty, and the judge showed leniency in sentencing because of his illness. Since 1936, Pendergast had suffered a heart attack and had endured major surgery three times. Boss Tom, for the first time in his and Harry Truman's lives, was out of politics. Now Truman would have to figure out how to get along without him.

As if that was not enough of a hindrance to his reelection chances, another obstacle presented itself in the person of Missouri governor Stark, a man whose ambition exceeded even his impressive résumé. His father, an associate of Luther Burbank, had developed a variety of apple, which he called Stark's Delicious and which made him a wealthy man. Lloyd Stark had taken over the apple business after graduating from the Naval Academy, then served in combat in World War I, helped to found the American Legion, and managed to expand his father's business and wealth even in the midst of the Great Depression. Getting to know Stark in the 1930s through American Legion activities, Truman admired him greatly, boosted his candidacy for governor in 1936, and helped him win Pendergast's endorsement.

As governor, Stark had gotten off to a strong start, expanding welfare and improving highway safety. However, Stark, mindful of Pendergast's legal problems, began distancing himself from the boss. He fired a crooked official close to Pendergast, and in 1938, he backed his own candidate to challenge and defeat Stark's choice for the State Supreme Court. This result further damaged Pendergast's already sagging prestige and helped clear the way for Stark's own advancement. Barred by statute from succeeding himself as governor, he wanted to be the next U.S. senator from Missouri—if he couldn't be president or vice president. In April 1939, in the wake of Pendergast's disgrace, *Life* magazine ran a six-page spread on Stark, linking him to an up-and-coming politician in the GOP, New York's famed racket-busting district attorney, Tom Dewey. The fall of the Boss, *Life* claimed, had catapulted apple grower Stark "right into the presidential ring." For the time being, with the onset of war in Europe in 1939, Stark decided to settle for the Senate and announced his candidacy for that office.

If Truman had heeded the political journalists and other savants, he would have spared himself the trouble and started planning his postsenatorial career. His party's leader in the White House hinted none too subtly that he could have the appointment to a cushy job on the Interstate Commerce Commission. "Tell him to go to hell," Truman responded.

"He is a dead cock in the pit," observed the *St. Louis Post Dispatch.*

However, Truman, except for one brief moment in the wake of his disastrous attempt to block Milligan's reappointment, never seems to have really wavered. On February 3, 1940, he announced his candidacy for renomination, facing the grimmest prospects since his failed 1924 bid for a second term as county judge. Still, he was not without assets, among them his many friends in the Senate. More than a score endorsed his candidacy, and several came to Missouri to campaign for him, thus contravening the suspicion among voters that the national party regarded him as a stepchild. Another big boost came from the Missouri branch of the railroad brotherhoods, with its 50,000 members, who, well remembering Truman's fight to prevent their wages being cut, pledged full-scale support. Still more help, though unintended, came from an unlikely quarter: prosecutor Milligan. Jealous that Stark was claiming credit for deposing Pendergast, and convinced that Truman would make only a token race for reelection, Milligan declared for the Senate, thus splitting the anti-Pendergast vote that otherwise would all have gone to Stark.

As much as Truman was absorbed by his struggle for political survival, he could not shut out the events across the ocean reshaping world history and Truman's own future. In May 1940, as Truman and his aides were mapping his strategy against Stark, the so-called phony war in Europe blew up in the face of the Western Allies. As Nazi armies swarmed across Europe, engulfing France and threatening to conquer Britain, Roosevelt moved to rally a nation suspicious of entering another European war to help the beleaguered British. Truman, drawing on his admiration for Woodrow Wilson and his own military experience, had already taken a stand in favor of supporting the Axis's enemies. In 1939, he voted to amend the Neutrality Act's embargo on U.S. arms sales abroad to allow Britain and France to buy military equipment in the United States. "I am of the opinion that we should not help the thugs among nations by refusing to sell arms to our friends," he declared.

In 1940, Truman backed Roosevelt's program to bolster the military by voting for the first peacetime draft in the nation's history. He also backed an amendment that the president would just as soon have done without. Black leaders did not forget that in World War I the military had extended the second-class citizenship blacks endured in much of civilian life to make them second-class soldiers too. With the new threat looming, the NAACP and other black leaders pushed through an amendment, which Truman supported, that banned racial discrimination in the administering of the draft. As it turned out, the amendment caused little change in the short term. Unwilling to abandon its long-established Jim Crow policy, the Army maintained that segregation did not amount to discrimination and continued to assign blacks to separate units. In the long run, though, the amendment and similar World War II legislative efforts probably contributed to the dramatic changes in armed forces racial policies instigated under the Truman presidency.

Whatever the practical consequences, the symbolic significance of Truman's casting his ballot against discrimination, along with other factors, helped him take advantage of Stark's blunders in dealing with Missouri's growing black population. Stark's first major trouble with Missouri blacks stemmed from the refusal of the University of Missouri law school to admit a black applicant, Lloyd Gaines, a graduate of Lincoln University, the state's black college, to its all-white law school. Gaines was told that he should apply for state financial aid to pay for his legal education outside the state. But in 1938, the U.S. Supreme Court ruled that Gaines had a constitutional right to a legal education in Missouri itself. To get around the ruling, Stark collaborated with the legislature in setting up a clearly subpar facility in an old beauty academy at Gaines's alma mater, Lincoln University. When Lincoln officials protested, Stark fired them. That infuriated many of the state's black leaders, notably Truman ally Chester Franklin, and led Franklin to commit himself to defeating Stark's senatorial bid and to encourage Truman to run against him.

Stark incurred further ill will that same year when black sharecroppers, protesting their eviction from their land in Missouri's southeast Bootheel region, camped out along a state highway to protest. The governor sent the highway patrol to roust them, angering blacks. Resentment of Stark reached a point where, in October 1939, a black political organization, the United Negro Democrats of Missouri, condemned Stark and pledged opposition to his candidacy. The Bootheel encampment had also stirred the ire of the local boss, a Pendergast ally, so Truman chose to exercise caution in dealing with this issue.

Nevertheless, the ill will Stark had generated created an obvious opportunity for Truman to reach out to the state's 250,000 black voters. Franklin offered Truman some typically cautious suggestions to exploit the opening in a letter written months before the senator announced his candidacy. If Truman attacked Stark directly, he might provoke a "clean government" backlash, since Stark had become a Pendergast foe and Truman was well known as a former Pendergast ally. Franklin also doubted the value of a black attack on the governor, which might trigger a racist backlash. Instead, Franklin urged Truman to make a positive appeal to blacks. "To keep up the good work we must now turn to selling you," the publisher wrote. "Be thinking of your points of contact with our voters so that when you come back home, we can map a course of action." His letter had a Polonius-like tone. He urged Truman not to be too outspoken on civil rights lest he be branded "a nigger lover." On the other hand, if he was too cautious, he might risk losing black support. Truman would have to walk a tightrope.

Truman responded with due courtesy. "In matters of this kind your judgment is always good," he wrote. As Franklin recommended, Truman did not publicly attack Stark for his handling of the controversies over the law school and the sharecropper protest. On a positive note, he did something that neither Stark nor Mulligan attempted: he appealed directly to black voters. For this, he used as the occasion nothing less than the kickoff of his campaign in Sedalia, an erstwhile cattle town in central Missouri, at the ground-breaking ceremony for a new hospital for blacks. The candidate spoke against a background of ever-darkening war news. Given the fact that Paris had fallen to the Werhmacht the day before, the turnout of 4,000 citizens, about 20 percent of the town's population, seemed to sixteen-year-old Margaret Truman, sitting on the platform, particularly impressive. Most Americans "were glued to their radios, listening to the greatest crisis of the century," she noted.

For the moment, though, her father could not afford to focus on anything but his battle to keep his job. Following Chester Franklin's advice and his own instincts, Truman began by citing his Senate record on civil rights. He mentioned not only his support for antilynching legislation and for the antidiscrimination amendment to the Selective Service Act, but his steady efforts to preserve the role of the office of recorder of deeds in the District of Columbia, which provided hundreds of jobs for blacks in the nation's capital. One reason for Truman's active support for the recorder's office was that it was headed by a longtime Missouri ally, William J. Thompkins, former editor of the black newspaper the *Kansas City American* and now president of the National Colored Democratic Association. Thompkins repaid Truman's help with interest in the 1940 campaign, when he traveled with Truman and also helped write his opening campaign speeches.

Truman followed his iteration of his own record with an important disclaimer. He was not, he stressed, advocating "social equality" for blacks. Truman was drawing on his own narrow experience; like most white middle-class Americans of that time, he had only limited contact with blacks as friends or on social occasions. But his remarks also reflected what was then regarded as a political imperative for advancing the civil rights cause. By disavowing social equality, Truman, like other civil rights supporters of the time, was trying to neutralize the primordial fears kept alive by supporters of segregation in the South and elsewhere. This was the argument that advancing the rights of black Americans would ultimately force whites to mingle with blacks on their jobs, in their neighborhoods, and in their schools. The worst racial nightmare for whites would come true: their daughters or sisters would fall prey to black men.

Having made the required rejection of the mixing of the races, Truman got down to business, citing the lack of job opportunities for blacks and the poor housing they were forced to accept. "I believe in the brotherhood of man," he declared, "not merely the brotherhood of white men; but the brotherhood of all men." The right of blacks to full citizenship, Truman contended, was not something whites could withhold, but rather was rooted as an entitlement in the founding principles of the Republic. "In giving to the Negroes the rights that are theirs, we are only acting in accord with ideas of a true democracy," he said. Then he pointed out that whites had a self-interest in seeing these ideas fulfilled. "If any class or race can be permanently set apart from or pushed down below the rest in political and civil rights, so may any class or race when it shall incur the displeasure of its more powerful associates, and we may say farewell to the principles on which we commit our safety."

A fuller statement of his views came the next month in Chicago, during the national Democratic convention in that city. Taking advantage of a break in the convention proceedings, Truman addressed Thompkins's Colored Democratic Association, whose members crowded into the Eighth Regiment Armory to hear him. Once again, he began with the denial intended to allay the fears of whites: "I wish to make it clear that I am not appealing for social equality of the Negro. The Negro himself knows better than that, and the highest types of Negro leaders say quite frankly that they prefer the society of their own people. Negroes want justice, not social relations."

Presumably when Truman referred to the preferences of "the highest types of Negro leaders," he was referring to the few he knew, men like Charles Franklin and William Thompkins, who probably would not have disputed his point, for the sake of political convenience if nothing else. In demanding political and economic equality for blacks while disavowing social equality, white liberals like Truman and many blacks seemed either unwilling or unable to recognize that the former would inevitably lead to the latter, or something close to it. Perhaps they refused to admit to themselves this relationship because that was exactly what the defenders of racism used as a battle cry.

Truman did not pledge himself to the support of specific proposals. He had already backed some such remedies when he endorsed anti-lynching legislation and voted against discrimination in the armed forces. He was not hiding what he had to say. His speech at Sedalia was made to a largely white audience, and even his Chicago remarks were part of the public record, where all citizens, regardless of color, could read them. What Truman did advocate was meaningful and clear. "We all know the Negro is here to stay and in no way can be removed from our political and economic life and we should recognize his inalienable rights as specified in our Constitution," he said at Sedalia. His condemnation of the unfairness blacks had to suffer in areas such as housing, as well as his full-throated commitment to redressing such grievances, not only for the sake of blacks but for their fellow white citizens, implied action against these injustices. Moreover, it would have been hard to find any other American politician of his stature acknowledging so bluntly the disadvantages imposed on black Americans—certainly none in Missouri, and certainly not the nation's incumbent president, Franklin Roosevelt.

In the weeks after the Democratic convention, the campaign tide in Missouri slowly began to turn in Truman's favor. His own grueling campaigning—stumping in every corner of the state, pausing at nearly every gathering of more than a few dozen voters, appealing to labor, to farmers, to city dwellers, and to everyone else he could reach—was a big reason for the shift. He had help, of course. To supplement his meager financial resources, the rail brotherhood chipped in with campaign workers and literature. A crucial assist came from St. Louis party chairman Bob Hannegan, not a boss in the Pendergast sense but more of a mediator among local leaders. Hannegan wielded enough influence so that Truman sought and gained his backing at the last moment by privately promising to support Hannegan's candidate for governor.

Even so, the outcome was desperately close. Truman trailed by more than 10,000 votes late on election night and wound up winning by barely 8,000 out of 665,000 votes cast. The general election was also a tough fight, but with FDR at the head of the ticket, it was not nearly as tough as the primary. Truman ran one percentage point behind Roosevelt, but he still beat his Republican challenger by nearly 3 percent. After the election, Truman, in a letter to Franklin, attributed his victory over Stark to the publisher's support.

That was probably overly generous. Blacks in Jackson County would probably have voted for Truman without Franklin's endorsement, and in St. Louis, Hannegan's organizing ability was a huge factor. Franklin's praise of Truman's aid to blacks probably did help a great deal with rural blacks, who had not voted for Truman in 1934 and who accounted for about one-third of the *Call's* circulation. Truman said his experience running for reelection reminded him of an old joke about a battered legal document that looked as if it "had been through hell three times with its hat off."

The main point, as he added, was that "I was still the United States Senator from Missouri." That he had gained the right to say that against all sorts of adversity meant that he could look forward to his second term in that office with greater confidence. This personal strengthening helped him later in the far-reaching challenges and unexpected opportunities that the future would offer.

5

ROAD TO THE TOP

So it was that the candidate for Jackson County judge who had paid a membership fee to the KKK would, sixteen years later, credit a black publisher with a major role in the victory that saved his political life. This metamorphosis was a slow and not necessarily steady process, and Truman would never completely outgrow the racism bred into him in childhood. In August 1939, he wrote to Bess Truman recalling that this date was "nigger picnic day" in Jackson County, remembering the chicken and catfish that he had enjoyed attending one such outing with the family washerwoman. A year later, in another letter to Bess, while he was in the midst of his Senate campaign in which two blacks played an important role, he mentioned having just killed a roach that had walked right out on the arm of his chair, "impudent as a Nigger."

Millions of other Americans at that time also casually used the "n" word, often, like Truman, without intended malice. Children all over the country innocently recited a nursery rhyme that started, "Eeny meeny miney moe, catch a nigger by the toe. . . . " But Harry Truman was not some youngster, or for that matter an average American. With his enhanced importance in the Senate, his attitudes on race would come under increased scrutiny, and his conscience would face new challenges. Such a conflict developed early in his second Senate term as a result of his assuming the most consequential role he had yet played as a politician, as chairman of the Senate War Investigating Committee. This rise to prominence was no accident. It stemmed from Truman's reformist inclinations, whetted by his involvement in the railroad finance probe, and also his ambitions for political gain and for becoming a significant part of history.

The moment would have been hard to miss. As anyone could plainly see, the economy, so dormant when Truman began his Senate career, was by 1941 coming back to life, sparked by the urgent efforts to prepare America for war. Inspired by a flood of mail complaining that the letting of construction contracts at Missouri's own Fort Leonard Wood was leading to a binge in profits for big companies, the senator set out to see the hanky-panky for himself. After an impromptu inspection of military posts in the South and Midwest, Truman concluded that Leonard Wood was no exception. Consistent with the history of American military preparedness, profligacy and fraud were pervasive.

On February 10, 1941, Truman proposed to the Senate an investigation of waste and inefficiency in the national defense program. "The policy seems be to make the big man bigger and put the little man completely out of business," he charged. Of course an inquiry into the war effort was not exactly what FDR wanted. But the president must have realized that if Truman did not do it, someone less friendly would. The senator assured the president that he would work closely with congressional leadership and avoid reckless muckraking. Absent Roosevelt's active opposition, the Senate created the committee Truman wanted, and not surprisingly, put him in charge.

This was an important enough mission to lead to tension between Truman and civil rights groups, who were less concerned about excessive profits than race discrimination against blacks seeking defense work. This was the issue that had prompted A. Philip Randolph to threaten a protest march on Washington. While Randolph's plans went forward, New York's Senator Wagner, who had sponsored the antilynching legislation two years earlier, proposed a committee to investigate the charges of discrimination. Senate leaders stalled and told the NAACP's Walter White that instead of creating another panel to probe national defense, racial complaints should be funneled to the Truman committee.

However, Truman told White that his agenda was already set for six months into the future, and even then, he would be able to cope with only three or four witnesses on discrimination. White had already lined up more than 100 witnesses and wanted a probe of discrimination not only in private industry, but also in the military and in the operations of selective service. Having been around long enough to know when he was getting the runaround, White joined Randolph on pushing ahead with the protest march, leading to Roosevelt's creation of the Fair Employment Practices Committee, or FEPC, empowered to cancel defense contracts with companies that discriminated. Another result was that Truman announced he would hold hearings on race discrimination in national defense after all, scheduling them for late June or early July.

But Walter White, concerned that not enough time was allowed to provide for a thorough probe, wrote the president and Truman asking for a delay. That suited Hugh Fulton, chief counsel of the Truman committee, fine. He wired White, "At your suggestion committee hearings on race discrimination have been postponed but no definite date has been determined for hearings." The delay set off a storm among black leaders outside the NAACP, some of whom accused White of "selfish leadership" for seeking a postponement so that the NAACP could play a more prominent role in the hearings. White answered back in a NAACP press release that charged that the proposed hearings represented "a frenzied and hasty attempt to dodge a real investigation into discrimination." They had only been scheduled to head off the threatened march on Washington, he argued, adding that the number of witnesses to be called was inadequate.

In mid-July, a group of black leaders organized by the *Pittsburgh Courier* met with Donald Lathrom, a Truman committee staffer, who assured them that hearings would probably be scheduled for August and would last three days. But August came and went with no hearings. All that the NAACP and other blacks got in response to their demands was hearings held by a subcommittee of the Truman panel in Kansas City and St. Louis to investigate racial discrimination in local defense-related employment. Those went smoothly, except that a few weeks later, word filtered back to Roy Wilkins, White's aide, that a Truman committee staffer, later identified as longtime Truman crony Harry Vaughn, had made provocative remarks after the St. Louis hearings. Vaughn had said, Wilkins was told, that the Truman committee did not intend to act on their concerns, adding, "If anybody thought the committee was going to help black bastards into $100-a-week jobs, they were sadly mistaken." "We have felt all along that the Truman committee was not going to do very much on this matter," Wilkins wrote to Ira Lewis, president of the *Pittsburgh Courier*. "This remark in St. Louis, if true, would seem to indicate that the committee does not take the whole business very seriously."

While Truman surely would have disavowed Vaughn's comments, he privately had no enthusiasm for probing discrimination because, as he claimed, he was skeptical of getting enough evidence to support any charges. "When we try to get the facts and the sworn testimony to prove it, it evaporates into thin air," he wrote a friend after a year of the committee's probe. "The people affected are afraid of assault and battery and you can't blame them much." The perpetrators, he said, were members of the "thug class and are very difficult to run to earth."

Despite the scrapes with the NAACP, the Truman committee

flourished. Its inquiries turned into one of the great success stories in the long and often dismal history of congressional investigations. In his public reports, chairman Truman lambasted not only big business but also self-interested labor leaders and inefficient federal agencies. After three years of high-visibility public hearings, Truman claimed to have saved the nation's taxpayers $15 billion. In the process, the erstwhile senator from Pendergast had refashioned himself as a champion of straight dealings. More importantly, he became someone Franklin Roosevelt could select as his running mate—and, as it turned out, his successor.

Meanwhile, though the newly created FEPC had worked for Roosevelt by getting Randolph to cancel plans for the protest march on Washington, it turned out to be an imperfect weapon against job discrimination. The FEPC was finding, as Truman had contended in refusing to press his own committee's investigations into bias, that discrimination was hard to prove. Moreover, even when the FEPC mounted a case, the government was reluctant to use its main enforcement weapon—revoking contracts—because the munitions that would be cut off were badly needed. Despite its ineffectiveness, the FEPC was targeted by many companies and Southern lawmakers as a source of bureaucratic intrusion into the war effort.

These circumstances did not improve after the United States officially went to war against the Axis powers in December 1941. Hoping to tamp down protests against the FEPC in the summer of 1942, FDR took away the agency's independent status and stuck it under the War Manpower Commission. As Walter White wrote later, "The conviction began to grow that the FEPC was being quietly shelved and that the government no longer was insistent that discrimination in employment be abolished." Indeed, in August 1942, a San Francisco–based antidiscrimination organization reported that government agencies, notably the United States Employment Service, were often themselves guilty of bias, and so were many labor unions, even though the labor movement had publicly backed the agency.

It became clear that while the huge black migration to the North to seek jobs in the war plants may have bolstered the Democratic Party in urban centers, it also created and worsened a multitude of problems for black soldiers and war workers. Because the Army ignored the antidiscrimination legislation passed by Congress, it exposed many blacks from the North who were stationed in the South to discrimination they had never encountered as civilians. But what blacks complained of as bias, many whites saw as a threat to their jobs, and in the South, to their whole way of life. The result was widespread hostility and often violence. In May 1943, the upgrading of black shipyard workers at a Mobile firm triggered a bloody brawl among several hundred workers, with eighty of them, mostly black, needing medical treatment. Early in June, set off by what turned out to be a false report of a black man raping a white woman, a mob of 10,000 whites roamed through Beaumont, Texas, for most of the day, beating blacks and burning their homes.

Many feared that even worse lay ahead, with overcrowded Detroit seen as the most dangerous spot in the country. War work was plentiful, but housing was scarce, and the situation was worse for blacks, who had fewer choices than whites. On June 20, 1943, the heart of the city whose leaders liked to call the arsenal of democracy, exploded in the worst race riot since a similar outbreak in Chicago in 1919. White mobs raged along Woodward Avenue, the city's main thoroughfare, pulling blacks from streetcars and beating them. Their fury was fed by mostly overblown stories of black looting and assaults in Paradise Valley, the city's black ghetto. By the time federal troops arrived, after more than twenty-four hours of bloodshed, the riot had claimed thirty-four lives, nine whites and twenty-five blacks, seventeen of whom had been shot by police.

In the wake of the riot, FDR's administration, preoccupied with the battlefronts abroad and war production at home, seemed insensitive to and baffled by the tensions in the cities. Attorney General Francis Biddle, after a cursory inquiry, told the president that a national study committee of some sort would be advisable, but added emphatically, "This is something that the government cannot do." All FDR should do, Biddle suggested, was to appoint an interdepartmental committee "to coordinate information work in the field and deal with the delegations who have been coming to Washington to see you."

Much less innocuous was a Biddle recommendation to consider limiting or ending black migration into overcrowded cities. When that was leaked to the press and stirred sharp protests, from, among others, the American Civil Liberties Union, Biddle denied that any such plan was under consideration. Though Roosevelt was famous in times of national stress for his fireside chats, Biddle recommended against that now, and the president did not disagree.

Roosevelt's only public comment on the summer's violence came in response to a letter from Representative Vito Marcantonio, a left-wing Democrat. The president said he had asked his attorney general to "give special attention" to the problem of race riots, adding his agreement with Marcantonio that the riots "endanger our national unity and comfort our enemies. "I am sure that every true American regrets them."

The NAACP publication *Crisis* reflected the frustration of many blacks with the administration's passivity when it published a bitter outcry by black poet Pauli Murray titled "Mr. Roosevelt Regrets":

What did you get black boy,
When they knocked you down in the gutter,
And they kicked your teeth out
And they broke your skull with clubs
And they bashed your stomach in . . .
What did you get when you cried out to the Top Man
And you asked him to speak out to save you?
What'd the Top Man say, black boy?
Mr. Roosevelt regrets.

That summer's rioting put an end to major outbreaks of racial violence for the time being, and also produced a quietus on agitation for advancement of civil rights. Blacks in the mean streets of the nation's cities
could read the casualty lists from Detroit and sites of other similar violent
outbreaks and realize that they had little to gain from violence, and much
to lose. Their political leaders saw slight opportunity for their cause in an
environment where any protests were viewed as inciting to violence or
disunity.

As for the junior senator from Missouri, though he avoided conflict
with the administration on race by steering away from his promised probe
of job discrimination, he did find himself at odds with the president on
another area that touched on minority concerns and morality. This controversy, if not under the rubric of civil rights, could certainly be defined
in broader terms as a question of human rights. It was the plight of Jews
trapped in Nazi-controlled Europe, which, like the cause of black Americans, was freighted with political significance. Jews were a powerful voting block in New York and several other of the nation's biggest cities. In
addition, for politicians anywhere, including Truman's Missouri, Jewish
campaign contributions could be a huge benefit. On the other hand, just
as support for civil rights risked stirring a white backlash, a politician
seeking special help for Jews when the nation was fighting for its survival
risked tapping into the strong vein of anti-Semitism that was rife in 1940s
America.

Jews, like blacks, were among FDR's sturdiest supporters. He maintained their backing by promoting economic and social reforms embody-
ing the Jewish cultural tradition. An unprecedented influx of Jews into the
federal government and into the ranks of his close advisers also bolstered
Jewish loyalty to the New Deal. But just as Roosevelt retained black support though he did not battle racism, he held on to the votes of Jews even
though he did not speak out against anti-Semitism, even after Hitler came
to power. Nor did he relax his firm opposition to revising immigration

policy to admit Jewish refugees as the Nazis steadily stepped up their persecution of the Jews during the 1930s. It fell to the so-called President's Jews, some particularly close Jewish American advisers, such as Harvard professor Felix Frankfurter and Roosevelt's chief speechwriter, Sam Rosenman, to cope with the Jewish pressure on the president to help the beleaguered Jews of Europe. As informal liaisons between the White House and the Jewish community in the 1930s, they explained to their coreligionists that Roosevelt was reluctant to relax immigration barriers to Jews because of the disastrous unemployment of the Depression. After war broke out, they argued that any help for the European Jews might impede victory over the Axis, which they contended was the Jews' best chance for salvation.

By 1942, as well-founded reports circulated that the Nazis had already begun carrying out a plan to exterminate the Jews of Europe, some Jews in the United States demanded faster action. Much of the pressure was initiated by an inspired agitator named Peter Bergson, whose zeal verged on fanaticism, and whose gift for organization and strategy approached genius. The leader of a militant Zionist bloc, he came to the United States from Palestine initially to fund a Jewish Army to take the field against Hitler. He soon shifted his focus to rescuing Jews facing annihilation through various schemes to persuade Germany and its allies to let Jews emigrate, while getting other nations to permit them entry. For this, he wanted government approval and funding from Allied countries, including the United States. By early 1943, Bergson had succeeded in drumming up the support of an imposing collection of notable Americans in the military, arts, and politics, including more than thirty members of the U.S. Senate, among them Harry Truman.

For Truman, his support for the Jewish cause came despite his occasional expression of ethnic stereotypes not unlike the feelings he privately voiced toward blacks. Writing to Bess Truman in 1939 during a visit to Miami, he said, "The principal product seems to be hotels, filling stations, hebrews and cabins." In July 1941, while staying at a military hospital in Hot Springs, Arkansas, he told her of a Jewish reserve officer from Little Rock taking him and a friend for an outing in his Cadillac. "He's a grand person," he wrote. "Name's Rosenbloom, but doesn't act it at all."

Truman never seemed to see a contradiction between his prejudices against Jews, the sympathy he felt for the plight of European Jews, and the friendships he formed with individual Jews. Max Lowenthal, a wealthy reformer and ardent Zionist who had helped write some of Truman's speeches on railroad financing, was one. Another was David Berenstein, a St. Louis lawyer who, though he occasionally irritated Truman, was chosen to manage his Senate reelection campaign in that city, whose vote had played a crucial role in his victory.

Speaking to a meeting organized by Bergson and his allies that packed a Chicago stadium in 1943, Truman called for action in terms that clearly conflicted with the stance of the White House. "Merely talking about the Four Freedoms is not enough," Truman said. "This is the time for action. No one can any longer doubt the horrible intention of the Nazi beasts. We know they plan the systematic slaughter throughout all of Europe, not only of Jews but of vast numbers of other innocent peoples." Truman was substituting for Illinois Democrat Scott Lucas, a close Senate ally who was unable to keep his scheduled date. At the last minute, Lucas had been appointed as a U.S. delegate to a hastily called international refugee conference in Bermuda. Soon after Truman's Chicago speech, the Bermuda conference concluded its secret deliberations, with nothing to report that might offer hope to the imperiled Jews.

Indignant, Bergson's group bought an ad in the *New York Times* bearing the headline, "To 5,000,000 Jews in the Nazi Death Trap Bermuda was a Cruel Mockery," and denouncing the conference's failure to act. Along with these charges, the ad included a long list of members of Bergson's Committee for a Jewish Army. Among them were prominent labor leaders, maestro Arturo Toscanini, journalist William Allen White, and an eclectic group of U.S. senators that included Southern segregationist Theodore Bilbo of Mississippi, Oregon Republican senator Charles Mc-Nary (his party's 1940 vice presidential candidate), and liberal Democrats Robert Wagner and Harry Truman.

Trouble was, while Bergson had indeed gained the support of these luminaries to back his Jewish Army idea, he had not taken the time to tell any of them about the ad attacking the Bermuda conference. This created a particular problem for Truman because he had to contend with an infuriated Scott Lucas, who took the Senate floor to denounce the Bergson group as "aliens" who were "taking advantage of the courtesy and kindness extended to them" to criticize U.S. governmental policies. Lucas also called on his friend Truman to let him know what he thought about the ad to which Truman's name was affixed. The next day, Truman wrote Bergson and quit the committee. "That does not mean my sympathies are not with the downtrodden Jews of Europe," he said. "But when you take it upon yourself without consultation to attack members of the Senate and House of Representatives who are working in your interest I cannot approve of that procedure."

Despite this flap, Bergson pressed on, now focusing on lobbying Congress to pass resolutions calling for "immediate action" to save the surviving Jews in Europe. He gained the support of Treasury secretary Henry Morgenthau, a Jew and a Hyde Park neighbor of FDR's whose role was critical. Morgenthau cleared the way for the United States to help ransom some 70,000 Jews from Romania for $170,000. Ultimately, Roosevelt, under pressure from Capitol Hill, created the War Refugee Board in January 1944 with a $1 million budget and the mission of assisting European Jews and other victims of Nazi persecution. The episode, like the aborted probe of job discrimination, reflected how Truman responded to the inevitable tensions between principle and practical politics at this stage in his career. Truman liked to think of himself as a fighter, and he certainly did fight hard in 1940 to win reelection when the odds were against him. But he was also at times a trimmer, particularly when he felt personally threatened or injured. He weaseled out of his agreement with the NAACP to investigate job discrimination when he realized that it would be a frustrating, thankless job that might make his committee look foolish. But even if he had been unable to make a firm legal case proving discrimination, the very fact of his hearings would have focused attention on the problem and given hope to blacks when that commodity was in short supply.

As for the Bergson group, Truman certainly had a just grievance against Bergson for using his name without permission. However, none of the other senators named in the ad resigned from the committee. Lucas's outrage seemed to have been overstated. The ad did not mention his name. Truman's heart had been in the right place when he joined the Bergson group, as it was most of the time when he supported civil rights, but in turning his back on the Bergson group, he overreacted by putting Lucas's wounded ego and his amour propre ahead of his concern for the fate of the refugees.

Like most men, Harry Truman liked to consider himself captain of his own fate. The truth was that so far as his political destiny was concerned, it had been largely shaped by someone else, namely Tom Pendergast. Now, with half of his second term in the Senate behind him, his future would once again be decided by someone else, in this case Franklin Roosevelt. As the end of Roosevelt's second term approached, his political future was clouded by uncertainty over his health. Though he was only sixty-three, the pressures of wartime leadership, combined with his disregard for his physical well-being, had taken a heavy toll. "His spirits were excellent," his vice president, Henry Wallace, wrote in his diary after a meeting with the president in the spring of 1944, "but it seems to me that his appearance was worse than I have ever seen it." Most Democratic party leaders shared that concern, along with a disaffection with the incumbent vice president. All of this led to increased interest in the choice of someone to replace Wallace as FDR's running mate in 1944.

One possibility often mentioned was South Carolina senator James Byrnes, an FDR Senate ally, but he had to be ruled out because he was a leading segregationist, an apostate Catholic, and a foe of labor. Among other candidates, Harry Truman's name seemed to have the broadest appeal—or at least raised the fewest objections. As New York Democratic leader and FDR confidant Ed Flynn put it, "It was agreed that he was the man who would hurt least." His assets included his steady support of the New Deal, his good relations with organized labor, and the distance he had put between himself and segregationists like Byrnes. He also had the vigorous endorsement of Bob Hannegan, the St. Louis party leader whom Truman had helped elevate to the national chairmanship of the party. There was one problem: Truman did not want to be vice president. He had made his position clear to Democratic senator Joe Guffey of Pennsylvania, who had broached the idea of the vice presidency to him in the summer of 1943. "I told him in words of one syllable that I would not," Truman wrote his wife. And why should he? His investigation of war production, which had turned him into a vice presidential possibility, also gave him every reason to stay on in the Senate, where he was riding high, and where he enjoyed the fellowship of his colleagues. Looking ahead to 1946, he was unlikely to face serious competition for renomination and would almost certainly be favored for the general election.

In the end, Roosevelt changed Truman's mind for him. On the day before the delegates to the 1944 Democratic National Convention would ballot for the vice presidency, national chairman Hannegan summoned Truman to his hotel suite to meet with party leaders. Then the phone rang, the first of two calls that would mark Truman's route to the presidency. FDR was on the line, and his booming voice could be heard throughout the room, demanding to know whether Hannegan had "got that fellow lined up yet."

"He is the contrariest Missouri mule I've ever dealt with," Hannegan replied.

"Well you tell him," Roosevelt bellowed loud enough for Truman to hear, "that if he wants to break up the Democratic Party in the middle of a war, that's his responsibility."

After a minute or two of thought, Truman said, "Well if that's the situation I'll have to say yes. But why the hell didn't he tell me in the first place?"

It was all over but the convention balloting, which did not take long. Wallace's liberal supporters gave him an early lead. When he failed to get a majority on the first ballot, his backers turned to Truman, who won the nomination on the second ballot.

With all the calculations that had gone into Truman's selection, party leaders had not taken into account the attitudes of black Americans. This had been considered in ruling out Senator Byrnes. But just as blacks would have been angered at the choice of Byrnes, they were deeply resentful of Truman because he was replacing a hero, Henry Wallace, a reaction that would complicate Harry Truman's campaign for the vice presidency and his service in that office. Wallace had begun denouncing racism both at home and abroad when he was FDR's secretary of agriculture. He echoed that theme in his signature address as vice president, the so-called Century of the Common Man speech, delivered in 1942, millions of copies of which the Office of War Information distributed around the world. He had solidified his heroic image with blacks in a dramatic speech to the Democratic convention that ultimately rejected him in favor of Truman. Wallace's call for economic and political equality between the races in postwar America assured his defeat at the convention. Among blacks, it also set a high standard for Wallace's replacement to adhere to, as Truman would soon find out.

A week after his nomination, the *Pittsburgh Courier*, one of the nation's most influential black newspapers, ran a page one story under the headline, "Democrats 'Sell' Race, Wallace to 'Buy' South." The story, written by the paper's managing editor, William G. Nunn, charged that Truman's nomination, combined with weak language in the party platform on civil rights, amounted to "an appeasement of the South which must rank in cowardice and short sightedness with the ineptitude shown by Chamberlain at Munich." To this overblown attack, Truman responded with an olive branch. He offered the paper an exclusive interview in which he sought to rebut the thrust of the article. "I have always been for equality of opportunity in work, working conditions and political rights," he told the *Courier*. He added a comment that held portent for the future: "I think the Negro in the armed forces ought to have the same treatment and opportunities as every other member of the armed forces." Then he made the point that he hoped would most shape black opinion: "Harry Truman isn't the important issue of the campaign. The real issue is the re-election of the greatest living friend of the Negro people, Franklin Roosevelt."

Asked his views on Henry Wallace's championing of the civil rights cause at the convention, Truman went all out to smooth over resentment of Wallace's ouster. "No honest American can disagree with Henry Wallace," he said. "What he said was gospel."

"The only thing I regret is that my nomination meant the defeat of Wallace."

Though the overall tone of the article was positive, citing Truman's support of antilynching and poll tax measures in the Senate and his black friends in Jackson County, it also mentioned Truman's reputed membership in the KKK and his longtime links to the Pendergast machine. If it were just a question of the vice presidency, the story said, there would be little reason to doubt Truman's abilities and good intentions. "But," the reporter added, "Negro voters have their fingers crossed on Truman as a potential president of the United States."

As he campaigned around the country, Truman tried hard to steer away from that possibility by stressing the point that he made to the *Pittsburgh Courier:* that the issue in the campaign was not his credentials, but the chance to continue Franklin Roosevelt's leadership. Even so, he could not avoid problems that reflected his inexperience in national campaigning and his occasional tendency to shoot from the hip.

Stumping in Southern California, he walked right into a local controversy over Democratic congressional candidate Hal Styles. After Styles was nominated, word got out that back in New York City, where he had lived before coming to California, Styles had been a Kleagle in the local branch of the Ku Klux Klan. The various explanations offered by Styles did not convince the Hollywood Democratic Committee, which, after investigating Styles's background, denied him its support. In the face of this, when asked whether he was endorsing Styles, all Truman needed to reply was that he did not know enough about Styles, but that he despised the Klan and all it stood for. Instead, he said breezily, "If he's ours, we're for him."

Styles could not have been more pleased. He plastered Hollywood with sixty billboards proclaiming, "Senator Truman says, 'I'm for Styles.'" Among those outraged in the movie industry was Hollywood dynast David B. Selznick, who wired the NAACP's Walter White in October challenging the organization's support of the national Democratic ticket in view of Truman's endorsement of Styles. Asked by White to explain his stand on Styles, Truman referred to charges made against him about his own link to the Klan. Because of "my own experience," he said, he was "reluctant to believe partisan charges coming from Republican quarters that a Democratic nominee is a Klansman." The problem with this explanation is that the controversy about Styles and the Klan did not stem from partisan charges. Styles himself had admitted membership.

Truman did not help himself by asserting he had been told that Styles had joined the Klan only so he could write an exposé series for a local newspaper. Styles had indeed offered that alibi, but it had been discredited. The whole bootless episode reflected an insensitivity to racial issues that was particularly disturbing for a politician who was vying to win an office only a heartbeat removed from the presidency—a timeworn phrase that gained particular salience in the present circumstances. Truman compounded his problems with jarring remarks made in an interview with Morris Milgram, a staffer for the left-wing Worker's Defense League and a longtime advocate for the cause of organized labor and the rights of minorities.

Given Milgram's background, Truman might have been cautious in dealing with him, but the vice presidential nominee seemed to hold little back, particularly when rejecting the notion of social equality for blacks. "If colored people behave themselves they get along," Truman remarked, a comment that seemed to set the tone for the interview. Asked whether he had ever had dinner with Kansas City publisher C. A. Franklin, or any other blacks, at his home, Truman was forthright. "No, I never have and I never will," he said. "I reserve the right to choose my guests. There are lots of whites whom I've never had to dinner and never would invite to my home." Milgram initially intended the article for the *American Mercury*, a monthly magazine of political and cultural commentary, but the *Mercury* turned it down. It was then published by the *Pittsburgh Courier* under the headline "South Has Little to Fear from Truman of Missouri." No sooner was the article published than Truman branded it a lie, contending that it had been intended to influence votes against him, though the attitudes expressed in the interview, if not the choice of words, seemed much like Truman.

Meanwhile, Truman was kept busy denying charges raised by Republicans and some old Missouri enemies about his ties to the Klan. It may have helped to undermine the credibility of these attacks when some right-wing extremists claimed he was really Jewish, a contention based on the fact that his maternal grandfather was named Solomon. Truman denied being Jewish, adding, "But if I were I would not be ashamed of it."

The Klan controversy was not so easily shrugged off, particularly in Boston, where the local Hearst paper, the *Boston Herald American*, gave it prominence, and where Democrats feared it might cost Irish Catholic votes. He got help on this score when he campaigned in the city from Congressman James Michael Curley, who had served three terms as mayor and whose popularity had scarcely been dented by a felony indictment against him. Speaking from the same platform as Truman, Curley said, "We have a very unusual candidate for vice president. He goes to California and word comes back to us he's a Jew. He arrives in the Midwest; the word comes back to us that he's a member of the Klan." Turning to Truman, he said, "Senator, I invite you to join my lodge, the Ancient Order of Hibernians. We'll be glad to have you as one of our members and I assure you we'll get out the vote." Elated, Matt Connelly, Truman's campaign aide and later his presidential appointments secretary, whispered to Truman, "That takes care of the Klan."

It surely helped in Boston, which the Democratic ticket carried handsomely, as usual. Truman may well have remembered that moment in 1950 when he gave a full pardon to Curley, who had been elected to a fourth term as mayor and then jailed on federal charges of influence peddling. Regardless of Curley's efforts on his behalf, Truman felt the need to defend his civil rights record, along with FDR's, in his last major speech of the campaign at New York's Madison Square Garden three days before the election. "More than six years ago President Roosevelt advocated a Federal anti-lynching law," Truman said, a claim that might have been technically accurate, though Roosevelt made sure few Americans were aware of this stand. At the same time, Truman said, he himself had voted in favor of an antilynching law. More than five years ago, Truman continued, Roosevelt had "gone on record" as favoring legislation to outlaw the poll tax, though again, the president's support had been sotto voce. He himself had voted to do just that. The senator went on to point out that Roosevelt had established the FEPC, and that he, Truman, had "on numerous occasions" voted to fund the embattled agency.

Meanwhile, the Republican National Committee gleefully pointed out that the GOP ticket of New York governor Tom Dewey and Ohio governor John Bricker had the edge over FDR and Truman so far as endorsements from black newspapers. The combined circulation of newspapers backing the GOP was 781,000, compared to 320,000 for papers supporting the Democratic ticket. High among the reasons mentioned by the pro-GOP papers were the dumping of Wallace and the choice of Truman and the fear that FDR would die in office. Some papers presumably were influenced by the stronger stance of the GOP platform on civil rights. The Republicans pledged a permanent FEPC, a federal ban on lynching, and a constitutional amendment abolishing the poll tax. The Democratic policy statement gave only hazy support to minority rights, urging congressional support for these principles. Some black papers may have been swayed by the generous advertising dollars provided by the GOP, which usually had more money to spend than its opposition.

Yet on Election Day, the endorsements and the platforms seemed to make little difference. The three largest-circulation black newspapers endorsing Dewey were the *Pittsburgh Courier*, the *Amsterdam News* of New York, and C. A. Franklin's *Kansas City Call*, despite Franklin's admiration for Truman as a Missouri politician. Yet FDR carried Pennsylvania, New York, and Missouri, as he had in 1940. Though Roosevelt won an electoral vote landslide with 432 votes to 99 for Dewey, the popular vote was much closer, particularly in some key states. In half a dozen or so of these states, the black vote arguably could be said to have made the difference.

Roosevelt's reelection did not dispel rumors and speculation about his health, which Truman tried to disregard. However, the seriousness of the president's condition was all too real to dismiss. Less than three months after Roosevelt took the oath of office, while Truman was enjoying a drink with a few Capitol Hill colleagues in Speaker Sam Rayburn's office, another phone call changed his life, this one even more momentous than FDR's message at the Democratic convention that pushed him into the vice presidency. This message was from presidential press secretary Steve Early, and it was short but urgent.

"Holy General Jackson," Truman blurted. "Steve Early wants me at the White House immediately." Then he added in a whisper, "Boys, this is in the room. Keep this quiet. Something must have happened." On arriving at 1600 Pennsylvania Avenue, Truman found first lady Eleanor Roosevelt waiting for him. She put her arm around his shoulder and said gently, "Harry, the President is dead." Ninety minutes later, Harry S. Truman was sworn in as the thirty-third president of the United States.

As his Senate career ended on a note of triumph and the influence and challenges of national leadership loomed, Truman could find reason for satisfaction and pride. He had served a rigorous apprenticeship, surmounting first the Pendergast stigma and then Pendergast's absence. Along the way, he had found a voice for himself, stemming in part from his inherent populist beliefs, first in the Senate hearings on railway finance and then in the investigation into the war effort. Whether or not his claim of $15 billion savings for the hearings could withstand an accountant's audit, there is no doubt that the Truman committee performed a service for the public as well as for the president by strengthening the idea that a Democratic government could be accountable to its citizens even when its own existence was threatened.

But on the issue of civil rights, his performance was ambiguous and, considering the hopes he occasionally aroused with his rhetoric, ultimately disappointing. In his speech at Sedalia, and then to black delegates at the Democratic convention in his 1940 Senate campaign, he spoke eloquently and with seeming passion to the concerns of black Americans. However, during his short Senate term, he rarely returned to those themes. What he did have to say about civil rights, aside from the awkward denials of his Klan membership and gratuitous remarks about social equality, was mostly perfunctory. It was true, as he said at Madison Square Garden, that he had been against lynching and the poll tax as a senator. The reality, as black Americans fully realized, was that Truman's Democratic

Party had controlled both political branches of the federal government for twelve years, and in ten of them, Truman himself had been in Washington. Yet next to nothing had been done about the poll tax and lynching, and what had been done to try to curb job discrimination had not lived up to its promise. Truman had shown little more than good intentions. He soon would realize that far more would be expected in his new status as the first officer of the republic.

6

★ ★ ★ ★ ★

THE TURNING POINT

At Truman's first White House press conference, less than a week after being sworn in as president, a black journalist began a question by telling him that FDR's loss was "very keenly felt by Negroes in America." They believed that they knew where the late president stood on such issues as the poll tax and the FEPC. Where did the new president stand on those issues, the reporter wanted to know.

"I will give you some advice," Truman shot back. "All you need to do is read the Senate record of one Harry S. Truman." That was the sort of glib response Truman had made during the 1944 campaign when challenged on civil rights. That helped him get by as a vice presidential candidate, but it was nowhere near adequate for his presidency. In fairness to Truman, he probably needed more time to reflect on where he stood and where he wanted to lead; it had been just five days since Eleanor Roosevelt had told him of Roosevelt's death.

"Is there anything I can do for you," the new president had asked FDR's widow.

"Is there anything *we* can do for *you*," the late president's widow had replied. "For you are the one in trouble now."

"Boys, if you ever pray, pray for me now," Truman asked White House reporters in his first full day as president. "I felt like the moon, the stars and all the planets had fallen on me."

As for civil rights, he would need more than prayers to set a course that would satisfy the demands of blacks without turning whites against him. His first test as president, over the status of the FEPC, demonstrated some of the difficulties he would face. For all its limitations, the agency represented FDR's most substantial contribution to the black struggle for justice. More importantly, it was uppermost in the minds of blacks and their leaders because it held the widest and most immediate significance for their lives. Much as blacks everywhere detested the poll tax and lynching, the truth was, blacks in the North did not pay poll taxes and were not threatened by lynching. However, a decent job at a fair wage, with a reasonable chance for a raise and promotion, were urgent needs for blacks everywhere, particularly in the unsettled economic climate of 1945.

The FEPC was beset by troubles that predated Truman's presidency. Mindful of Southern opposition to the agency when he created it in 1941, FDR had decreed that it get its budget from the president's emergency fund. But in 1945, Congress circumvented the president's circumvention by banning that practice. Now financing for all independent agencies, such as the FEPC, would require congressional approval. Truman fought back on two fronts, striving to restore the agency's budget while pushing for a permanent FEPC that would be less dependent on congressional whims for funding. A flock of bills to establish a new agency had been introduced in the House, where they were awaiting action by the House Rules Committee, and two more bills were in the Senate when the Seventy-ninth Congress began.

Truman wrote key lawmakers in both chambers urging action and promising support. But Southerners resisted. In the House, they mustered enough votes on the Rules Committee to keep the permanent FEPC bill bottled up. In the Senate, they used their tried-and-true weapon, the filibuster, to block funding for the existing agency. Leading the Senate battle was Theodore Bilbo of Mississippi, the most notorious defender of racism in Congress, who, together with his like-minded House colleague John Rankin, was lampooned in the satirical musical comedy *Finian's Rainbow* as Senator Billboard Rawkins. In real life, Bilbo's s rhetorical barrage brought to a dead stop an appropriation bill to fund not only the FEPC but also fifteen other independent agencies. When the *Washington Post*, edited by Eugene Meyer, attacked him, Bilbo retorted, "I had forgotten that the editor of the *Washington Post* is a Jew, and I presume that his wife is a Jewess. The Negroes and the Jews in New York as well as others who are working with them hand in hand are the ones who have been back of this vicious legislation."

To get the bill through and prevent all the agencies from being starved for funds, Senate majority leader Alben Barkley of Kentucky patched together a compromise that cut the initial FEPC's $500,000 budget request in half, to $250,000. That kept the FEPC alive, but barely. The compromise stipulated that none of the $250,000 could be spent after June 30, 1946, thus signaling the intent of Southerners to bury this nettlesome agency for all time. "During the next fiscal year the committee will exist largely in name only," wrote George McCrary, labor columnist for the black newspaper *Atlanta World.* McCrary professed to see a silver lining. "In making war on the committee the opposition will run into a barrier almost impossible to overcome," he predicted. "President Truman and Democratic Chairman Hannegan must soon realize that something has to be done and done fast to hold labor and the Negro vote in the Democratic Party."

That turned out to be too rosy an appraisal. Much as he wanted to maintain black support, Truman could not overcome Southern resistance. On September 6, 1945, a month after victory over Japan, as the FEPC remained mired on Capitol Hill, Truman sent Congress a twenty-one-point message asking for action on social and economic issues, including the FEPC, but his words made little impression on Capitol Hill and left A. Philip Randolph fuming. In a letter to Matthew Connelly, Truman's appointments secretary, Randolph warned that unless Truman mobilized support for the FEPC in the Congress, the opposition, as in the past, "will make a farce out of this whole thing." However, when Randolph sought to meet with the president to press his case, Truman turned him down.

Though Truman's rhetoric was vigorous in support of the FEPC, his actions fell short. In November 1946, when the Capitol Transit Company, whose buses carried Washingtonians where they needed to go, was shut down by a wildcat strike, Truman, using still-existing wartime authority, seized the company. The FEPC, which had long tried in vain to persuade the company to hire blacks, now took advantage of its coming under federal control to draft an order directing the firm's management to stop discriminating. However, the White House got wind of the plan and overruled the agency. Charles Huston, one of two black members of the committee, wrote Truman on behalf of the panel, asking him to endorse the draft order, but Truman did not respond. After waiting a week, Huston resigned in protest, telling Truman in a letter that the president's attitude reflected a persistent course of conduct of giving "lip service" to the battle against discrimination "while doing nothing substantial."

Three days later, Truman wrote back to contend that he did not have the legal authority to change the practices of a seized corporation, a conclusion based on the opinion of Sam Rosenman, who had been chief speechwriter to FDR. It was of a piece with the cautious advice Rosenman had offered FDR when the president was asked to help European Jews escape Nazi persecution. In 1938, in the wake of *Kristallnacht,* Hitler's first massive pogrom, Rosenman, in an unsolicited memo, warned FDR that any increase in immigration quotas for Jews would worsen unemployment and produce a "Jewish problem." Rosenman's forte in the Roosevelt White House had been as a ghostwriter and political handyman, not a legal authority. In time, Truman would find different sources for guidance on dealing with the law. Meanwhile, his reliance on Rosenman signified his uncertain course on civil rights.

Despite his stand in the Capitol Transit case, Truman continued to make the case for a permanent agency to deal with job bias. In a radio address, as part of a general discussion of domestic issues, he blamed a "small handful" of lawmakers on the House Rules Committee for preventing the legislation he sought from getting to the floor. Later he took revenge on one of these congressmen, Roger Slaughter. The FEPC vote was only one of the grudges Truman held against Slaughter. The congressman happened to be from Truman's own home district and had become a leading Democratic foe of administration proposals. Truman worked to defeat him in the Democratic primary that fall, with the aid of the remnants of the Pendergast organization. However, the Truman-backed candidate, Enos Axtell, lost out to the Republicans in the general election. Meanwhile, Slaughter charged vote fraud in the primary campaign, leading to indictments that failed to reach trial because the key evidence was mysteriously stolen.

There was to be no happy ending for the FEPC either. In June 1946, following official notification from the White House that no funds were available to keep it alive, the agency went out of existence. Frustration among blacks was mitigated by several presidential appointments. Besides selecting Harold Burton, a former Senate comrade of his who had been an FEPC supporter, to the Supreme Court, Truman gave appointments to three well-thought-of blacks, Irvin C. Mollison, a Chicago lawyer, as a customs court judge; William Hastie, a war department official, as governor of the Virgin Islands; and Howard University professor Ralph Bunche as a member of the Anglo American Caribbean Commission, a stepping-stone toward an eminent career in international diplomacy and ultimately the Nobel Prize.

Not surprisingly, as Truman's presidency passed the one-year mark, his record received mixed grades from black leaders. He was credited with doing better than expected and for good intentions, as the *Pittsburgh Courier* observed. "But the weak and underprivileged need a rugged militant champion," while Truman, the paper complained, "lacked the force and influence" to get congressional approval of such items as a permanent FEPC and anti–poll tax legislation.

Reasonable as such reaction was, it did not fully take into account Truman's political circumstances and the dysfunctional nature of the governing system in which he was operating. The Madisonian hamstrings of pitting the ambition and interests of one political branch against another meant, barring a war or similar crisis, a hard time for most presidents in getting Congress to respond to their proposals. Blacks and others of that era whose main goals required decisive federal action wanted a rerun of FDR's early accomplishments. As a result of the Great Depression and his own cunning, Roosevelt was able to achieve imposing social and economic reforms in his first term. But partly because of his own blunder with the Supreme Court, then the onset of war, the surge of liberalism that marked the New Deal turned out to be little more than a splendid spasm. In his last two terms, FDR could count only one significant domestic achievement, the GI Bill, which was more a product of patriotic fervor combined with fear of postwar unemployment than a product of progressive zeal.

A fair judgment of Truman's performance required remembering that no one had elected him president. His accidental ascension lacked any mandate or program, certainly not in civil rights. The political reality was that even if he had been more vigorous in hectoring Congress about the FEPC or other matters important to black Americans, there is little reason to think he would have gained any ground. Lawmakers would pursue what they regarded as their own best interests. As Walter White remarked in exculpating Truman from blame for the House Rules Committee not clearing the way for a permanent FEPC through Congress, "It was not his fault a tie vote prevented action."

Civil rights remained a crucial issue for Truman—and was becoming increasingly more so. For the sake of his presidency and his party, as well as for the benefit of black Americans, Truman needed to develop a better strategy than simply muddling through. His hand was forced by the violence and discord triggered by the rising tide of black expectations crashing against the implacable will of the white South. The result bore out the warning of Virginius Dabney two years earlier in his *Atlantic Monthly* article forecasting "a racial explosion." Dabney recalled the bloody clashes in the summer after the end of the Great War, a period that came to be called Red Summer. By some reckonings, at least twenty-five major riots erupted across the country, bringing about the lynchings of more than fifty blacks. In Houston, after black soldiers responding to the goading of white hoodlums went on a rampage, killing seventeen whites, nineteen of the doughboys were hanged and fifty-one were jailed for life. After an inquiry into the summer's worst outbreak, a week of disorder in Chicago that took thirty-eight lives, a gubernatorial commission declared, "The moral responsibility for race rioting does not rest upon hoodlums alone but also upon all citizens, white or black, who sanction force or violence in interracial relations or who do not condemn and combat the spirit of racial hatred this expressed."

Whatever impact this conclusion might have had on Americans faded under the pressures of the home front tensions of World War II, as the riots in Detroit and elsewhere in 1943 had demonstrated. Soon after the war ended, the violence resumed, mainly in the states of the Old Confederacy. The spark, as Dabney had foreseen, was provided by indignation at blacks refusing to stay in the place assigned to them by Southern law and custom. Georgia, where the Ku Klux Klan had been reborn in 1945, was the scene of some of the worst incidents in reaction to a rise in black voting strength in the state. Aroused by the candidacy of Herman Tallmadge, the scion of a racist dynasty founded by his father, Gene Tallmadge, known for snapping his galluses and spewing invective, a record 100,000 blacks voted in the Democratic gubernatorial primary. Tallmadge won anyway, and retribution against blacks was swift. Within three days of the election, Mario Snipes, the only black man to vote in his district, was shot and killed in his own front yard. A sign posted on a black church warned, "The first nigger to vote will never vote again."

In that same summer of 1945, and in that same state, a black man just released from jail on bail was lynched, and three other blacks who happened to be with him were also shot and killed. Meanwhile, as new Klan chapters sprouted around the South, a half dozen cases of lynchings were reported in small Southern communities, places where the Klan typically found its greatest support. In May 1946 in Columbia, Tennessee, in an apparent celebration of a decisive setback to the FEPC in the Senate, Klansmen, local police, and National Guardsmen stormed through the town terrorizing its black citizens. Trumped-up charges brought the arrest of thirteen, some of whom were slain in jail. On June 14, the American Federation of Labor filed a complaint with the justice department charging that a black trade unionist, Willie Dudley, had been abducted and beaten by masked Klansmen in Gordon, Georgia.

Adding to the anger and frustration of blacks and their white allies was the failure of the legal system to respond to this crime spree. Indeed, in Alabama, which ranked close to Georgia as a trouble spot, law enforcement was part of the problem. In Birmingham, the state's industrial center and its largest city, where Eugene "Bull" Connor presided over the police department, his officers were alleged to have killed five black war veterans in separate incidents in the first six weeks of 1946. Police committed similar mayhem in Louisiana, Texas, Tennessee, and South Carolina in February.

Protests to President Truman and other political leaders were lodged by every black and civil rights organization of consequence. Max Yergan, president of the National Negro Congress, led a march of 1,000 to the White House and condemned Truman for not denouncing the racial violence. These sorts of demonstrations led to Truman's September 19 meeting with Walter White and his emotional pledge to "do something."

But black Americans had heard promises before from white leaders, pledges that had always been forgotten. If Walter White seemed willing to give Truman the benefit of the doubt, other black leaders were more skeptical and demanding, among them Paul Robeson. All-American athlete, star of film, Broadway, and the international concert stage, and left-wing militant often accused of being a card-carrying communist, Robeson now headed an organization called the American Crusade against Lynching. When he met with Truman a few days after the session with White, he brought with him the publisher of the *Chicago Defender,* as well as other civil rights activists. Things did not go well from the start. When Robeson asked Truman to issue a formal statement against lynching and to propose a full-scale program against mob violence, Truman told him no. Such pronouncements were political issues that had to await the right time, which was not the present, the president said. One member of Robeson's group suggested that "it seemed inept" for the United States to take the lead at the Nuremberg war crimes trials then going forward, "and fall so far behind with respect to justice for Negroes in this country." Truman snapped that one thing had nothing to do with the other. That was the end of the meeting. The reaction to this encounter in the black press detracted from whatever aura of interracial amity the president might have achieved with Walter White. "Truman and Robeson in Word Battle at White House," headlined the *Pittsburgh Courier* over its page one account of the meeting. The *Chicago Defender* was just as blunt: "Truman Balks at Lynch Action," it declared.

The president's meetings with White and Robeson suggested how far he had come in developing a working relationship with black leaders, and how far he still had to go. With White, the president was patient and empathetic. His encounter with Robeson turned into a blunder. Robeson got Truman's back up, but his behavior was predictable. He wanted attention for himself and his Crusade, and he concluded that the surest way to get it was to provoke the president. Truman should have understood that. Once he had agreed to the meeting with Robeson, Truman would have been wise to counter his demands with a soft answer, which would have avoided the hostile reaction in the black press.

Adding weight to the impact of his confrontation with Robeson was that the encounter coincided closely with the ouster of former vice president Henry Wallace from his cabinet. Indeed, the same issue of the *Chicago*

Defender that reported Truman's spat with Robeson carried a headline declaring, "Nation's Liberals Back Wallace Peace Stand." The story made a point of stating that "Negro and white progressive leaders" were launching a mass movement to support Wallace in his future endeavors, not just because of his foreign policy stance but also because of his commitment to civil rights.

In truth, civil rights was only one of a series of seemingly intractable problems Truman faced that autumn, which the 1946 congressional campaign had brought into bold relief. Labor strife, unreasoning consumer demands, greedy corporations, and other griefs of the postwar economic conversion put Truman's party behind the eight ball and added to the historically grim outlook for the party in power in off-year elections. For their part, the Republicans mounted a massive publicity campaign focusing attention on the discomforts of the past war period, neatly summed up in their campaign slogan: "Had Enough? Vote Republican."

The huge Republican gains on Election Day matched the GOP's great expectations: fifty-five seats in the House and twelve in the Senate, giving the president's opposition majorities in both houses. Truman was silent for nearly a week in the aftermath, and when he finally spoke, his words were a long way from the feisty rhetoric the public had become accustomed to. The people had spoken, he said. "I accept their verdict in the spirit in which all good citizens accept the result of any fair election." His subdued tone reflected his descent from a public approval rating in the mid-seventies to under 20 percent by election time. There was certainly no poll pointing to broad public support for action on civil rights. These circumstances hardly seemed favorable for Truman to take on the most controversial domestic issue of the time. However, during months of continuing lawlessness and brutality in the South, as well as increasing demand for action from civil rights supporters, Truman's attitude had hardened from concern to resolve. He had come to a turning point and had decided to act on his promise to "do something."

The closest that idea had come to a specific formulation was a suggestion by White House aide David Niles at the meeting with Walter White for a committee to find ways to ease racial tension. Along with his deputy, Philleo Nash, Niles bore the main responsibility for dealing with the various interest groups, particularly unions, Jews, and blacks, which FDR had pulled together into the coalition that four times elected him president. Creating a committee to deal with racial problems was certainly not a new idea. When he headed the NAACP, James Weldon Johnson had made a similar proposal to Warren Harding in 1921, before black leaders abandoned the hopes that Harding had fanned as a candidate.

After the Detroit Race Riot in 1943, FDR aide Jonathan Daniels had suggested something of the sort, and so had David Niles. However, FDR put off any such action until after the war.

When Niles sought to revive the idea at the meeting with White, no one was bowled over. White pointed out that getting congressional approval for such a panel would inevitably run into the sort of resistance that had smothered the FEPC. Even if no firm agreement came out of that meeting, Truman clearly wanted some action. He wrote to his attorney general, Tom Clark, mentioning the beating and blinding of black veteran Isaac Woodward by a South Carolina police chief, which White had told him about. "I have been very much alarmed at the increased racial feeling all over the country and I am wondering if it would be well to appoint a committee to analyze the situation and have a remedy to present to the next congress," the president said.

Not content to wait for the committee, a week after Truman's note, Clark filed criminal charges against Woodward's assailant, Batesburg, South Carolina, police chief Lynwood Shull, relying on a federal statute prohibiting police from depriving a citizen of constitutional rights. When brought to trial, Shull admitted hitting Woodward. But he claimed that he was just trying to quiet the black man because he had been disorderly on the Greyhound bus that took him to Batesburg. Medical evidence showed that Woodward had been bleeding from both eyeballs and that the cornea of his right eye had been broken. Despite this, it took just thirty minutes for the all-white jury to acquit Chief Shull. Aside from showing the administration's goodwill toward blacks, about all the case accomplished was to demonstrate the need for more effective federal weapons against racial violence—a point Truman seemed to fully realize. In sending David Niles a copy of his letter to Clark, Truman added a note to Niles: "I am very much in earnest on this thing and I'd like very much to have you push it with everything you have."

Niles, who had more experience dealing with organized labor and Jews among key Democratic interest groups than with blacks, turned the assignment over to his second in command, Phileo Nash. With a University of Chicago PhD in anthropology and a wife, Ethel, who had headed the first racially integrated school in Washington, D.C., Nash seemed to possess the right profile for the job. A native of Wisconsin, the thirty-three-year-old Nash had lingered in academia long enough during the hard times of the 1930s that he feared becoming "a research bum." He came to Washington in 1941 with the Office of Facts and Figures, the precursor to the Office of War Information, the administration's war propaganda agency. At OWI, he became the eyes and ears on racial tensions for Jonathan Daniels, aide to FDR and later Truman. In addition, Nash had helped to organize the American Council on Race Relations, aimed at easing racial tensions during the war.

Meanwhile, Truman had concluded that the way to avoid congressional resistance to a civil rights committee that White had worried about was to create it by executive order and to finance it from his own contingency funds, the same way FDR had set up the FEPC in 1941. With that plan in mind, Nash set about recruiting committee members, guided by Walter White's advice that the committee should be "broadly representative" of American life and not rely just on "especially interested persons like myself." Chosen as chairman, at White's suggestion, was General Electric president Charles E. Wilson. White had been told by a friend that Wilson, when asked to mention the most important issue facing the nation, had cited not foreign affairs or labor problems but race relations. Hard-driving and firm in his convictions, Wilson had butted heads with the military while overseeing wartime production on the war production board and had quit the post. He also bucked union pressure for postwar wage increases, but he came to believe that management was partly to blame for union demands. He was "a man with no great experience in race relations," Nash acknowledged later. "But nobody could say that with him as a chair that you were prejudging."

For the rest of the committee, Nash was guided largely by White's stress on broad backgrounds, so much so that some later referred to the panel as the "Noah's Ark Committee." "We wound up with two of everything," Nash said with only moderate exaggeration. There were two women, two Southerners. two businessmen, two labor leaders, two blacks, and several representatives of the clergy. Rounding out the fifteen-member panel were two almost obligatory selections: Morris Ernst, cofounder of the ACLU, a cornerstone of civil rights and civil liberties activism, and Franklin D. Roosevelt Jr., whose appointment established a link to the New Deal. Dartmouth University political scientist Robert Carr served as staff director.

In setting up the committee, the president's aides had thought of President Hoover's Wickersham Commission, which had been assigned to study the problems of law enforcement, as a template . It was an unfortunate model. Chaired by Hoover's attorney general, George W. Wickersham, and loaded with prestigious names, the committee offered almost as many judgments as it had members. This inspired the *New York World's* popular columnist, Franklin P. Adams, to a bit of doggerel that reflected the overall public reaction to the report:

Prohibition is an awful flop.
We like it.

It can't stop what it's meant to stop.
We like it.

That was not the sort of result Truman wanted. He made that clear in his marching orders to the fifteen-member President's Committee on Civil Rights on December 5, 1946, when he officially created the panel. Truman did not merely ask the committee to find out whether civil rights were being violated. That was taken as a given. "Today, Freedom from Fear and the Democratic institutions which sustain it, are again under attack," he told the panel. "In some places, from time to time the local enforcement of law and order has broken down, and individuals—sometimes ex-servicemen, even women—have been killed, maimed or intimidated." Moreover, he wanted the committee to do more than simply look into and lament these conditions. Its main task was to deliver recommendations for action by the federal government "for more effective means for the protection of the civil rights of the people of the United States."

That was backed up with a pep talk personally delivered by the president. "I want our Bill of Rights implemented in fact," Truman told the panel at its first meeting in January 1947. "We have been trying to do this for 150 years. We are making progress but we are not making progress fast enough." The federal government, he acknowledged, should not be called upon to exercise dictatorial powers in the nation's state and cities. "But," he added, "there are certain rights under the Constitution of the United States which I think the Federal Government has a right to protect. It's a big job. Go to it."

In an embarrassing sign of the gap between Truman's lofty goals and the state of race relations in the country he governed, particularly in its capital city, a week after he met with the new committee, he himself was accused of racial insensitivity. On January 22, 1947, the president, the first lady, and daughter Margaret went to Washington's National Theater to see the revival of Sigmund Romberg's schmaltzy musical, *Blossom Time*. As it happened, the theater had been picketed since the show opened earlier that month by a local civil rights group, the Committee for Racial Democracy, because of its long-standing refusal to admit blacks. Learning of Truman's plans, the group had wired him, urging him to respect their protest and not attend, a telegram Truman later claimed he never saw.

When the president's limousine pulled up in front of the theater, Secret Service agents shooed away the eight pickets from the entrance, though they hovered near enough to be easily seen. Asked about the episode the next day at his regular press conference, Truman was abrupt, claiming that he first learned of the picketing from that morning's newspaper. "I wanted to see the show," he added. "I wanted to see it for 20 years. So I went down there and saw it." His dismissive tone drew laughter from the assembled correspondents.

As the *Baltimore Afro-American* pointed out, no one asked Truman how he would have reacted if he had known of the picketing. Based on his past statements, it would have been a hard question for him to answer. In his 1940 campaign speech and after, the president had been at pains to distinguish between the constitutional rights of black Americans, which he was prepared to defend, and social equality, which he rejected. He might well have reasoned that admission to a theater, even in the capital of their country, was not a constitutional right for blacks but rather a function of what he would regard as social equality. In other words, Truman wanted to define civil rights for black Americans in his own terms, not theirs. He had asserted in his Sedalia campaign speech that blacks themselves did not want "social equality," though he did not say how he knew this. At any rate, he might have realized that the more he championed what he regarded as civil rights, the harder it would become for him to ignore the rights that blacks claimed for themselves.

Whatever Truman's rationale, his actions plainly angered many blacks. "It has become difficult for some people to accept President Truman's explanation," the *Baltimore Afro-American* asserted. The paper could not resist pointing to the contradiction between Truman's attendance at a theater that closed its doors to Washington's blacks and his creation of a committee to help redress the injustices inflicted on blacks around the country. Moreover, the *Afro-American*'s editorial writer also recalled another example a year earlier of Truman's civil rights solipsism. This was the controversy over Bess Truman's attendance at a tea in her honor hosted by the Daughters of the American Revolution at Constitution Hall. Soon after she had been invited to that event, word got out that the DAR had refused permission to Hazel Scott, the celebrated black pianist and wife of Harlem congressman Adam Clayton Powell, to perform at its hall. That rejection naturally recalled the DAR's refusal in 1939 to allow the renowned contralto Marian Anderson to appear at the ball. This refusal led Eleanor Roosevelt to quit the DAR and help arrange for Anderson's memorable Easter Sunday concert at the Lincoln Memorial.

In closing its doors to Hazel Scott, the DAR had snubbed the wrong husband. Powell, a flamboyant clergyman and son of a wealthy Baptist minister who turned to politics, came to Congress in 1945, the only other representative of his race besides Chicago's William Dawson. Dawson was considered a party regular. Powell soon made a point of challenging the establishment at every turn, beginning with the ban against blacks using the House restaurant. In view of the DAR's treatment of his spouse, Powell wired Bess Truman reminding her of Eleanor Roosevelt's protest and urging her not to attend the tea. When she went anyway, he lashed out at the first lady as the "Last Lady." Typically indignant at any slur aimed at a member of his family, Truman, when talking to his staff, referred to Powell as a "Nigger preacher." Truman also saw to it that for the rest of his presidency, Congressman Powell was never invited to the White House, even for annual receptions for members of Congress. Truman's use of the "n" word in a conversation with an aide remained private for years after his presidency, but the divergence between his views on civil rights and the broader expectations of many blacks would continue to plague him.

As Truman should have realized, having lived and worked in the nation's capital for more than eleven years, the potential for such contretemps as his attending the picketed National Theater and the Hazel Scott controversy was rife. Washington was a Southern city, and racial segregation in its environs was very much like that of any other Southern city. The major difference was that, thanks to the presence of the federal government, blacks could more readily find employment there than elsewhere in the South, though rarely above the level of clerk. Another difference was that unlike the rest of the South, segregation of the 300,000 blacks who made up more than a third of the capital's population was achieved not by statute but rather by culture, custom, and political clout. Indeed, back in 1872, when Washington briefly functioned under home rule, its lawmaking body had banned racial discrimination in hotels, restaurants, barbershops, and other public places. That statute remained on the books and in force until 1901, when Congress, in the process of abolishing home rule, adopted a new set of laws for the district and simply deleted, though it did not repeal, the anti–Jim Crow law.

However, the Southern lawmakers who dominated the congressional committees that managed the capital's affairs combined with real estate and other business interests to ensure that barriers to blacks were as high and as rigid as anywhere else in the country. Being barred from the National Theater and movie houses outside their own neighborhoods was the least of the problems for blacks. The ghettos in which blacks were confined were as crime-ridden, overcrowded, and decrepit as any in the nation. Their neighborhood schools were dilapidated, crammed, and understaffed. Blacks could get served at lunchrooms, but they had to stand and eat. They might enter a department store, but they often could not get waited on.

Though liberals seeking to combat discrimination cited Washington as a shameful example, a particularly dramatic one because Americans liked to refer to it as the "capital of the free world," the reality was that conditions in Washington differed only in degree from those in cities in the North. In New York and the nation's other Northern big cities, blacks had an easier time getting into restaurants and theaters, but most lived in ghettos, often in run-down dwellings, and white flight to the suburbs had become one of the dominant phenomena of American postwar existence. Some unions had helped blacks find work, and decent pay, in a range of industries. Just as the federal government was a relatively accessible employer for blacks, so too were city and state governments in the North—though again at lower levels in the pecking order. In the professions, notably medicine and law, as in the upper echelons of big corporations and in many other desirable occupations, such as finance, entertainment, and professional sports, opportunities for blacks were all but nonexistent. This was the broad sweep of the wrenching problems Truman had committed himself to address.

In the face of these bleak circumstances, blacks had to struggle to find reason for hope. In the NAACP's annual report, presented just as the civil rights committee was starting its work, Walter White looked back on 1946, with all its antiblack violence, as one of the "grimmest in history." Yet he pointed to "the burning core of resistance" to racism as a positive portent for the future.

For once, a branch of the federal government had provided the NAACP with grounds for optimism. White cited the U.S. Supreme Court's 1944 decision in *Smith v. Allwright*, which struck down the all-white Democratic Party primary in Texas. Like a number of other Southern states, Texas relied on this device as its shield against black voting. In the case before the Court, the Texas Democratic Party contended that as a private organization, it was free to limit voting according to its own preference. The justices saw through that claim. Their opinion pointed out that the Democratic primary, which in most places in the South was tantamount to election, was an integral part of the political process, and that the color ban amounted to a denial of the Constitution's guarantee of equal rights. The case, argued before the Court by the NAACP's chief counsel, Thurgood Marshall, represented perhaps the most significant victory the justices had ever granted to the cause of civil rights. The results were immediate and significant, as reflected by the increased black turnout in Georgia in 1946 to vote against Herman Tallmadge, and also in Texas and Florida.

Responding to the increased energy of the civil rights movement and encouragement from some white politicians, blacks were voting in growing numbers in many places in the North too. Indeed, after the 1946 elections, dismal as they were in general for Democrats, Truman aide David Niles found some bright spots in black districts. "The Negro vote in New York City was decisively pro-Democrat," Niles reported to Matthew

Connelly. GOP governor Thomas E. Dewey, a likely Truman opponent in 1948 who was considered a relative civil rights liberal, was unable to win a single Harlem district. The returns also showed that black support for Democrats was by no means automatic. It depended, as with other voting groups, on efforts made by the party and its candidates. In Ohio, a critical battleground in any presidential election, Cleveland voters elected three black Republicans to state office.

"The Cleveland Democratic organization, however," as Niles pointed out, "failed to place a Negro on the ticket." Moreover, in Columbus, the state capital, "the heavy Negro vote was all Republican." In Pennsylvania, another swing state, Philadelphia sent five blacks to the state assembly, all of them Republicans. What's more, one of them was a dentist who had served several terms as a Democrat and then jumped to the GOP.

With the Republicans in control of the Congress for the first time in sixteen years, blacks looked eagerly to the newly empowered GOP for gains that the Democrats had denied them. Their hopes had been fostered by the 1944 Republican platform, which pledged itself in no uncertain terms to establish a permanent Fair Employment Practices Committee. The Republican Speaker-designate of the House of Representatives, Representative Joe Martin of Pennsylvania, punctured that bubble even before he had officially taken his office by letting black Republican leaders know that the GOP would not fulfill that promise. Acknowledging that the FEPC platform pledge was a bid for the black vote in the 1944 presidential election, Martin bluntly noted that blacks did not take the bait. But as Martin explained, the Republicans had another, more fundamental reason for not acting against employment discrimination. Speaking with notable candor, Martin said many businessmen who helped finance the party would rebel if they were subject to a ban against racial and religious bias in their hiring.

Questioned about these remarks, Martin later denied saying any such thing, branding the story "Democratic propaganda." However, when asked what the prospects for an FEPC were in the new Republican Congress, Martin said he had not had time to think about that. All of this served to underline the main point Walter White wanted to make as he surveyed the political landscape at the start of 1947. "In seventeen Northern and border states with a combined electoral vote of 281 it should be remembered by both major parties the Negro vote could swing the balance of power." In the wake of the Democratic defeat in 1946, as Truman and his aides looked ahead to 1948 and the contest for the White House, this was a reality they could not afford to overlook.

As he began his presidency, Harry Truman looked ahead to gaining victory over the Axis powers. But another challenge loomed at home: the conflict between the demands of black Americans for equality and stubborn white resistance. (Courtesy Harry S. Truman Library)

Tom Pendergast gave Truman
his start in politics. Boss Tom's
unsavory reputation in Kansas
City clouded Truman's image in
Washington. But Truman owed
Pendergast for teaching him
the value of black support in
seeking office. (Courtesy Harry S.
Truman Library)

A long-time stalwart in the party
of Lincoln, Chester A. Franklin
was an unlikely ally for Democrat
Truman. But fed up with GOP
indifference on racial issues,
Franklin was impressed by Judge
Truman's efforts on behalf of
local blacks. (Courtesy The Black
Archives of Mid-America, Inc.)

The racial problems facing President Truman were foreshadowed by wartime violence, notably in Detroit, where thirty-four died in 1943 rioting. In 1944, blacks in the Motor City paraded to show their determination to bury segregation. (Courtesy Library of Congress)

Pledging to support the black drive for racial justice, Truman became the first president to address the NAACP in June 1947. Some 10,000 heard him speak at the Lincoln Memorial, and worldwide radio carried his speech to millions more. (Courtesy Harry S. Truman Library)

Soon after he urged Congress to enact his civil rights program, the touring president was hailed by Virgin Islanders, among them William Hastie (left), whom Truman had named the territory's first black governor. (Courtesy Harry S. Truman Library)

Not everyone was pleased with Truman's civil rights message. South Carolina's Strom Thurmond (second from right) led Southerners in protesting to Democratic national chairman J. Howard McGrath (seated). He politely brushed them off. (Courtesy Library of Congress)

NAACP head Walter White (center) and aide Roy Wilkins (left) sparked the black drive for equality. Chief Counsel Thurgood Marshall (right) won the epochal Supreme Court ruling ending school desegregation, with an assist from Truman's justice department. (Courtesy Library of Congress)

In 1941, A. Philip Randolph's threat to stage a mass march on Washington protesting job bias prodded FDR to create the FEPC. In 1948, Randolph's warning that blacks would resist serving in a Jim Crow army spurred Truman to integrate the armed services. (Courtesy Library of Congress)

EXTRA — By Executive Order

PRESIDENT TRUMAN WIPES OUT SEGREGATION IN ARMED FORCES

2nd Order Sets Up FEPC In All Government Jobs

NATIONAL Edition

Chicago Defender

WORLD'S GREATEST WEEKLY

Copyright 1948 by Robert S. Abbott Pub. Co., 3435 Indiana Ave., Phone: Calumet 9650

VOL. XLIV., No. 16   CHICAGO, ILL., SATURDAY, JULY 31, 1948

10c PAY NO MORE

In a dramatic and historic move, unprecedented since the time of Lincoln, President Harry Truman issued Monday afternoon two executive orders which doom forever Jim Crowism in the Armed forces of the United States and guarantee equal job opportunities in the Federal government and all of its branches.

Executive Order No. 1

Establishing President's Committee on Equality of Treatment and Opportunity in the Armed Services.

services in order to determine in what respect such rules, procedures, and practices may be altered or improved with a view (See, WIPES OUT, Page 3)

Under 'States' Rights'

Posse, Bent On Lynching, Searches Woods For Prey

Rumor Negroes Would Resist Scatters Mob

Intended Victims Escape; 2 Whites Shot As Prowlers

HAZELHURST, Miss.—A mob of 200 armed whites, including highway patrolmen lined up on the hunt of Turkey Creek, at Dentville, all night Friday afraid to cross because one of their number said that some of the 75 Negroes who took refuge in a woods across the creek were armed.

SAVE This PAPER It Marks HISTORY

Aubrey Williams Bids Dixie Demos Farewell: 'Get Out And Stay Out'

By JOHN LEFLORE

Come Back And Do A Job Is Truman Edict

GOP Must Decide What Comes First, Party Or Nation

Dustin' Off the NEWS
By LUCIUS C. HARPER

South Doesn't Know About The Old Constitution

Baltimore Sidesteps Court Order Ending Golf Link Jim Crow

Wallace Says He'll Stay In Race, But Won't Predict Victory In '48

By VENICE T. SPRAGGS

PHILADELPHIA—Henry A. Wallace has no intention of abandoning his "peoples movement" whose followers approved his presidential candidacy at the founding convention of the new Progressive Party which attracted a wide-and eye-opening attendance.

Asks Integration In U. S. Department

Leaders To Help Raise Funds For Demo Campaign

CIVIL RIGHTS IN PRACTICE is shown here as

Demand Return To Dixie Of Coast Businessman Freed 21 Years Ago

OAKLAND, Calif.—Following unusual procedure, Gov. Earl Warren last week slated for July 27 a public hearing of the case of Wiley King, 45, well known local businessman and churchman, whom the state of Mississippi demands be extradited for what King supporters claim was a self-defense slaying performed many years ago.

Hint L. Lomax Jr. To Marry Writer Almena Davis Soon

Snub Truman's Wife; Friends Are Too Dark

Klan Increases Members To Scare Negroes From Voting

STONE MOUNTAIN, Ga.—Garbed in bedsheets presumably designed to strike fear into the hearts of Jim Crow's faithful voting.

6 Killed, 19 Hurt As Trucks Collide On Memphis Highway

FRENCHMAN'S BAYOU, Ark.—Six workers, including two women, were killed, and nineteen others were injured, near here Wednesday morning in a collision between a truck bearing 50 colored cotton choppers and a large highway transport.

Judge Moore's Reappointment Wins Bar Nod

WASHINGTON—The Bar association has unanimously approved the reappointment of Judge Herman E. Moore to the bench of the U. S. District Court of the Virgin Islands.

WRITE YOUR CONGRESSMAN—TODAY

— Urge Him To VOTE FOR —

PRESIDENT TRUMAN'S CIVIL RIGHTS LEGISLATION

Civil Rights Mean A Guarantee of Human Rights To You!

WRITE YOUR Congressman In Washington TODAY!

Blacks viewed Truman's 1948 edict banning segregation in the military as the most important presidential action on their behalf since the Emancipation Proclamation. He also ended segregation for federal civilian workers. (Courtesy of the *Chicago Defender*)

Charles Fahy, a former top New Deal lawyer, led a long battle against military foot-dragging to make Truman's integration decree a reality. Korean war casualties bolstered the effort forcing assignment of black troops to combat units. (Courtesy Franklin D. Roosevelt Presidential Library)

7

★ ★ ★ ★ ★

MORE THAN A DREAM

Truman's decision to create the President's Committee on Civil Rights would ultimately give new focus to his presidency and lead to a transformation of race relations in the country. However, this was not evident at first, to either supporters of civil rights or their opponents. After all, the pages of American history were strewn with the names of presidential committees, such as the Wickersham commission, whose output usually amounted to no more than attempts to sweep problems under the rug. Despite Truman's vigorous instructions to the new panel, no one knew where all this would lead.

In June 1947, six months after the executive order establishing the committee, Truman himself provided a powerful hint about what he wanted to accomplish in a speech to the annual meeting of the NAACP in Washington. Truman's acceptance of Walter White's invitation to address the gathering carried historical significance because he would become the first president to address the most important organization advocating for black Americans. David Niles, Truman's chief liaison to Democratic interest groups, and who seemed personally less concerned with blacks than with Jews and organized labor, apparently concluding that this symbolism was sufficient, recommended that the subject of civil rights should be restricted to "the closing paragraph of the speech, not to exceed one minute." However, Truman had no intention of shrinking the message he wanted to deliver to a few sentences. Instead, when accepting White's invitation, he asked him for a memorandum "emphasizing the points you think I ought to emphasize." White told him, as he later recalled, that if Truman included even half the things the NAACP head thought he ought to say, "the Southern Democrats would probably want to run him out of the country." White and Truman both laughed, but the truth is that Truman was well aware as he worked on his speech with the help of staffers from the Committee on Civil Rights that what he had to say would be no laughing matter to many people, including members of his own family.

On June 28, 1947, the day before he delivered his speech, he wrote to his sister, Mary Jane Truman, to alert her and their mother, whose health was failing. "I've got to make a speech to the Society [sic] for the Advancement of Colored People tomorrow and I wish I didn't have to make it," he began, then made an unfavorable reference to another speaker at the event, the former first lady. "Mrs. Roosevelt has spent her public life stirring up trouble between whites and blacks—and I'm in the middle," he added. "Mamma won't like what I say because I wind up quoting Old Abe. But," he concluded, "I believe what I say and I'm hopeful we may implement it."

A crowd of more than 10,000 saw him at the Lincoln Memorial. Millions more heard him in the United States and by shortwave radio around the world. Truman's oration conveyed a passion and commitment that belied the ambivalence of the private comments he had made to mollify his sister and mother. Indeed, Walter White later compared Truman's speech to the Gettysburg Address. Truman declared that by civil rights, he meant "not protection of the people against the government, but protection of the people by the government," a concept far broader and stronger than any other president had conceived. For the first time, he linked the battle to advance these rights at home to the cold war struggle against the Soviet Union, thus adding a powerful pragmatic weapon to the civil rights arsenal. Referring to the contest with communism to win allegiance of "desperate populations" across the globe, Truman said, "Our case for democracy should be as strong as we can make it. It should rest on practical evidence that we have been able to put our own house in order."

The main justification for his advocacy was based not on international relations but on the bedrock principles that defined the country he led. "As Americans, we believe that every man should be free to live his life as he wishes," Truman declared. "If this freedom is to be more than a dream, each man must be guaranteed equality of opportunity. The only limit to an American's achievement should be his ability, his industry, and his character." He concluded, as he had warned Mary Jane Truman, with a prayerful quote from Lincoln urging national unity "in pursuing benefits for all classes and conditions of mankind."

When he was finished, he returned to his podium seat next to Walter

White and told the NAACP leader, "I mean every word of it and I am going to prove that I do mean it." Significantly, the president did not feel the need to burden his audience with a restatement of his opposition to social equality for blacks, as he had articulated in the Sedalia speech opening his 1940 reelection campaign. Evidently he had come to realize that this opinion, assuming he still held it, would not advance the cause that was now his immediate priority.

What the president did say at the Lincoln Memorial was enough for the NAACP's *Crisis* to describe his address as "the most comprehensive and forthright statement on the rights of minorities in a democracy and the duty of the government to secure safeguards that has ever been made by a President of the United States." Still, blacks and other civil rights supporters wanted to see more tangible gains, and for this, they looked to the report of the Committee on Civil Rights. However, this was taking time—more time than the White House had planned. The longer the committee worked, the more work it found. The full committee met ten times, and members also met in subcommittees assigned to specific issues. In addition to reviewing drafts of proposed civil rights laws submitted by the justice department, the committee heard testimony from scores of witnesses and studied relevant material from more than 100 organizations. As the committee moved ahead, disagreements surfaced over what to recommend and what to leave out. Discarded as impolitic or beyond the committee's jurisdiction were proposals for antilynching laws aimed at entire communities, for repealing the sedition laws, and for denying congressional representation to states where voting laws hindered minorities from casting their ballots. Mid-March of 1947 was the initial target date for the submission of the report, but that was postponed more than once.

The committee reached basic agreement on its proposals at a July meeting in Dartmouth, and a draft prepared by staff director Carr was circulated among members. One of its members, Methodist churchwoman Dorothy Tilly, worried that Truman would reject the report because it denounced segregation. However, her arguments were overridden by the majority, which wanted to do just that. Finally, Carr set the date for submission to the president in late October 1947.

This was too long to wait for some NAACP militants, particularly W. E. B. Du Bois, who sought international support for black demands. On October 23, 1947, Du Bois, now the director of special research for the NAACP, submitted to the United Nations under the aegis of that organization *An Appeal to the World*, a 155-page chronicle of the long and troubled history of black Americans. What it amounted to was an indictment of the government of the United States on the charges of pervasive discrimination and injustice against black Americans. The Soviet Union had called on the UN to investigate the petition. However, with the backing of other nations that feared international scrutiny of their domestic affairs, the United States persuaded the United Nations to table the NAACP petition. Du Bois, who was suspected by his critics of communist affiliation, was charged by Jonathan Daniels, a member of the UN's committee on discrimination against minorities, with aiding the Soviets against the United States in the cold war. He responded that the NAACP was not "defending Russia," but rather was "trying to get men like Mr. Daniels to stand up and be counted for the decent treatment of Negroes in America."

Despite such complaints, the NAACP's manifesto attracted worldwide attention. Attorney General Clark told the National Association of Attorneys General that he felt "humiliated" that the NAACP believed it had to go beyond America's borders to present its grievances. To demonstrate the federal government's concern, Clark said, the civil rights unit of the justice department was being strengthened to act where states failed to meet their obligation to protect the rights of citizens.

The plea to the international community served as a preamble of sorts to the long-awaited report of the President's Committee, submitted on October 29, 1947, and pointedly titled with a memorable phrase from the Declaration of Independence, "To Secure These Rights." First laying out what it considered essential rights for all Americans, notably the right to equal treatment, the report went on to recount, sometimes in brutal detail, the ways in which these rights were often denied to blacks and other minorities. And finally, as the president had directed, it set out proposals to correct these abuses—goals that in many ways anticipated the accomplishments of the civil rights movement more than two decades later. Among them were expanding the justice department's civil rights section; enacting federal laws punishing lynching and police brutality; banning the poll tax; safeguarding the right to cast ballots in primaries and general elections; and outlawing discrimination in private employment. Not only did the report take aim at racial discrimination, but it also denounced segregation, calling for the denial of federal funds to any public or private program that drew a color line. If the report had its way, the nation's capital, where Jim Crow was pervasive, would become a model for the country by integrating all its public facilities, including its public schools.

When President Truman received his copy of the report, he remarked that "this committee has given us an American charter of human freedom and a guide for action." Three months later, on February 2, 1948, Truman sent a special message to Congress calling for enactment of a broad range of the report's recommendations, most notably a lynching ban, an end to the poll tax, creation of a permanent Fair Employment Practices Committee, and safeguards for the right to vote. He shied away from attacking segregation directly, as the report advocated, except in interstate travel, perhaps because the government he led was in itself a prime culprit, particularly in the civil service and the armed forces. However, he promised executive action to change these policies.

Reaction from the Northern press and civil rights organizations was by and large favorable. But there were a few carps. The *New York Herald Tribune,* a voice for moderate Republicanism, chided the president for asking too much, suggesting that he should have set aside the most controversial items. A more common criticism was that the president was simply playing politics to avoid losing black votes to Henry Wallace, who, as many had anticipated, had announced his presidential candidacy on an independent ticket two months earlier. The plan did indeed win general approval from the black press, including the *Norfolk Journal and Guide,* which provided a rebuttal to those who questioned Truman's motives. How much political benefit would Truman reap in the long run, the paper asked, since he had "alienated the vast majority of the white South" in doing "a great and selfless thing"?

Many white Southerners did not need to hear the president's words to sense the threat. The committee's report had been enough to tell them that the political winds from the White House were gusting against them. The first significant sign of what was to come emanated from the heart of the Old Confederacy, Jackson, Mississippi, where Fielding Wright, a more restrained version of his state's best-known politician, Theodore Bilbo, took office as governor on January 20, 1948. Whatever stylistic differences he may have had with Bilbo, when it came to race, in substance, Wright's racial views were scarcely different. The direction of Truman's policies, Wright contended, was designed "to wreck the South and its institutions," which the new governor pledged himself to defend. "Vital principles and eternal truths transcend party lines," he warned, adding ominously that "the day is now at hand when determined action must be taken."

Such sentiments were not limited to the Magnolia State. Southern governors meeting in Wakulla Springs, Florida, just as Truman delivered his civil rights message to Congress debated a proposal from Wright to immediately plan for a new political party. Alabama governor James Folsom wanted more time. He proposed that the governors wait until the Democratic convention in July to challenge the president and his proposals. They finally agreed, as a compromise of sorts, to send a delegation to meet with the Democratic Party's national chairman, J. Howard McGrath, and then report back.

What was particularly surprising about this idea was the identity of its author, Strom Thurmond of South Carolina, who, with this gathering of Southern leaders, began to move toward a destiny even he would hardly have imagined. Until that moment, Thurmond was no better known outside Dixie than a dozen other obscure Southern governors. Indeed, he had been chief executive of his own state little more than a year. A farmer's son and decorated World War II veteran of the Eighty-second Airborne Division, he had worked his way up the political ladder from school superintendent to state senator to county judge to winner of a ten-man race for governor. In South Carolina, what called more attention to Thurmond was the forty-four-year-old governor's marriage near the end of his first year in the statehouse to the former Jean Crouch, a woman twenty-three years his junior who had recently been crowned queen of the state's Azalea Festival.

Adding an intriguing, if generally unspoken, element to Thurmond's background were the persistent rumors that at twenty-two, he had fathered a daughter with a black teenager, Carrie Butler, who had been a family maid. The rumors were steadfastly denied by Thurmond, but they gained support from those who saw the supposed offspring, Essie May, riding the elevator to Governor Thurmond's office in the statehouse, and were finally confirmed after Thurmond's death in 2003. Even as he refused to acknowledge paternity, Thurmond secretly helped to support his daughter, a not uncommon behavior in the South since the days of slavery perhaps most famously illustrated by Thomas Jefferson's affair with his slave Sally Hemings.

Perhaps because of this hidden episode, the new governor, while always adhering to Southern customs, had never been as flamboyant in exploiting racial tensions as some colleagues. In February 1947, barely a month after he took office, he won wide praise for his response to the most brutal lynch murder his state had seen in years. An armed mob of whites hauled a Greenville black man, Willie Earle, charged with stabbing a white cab driver, from his jail cell, beat him beyond recognition, and shot him. Thurmond reacted immediately, calling the crime "a blot on the state of South Carolina" and an offense against "decency, law and the democratic way of living." He ordered the state police to commit all their resources to solve the case. Within two weeks, thirty-one men, most of them cab drivers, were arrested for their involvement in Earle's murder. Thurmond was praised by the *New York Times* and local black leaders. However, two months later, an all-white jury acquitted all defendants. Still, Thurmond wrote one citizen that "great good was accomplished" because the fact that charges had been brought at all had set a useful precedent for the conduct of law enforcement.

In addition to condemning racial violence, Thurmond had not been among the many Southern leaders who grumbled about the Democrat in the White House. To the contrary. Only a few months before the Southern

storm broke over civil rights, in a speech at a public affairs forum in Louisville, Kentucky, carried over the radio, Thurmond gave the president a
strong vote of confidence. Looking ahead to the 1948 election, Thurmond
declared, "We who believe in a liberal political philosophy, in the importance of human rights as well as property rights will vote for the election
of Harry Truman and I believe we will win." Thurmond had focused on
Truman's record in foreign affairs in making his assessment. But whatever his reason, his conclusion was much different, even in October 1947
when the forum was broadcast, than the views of most in his party and
his region.

What changed his mind was Truman's civil rights proposals, which
Thurmond recognized as the knock of political opportunity. These had
created a storm of protest in Thurmond's South Carolina, where politicians practically lined up to denounce what the Committee on Civil Rights
had brought forth and what Truman had backed. Viewing the governor's
caucus as a way to get on the national stage, Thurmond prepared for the
forthcoming session with his aides, and he had a draft of a resolution calling for the meeting with McGrath in hand when he arrived. To complete
his triumph, the governors not only endorsed Thurmond's plan, but they
also chose him to head the mission to McGrath on February 23, 1948.

Four days before that meeting, Southerners got a chance to vent their
resentment at one of the ritual feasts of the national Democratic Party, the
annual Jackson Day dinner in Washington. The 2,100 guests filled two of
the capital's grandest banquet halls, where they dined on terrapin soup
and breast of capon and toasted their nineteenth-century patron saints
in champagne. The distinguished company included the president of the
United States, Harry S. Truman, and the first lady, members of the cabinet, and sundry senators and representatives. Conspicuous by their absence were a number of prominent Southerners, who chose skipping the
dinner as a way to demonstrate their disapproval of Truman's civil rights
initiatives. Senator Olin Johnston of South Carolina, Strom Thurmond's
home state, had reserved a table right in front of Truman at the head table
with instructions to keep all eight chairs empty.

In anticipation of the forthcoming July nominating convention,
though the president himself had yet to publicly make known his intentions, the after-dinner entertainment featured a Draft Truman rally, complete with placards reading, "Harry Is Our Date in '48." Later, Truman
would spell out his vision of progressive liberalism, which he promised
would draw on the Democratic heritage to brighten the future for all
Americans for at least four more years.

He made no mention of his civil rights proposals. But that omis-
sion did little to mollify Thurmond and his fellow Southerners at their

February 23 meeting with McGrath. McGrath, a native of Rhode Island, which three times had elected him governor before sending him to the U.S. Senate, had a grasp of political reality appropriate for a national chairman and old-fashioned Irish pol. He knew that presidents do not commonly kowtow to senators, an insight that Truman had reinforced in advance of the meeting with Thurmond's delegation and that McGrath demonstrated at this get-together. The governors wanted Truman to withdraw the proposals in his civil rights message to Congress. No, said McGrath. The governors also wanted the party to reinstate the requirement for a two-thirds majority for nominating a president at its national convention, a rule that amounted to a Southern veto over the nomination. "That would be a step backward," McGrath told them. The chairman also turned down their request that the president scrap his proposal to establish a civil rights division in the justice department. In only one respect did McGrath offer the Southerners anything representing an olive branch, and that was with respect to the party platform. The civil rights plank in the 1944 platform, which black leaders had derided as vague and toothless, McGrath said might be "adequate" for 1948.

At the moment the Southerners were far more concerned with Truman's legislative agenda than with the platform. McGrath himself probably thought he was offering the South a concession that would not matter much when push came to shove. After all, the Democrats had not had a battle over their party platform since the memorable 1924 convention, when passionate debate over the Klan and Prohibition tore the party apart. But the convention and the platform debate were still four months off. As McGrath and Truman would discover, what might have been a reasonable assumption in years past turned out not to fit 1948. The debate over civil rights, instead of subsiding as McGrath no doubt hoped, would, as spring turned into summer, reach a new crescendo of discord.

As for Thurmond's delegation and other Southerners, in the aftermath of their meeting with McGrath, there was not much for them to do but sulk in private and threaten in public. National party leaders would soon be forced to realize, the Southern governors declared in a joint statement, "that the South is no longer in the bag." A "vast majority" of Southern Democrats, they warned, intended to force the party to return to its original principles "and will resort to whatever means are necessary to accomplish this end."

Democrats could not discount the impact of a Southern defection on the national political balance of power. Until the advent of FDR, their party's chances of winning the White House and majorities in Congress had been heavily dependent on the backing of the Solid South, with its 100 or so electoral votes. It was true that in his four presidential victories, each time garnering more than 400 electoral votes, FDR marginalized the impact of the South because he would have won even without its support. However, not many Democrats believed that Truman could match that performance in 1948, and so the South's support seemed once again likely to be critical.

Whatever Southerners decided to do about the political future, Truman soon made clear that he was not going to be held hostage to their plans. On March 8, 1948, the president instructed Chairman McGrath to tell the country, including the South, that he was prepared to accept the nomination of his party to seek a full term in his own right. To make plain Truman's disregard of the South's not-so-veiled threats to defect, McGrath volunteered that on civil rights, "the president's position remains unchanged."

But as Truman and the Democrats looked ahead to their July convention, the struggle of black Americans for equity was not the only moral dilemma on the president's mind. Indeed, in the same press briefing in which he underlined Truman's determination to push ahead on civil rights, McGrath brought up another concern that he said affected the security of the nation and the world. This was the fierce international controversy over the future of Palestine and the aspirations of Jews to make a part of that disputed Holy Land a national homeland for their people. It was not just their both being mentioned by McGrath almost simultaneously that linked civil rights to Palestine. The two issues were connected in more fundamental ways. Both challenged the nation's conscience. The civil rights debate dealt with the struggle to redeem the American promise of equality and justice for a group of citizens who had been betrayed for all the three centuries they had endured on American soil. At the heart of the controversy over Palestine was the quest for peace and security by a people who for centuries had been denied a land they could claim as their own, and who had suffered a crime as infamous as any in recorded history. But as much as these were matters of high principle, both were linked to the struggle for political power.

Both civil rights and a Jewish homeland were causes that attracted support from the core constituencies of the Democratic Party. Most of the elements of the American Jewish community who sought a new country for displaced Jews also were vigorous supporters. They backed banning the poll tax, ending lynching, and other priorities on the civil rights agenda, along with contributing financially to such causes. Organized labor also backed both a Jewish homeland and the cause of civil rights, as did the leading liberal publications. *The Nation,* for example, in the February 1948 issue, published an editorial warning that if Truman backed away from the Jewish cause in the face of Arab pressure, "the course will be set for war." This was followed with an editorial urging Truman to defy Southern threats against his civil rights program.

Yet viewed in political terms, both issues offered risks that at least matched their potential rewards. Truman's response to the crisis that in the spring of 1948 developed over Palestine would illuminate his emerging approach to civil rights. By the time Truman ascended to the White House, the fight for a Jewish homeland had waged for all of the twentieth century. It had reached a milestone near the end of the Great War, with the Balfour declaration, Britain's pledge to establish a Jewish homeland in the Mideast. However, the issue came to a head near the end of World War II, when FDR, on his way home from the Yalta conference, met with Saudi Arabian monarch Ibn Saud and asked the monarch to endorse the idea of a Jewish homeland. When Saud turned him down, Roosevelt promised that the United States would never aid the Jews at the expense of the Arabs. Moreover, Roosevelt had followed up his verbal promise to the king with a written pledge.

Truman, although a relative naif on some complex foreign policy issues by the time he became president, already held a position on Palestine. As a senator, he had backed the goals of Zionism and its ultimate objective of reopening the biblical Promised Land to the Jewish diaspora, a position he reinforced by his endorsement of efforts to rescue those trapped in Hitler's Europe until his falling-out with the Bergson group. He had many Jewish supporters and friends in Missouri, notably Eddie Jacobson, his erstwhile Camp Doniphan comrade and partner in the haberdashery business. For him, as with many other members of Congress, this was not a hard choice. In the aftermath of Nazi persecution and the final solution, Jews had the sympathy of much of the world. In more pragmatic terms, American Jews were famous for their generosity in making political contributions, and equally well known for their tendency to vote in a bloc for whichever candidate or party supported the causes closest to their hearts.

Truman certainly was mindful of all this. But other, more personal aspects fostered his sympathy for the Zionist cause. His religious beliefs and his childhood reading of the Old Testament enhanced his view of the Jewish claim to the "land by the River Jordan," celebrated in song and Gospel. He later explained that it was not just the biblical chronicles but rather the "whole history of that area" that captured his attention. As he recalled telling Rabbi Stephen Wise, who was among the first American Jewish leaders to try to sway the new president, he "knew all about the history of the Jews" and had read the Balfour declaration. Finally, as Truman reminded a group of American diplomats who warned him of the dangers for the United States if he backed a Jewish homeland, hundreds of thousands of his constituents favored the Zionist cause. "I do not have hundreds of thousands of Arabs as constituents," he added.

Actually, the political environment for Zionism was not quite as one-sided as that. Although there were few Arab constituents, the two most prominent leaders of the American foreign policy establishment, Defense Secretary James Forestall and, even more important, Secretary of State George C. Marshall, were firmly opposed to Zionist demands. They regarded the Jewish push for a homeland as jeopardizing U.S. relations with the Arab states, thereby threatening their country's access to oil and to strategic bases in the Mideast. With cold war tensions mounting steadily, the political significance of their opposition could not be dismissed by any president, and certainly not by a new, unelected chief executive whose foreign policy credentials were as slim as Truman's appeared to be.

Caught between pressure from American Jews mourning the victims of the Holocaust and his top military and diplomatic advisers, who warned that yielding to the Zionists would harm the country he was sworn to protect, Truman turned for guidance to his aide, New Dealer David Niles. Born David Neyhus in 1890 to Russian Jewish immigrants, Niles was raised in near poverty in North Boston. He never advanced beyond high school, but the tumult of the Great War allowed him to get a white-collar government job in the information office of the department of labor. With the return of peace, Niles bent his energies to a range of liberal causes, and ultimately to the New Deal and the White House. He never married and seemed completely absorbed by his work. In the 1930s, Niles had been a member of the American Jewish Committee, which then represented the Jewish establishment and which frowned on Zionism. "Before Hitler came to power I was an anti-Zionist, then after that I became a non-Zionist," he explained. "After the war I became a full believer in the idea of political Zionism." His allegiance was cemented by his long-time secret love affair with Justine Wise, the daughter of Rabbi Stephen Wise, an ardent Zionist.

Niles's task was made more difficult when, as Truman began to incline toward the Zionist position on Palestine, Saudi Arabia protested, arguing that FDR had given his word not to support the Jews. Truman was nonplussed, knowing nothing of the exchange of letters earlier that year between FDR and the king. Embarrassed, the administration was forced to release the correspondence, which the state department argued fell short of an ironclad commitment to opposing a Jewish state. After some further protests, clinging to the hope of future economic aid from the United States, Saudi Arabia let the matter drop. But the unwelcome surprise caused problems for Truman by undermining the rapport he was trying to build with American Zionists.

They did not make it easy for him. Supporters of the Jewish home-land flooded the White House with letters and petitions as the fate of Palestine was being decided by the United Nations, to whom great Britain had turned over the problem of its former mandate. The pressure irritated Truman. But he realized that he was competing for Jewish favor with Republicans trying exploit Jewish dissatisfaction with what many perceived as Truman's indecisiveness. As the 1946 congressional elections approached, Truman chose Yom Kippur, the solemnest of Jewish holy days, to issue a statement that not only called for "substantial" Jewish immigration into Palestine, but also for the first time spoke favorably of the idea of creating a "viable Jewish state" in Palestine, the basic Zionist goal.

It was true that during the next eighteen months, Truman's backing for a Jewish state sometimes seemed to waver. However, in November 1947, he was swayed in a meeting with Chaim Weizman by the idealism of the future first president of Israel. On his orders, the United States then voted in a crucial United Nations vote to partition Palestine, setting the stage for the establishment of a Jewish state.

The state department fought back, warning of violence in Palestine and promoting the idea of a trusteeship, which would postpone the birth of a Jewish state indefinitely. Out of patience with Jewish lobbying, Truman himself seemed to be leaning in favor of the trusteeship plan and cut off contact with Zionist leaders. At the pregnant moment, Truman's ex-partner, Eddie Jacobson, wangled his way into the Oval Office and begged his old friend to meet with Weizmann again. Tearfully, Jacobson told Truman that he was shocked that Truman had refused even to talk to any of the Zionists: "It doesn't sound like you, Harry, because I thought you could take this stuff they have been handing out."

With his back to his visitor, Truman stared out at the White House Rose Garden for a moment. Then he turned to face Jacobson with his answer: "You win, you bald-headed son-of-a bitch. I will see him."

Within the week, Truman met with Weizmann, who once again, as in their first meeting the previous fall, adumbrated the Zionist dream of making the desert bloom. When their talk ended, both men realized that they had reached a common understanding on U.S. support for a Jewish homeland in Palestine. Still, there was continued resistance from the state department, particularly from Marshall. To the public, George Catlett Marshall, who had been America's top soldier before Truman made him the country's top diplomat, was the very embodiment of restraint and self-discipline. The term "military bearing" might have been invented to describe his presence. Stern, unbending, and humorless, his aloofness kept even presidents at their distance. Neither Franklin Roosevelt, who had made him Army chief of staff, nor Harry Truman, who had named him secretary of state, called him by his first name. Marshall had on more than one occasion shown no qualms about standing up to FDR when the president was at the height of his prestige and power.

He certainly felt no restraint about challenging Harry Truman as he struggled for public respect. The decisive moment came on May 12, 1948, little more than forty-eight hours before the Palestinian Jews were scheduled to declare their nationhood. On hand in the Oval Office along with Marshall and the president were Marshall's deputy Robert Lovett, David Niles, and Clark Clifford, who had become Truman's chief adviser on domestic matters, including politics. The forty-one-year-old Clifford's presence at this high-level parley illustrated his rapid rise since this former St. Louis lawyer and Navy captain had joined Truman's staff as his assistant naval aide in 1945. Clifford soon found opportunities to help out Sam Rosenman, the FDR aide whom Truman kept on with the title of special counsel, a job that included speechwriting and political troubleshooting. When Rosenman left, Clifford assumed his responsibilities and soon gained even greater influence. Tall, handsome, and patrician, he operated with a silky self-assurance generating the notion that his success in any particular endeavor was inevitable.

Clifford opened the meeting, arguing for swift recognition of the new government-to-be. Arab and Jewish forces were already shooting it out, Clifford reminded Truman, and unless the United States moved promptly, the Soviet Union would use that opening to enlarge its influence in the Mideast. Practical considerations aside, the United States had a "great moral obligation" in the wake of the Holocaust to help bring the "ancient injustices" inflicted on the Jewish people to an end. While he talked, Clifford noticed Marshall's face growing red with anger. Then the secretary got the floor. "I don't even know why Clifford is here," he told Truman. "He is a domestic adviser and this is a foreign policy matter."

"Well, General," Truman responded, "he is here because I asked him to be here."

Marshall's response was to accuse Clifford of trying to inject politics into the issue. Defense Secretary Lovett picked up the attack, charging that quick recognition of the Jewish state was buying a "pig in a poke." It was Marshall who got everyone's attention when, looking at Truman directly, he said, "If you follow Clifford's advice and if I were to vote in the election I would vote against you."

For a moment, no one said anything. Clifford later remembered thinking that if Marshall made his views public and quit in protest, it "could virtually seal the dissolution of the Truman Administration" and break up the Western Alliance, not to speak of the damage that would be wrought on Truman's prospects in the forthcoming election. Truman himself offered some placating words to Marshall and ended the meeting. "Well, that was rough as a cob," he said to Clifford.

But the president refused to budge. Marshall, while maintaining his opposition to recognition in private, abandoned any thought of a public protest after friends reminded him that after all, the question of recognition was reserved by the Constitution for presidents to answer. That cleared Truman's way to do what he was determined to do: give the U.S. imprimatur to the Jewish homeland-nation, an action he took only minutes after Israel had declared itself in existence. Defenders of Truman against charges that he had been overly solicitous of American Jewry could point out he granted only de facto recognition, simply acknowledging the reality of Israel's existence, limiting the U.S. commitment to the new country, as distinguished from de jure recognition. Moreover, he refused to sell arms to Israel even as the new country was under sustained assault by the surrounding Arab nations. However, the practical and symbolic significance of Truman's action was clear and enduring; it was evident that the United States was underwriting Israel's survival.

As might be expected, initial reaction was mixed. The 9,000 delegates to the Southern Baptist Convention, members of Truman's own faith, overwhelmingly voted down a motion of approval as a way of rebuking him "for playing politics with the Jewish vote." Delegates told the reporters that their action also reflected discontent with his civil rights proposals, further evidence of the linkage of the two issues, at least in the minds of many Americans. The *Chicago Tribune*, no friend to Democratic presidents, suggested that Truman "had set a record for diplomatic haste" and demonstrated that "there is little he won't do to pick up votes in closely contested states this autumn."

But so far as Truman's political future was concerned, the most significant and hopeful response was that of Republican Michigan senator Arthur Vandenburg, who called Truman's action a "logical and proper step." Coming from the chairman of the Senate Foreign Relations Committee and the unofficial voice of bipartisan foreign policy, that judgment would make it hard for any other Republican to use this issue against the president.

Political calculus entered into Truman's decision making, as it did in his dealings with civil rights. Just as anything he did to advance civil rights would cost him with Southerners and other defenders of the status quo, whatever he did for the embattled Jews of Palestine would leave him vulnerable to the accusation of playing politics with the nation's security. The positive side had to be examined closely. The richest prize the Jewish vote had to offer was the state of New York, with its forty-seven electoral votes, the most of any state. However, in 1944, Roosevelt, running against

New York's own governor, Tom Dewey, had carried New York by only 300,000 votes out of six million cast, helped by the Jewish vote. With Dewey, still governor and favored to again be the Republican standard-bearer, and Henry Wallace on the ballot, likely to pull substantial Jewish votes, Truman probably realized that not even his stance on recognition could assure that New York would wind up in the Democratic column in November.

Presidential politics aside, in helping out the Palestinian Jews, Truman was able to serve his own institutional purposes by in effect putting the state department in its place. As he noted in his memoirs, "I wanted to make it plain that the President of the United States and not a second or third echelon in the State Department is responsible for making policy." By doing so, Truman enhanced his stature in the eyes of others and bolstered his own self-confidence as he moved toward difficult decisions on racial issues.

The parallel between Truman's handling of Israel and civil rights is striking. On both issues, he hesitated and equivocated while measuring the consequences. In the end, in both cases, he faced up to the challenges and the risks and took the high ground. The importance to Truman of the "moral obligation" to which Clifford referred was dramatically underlined when, a year after recognition, the chief rabbi of Israel, Isaac Herzog, visited the United States. Meeting with Truman, he expressed his gratitude on behalf of his country. The rabbi did not mince words. "God put you in your mother's womb," he told the president, "so you would be the instrument to bring the rebirth of Israel after two thousand years." Among the witnesses was David Niles, who said later, "I thought he was overdoing things but when I looked over at the president, tears were running down his cheeks."

Back when he had actually made the decision in favor of Israel, Truman had little time to commemorate his accomplishment with either tears or celebration. He had to try to win an election, an enterprise in which, by the verdict of all political pundits and most practitioners, his chances of success fell in a narrow range from slim to none.

8

RUNNING FROM BEHIND

Despite all the gloom and doom surrounding his prospects, Truman was eager to get started taking out after the Republicans, and he decided not to wait until the nomination was actually his. Weeks before the Democratic convention in June 1948, he seized upon a long-standing invitation to receive an honorary degree from UCLA and set out for the West Coast, stumping all the way. The two-week train trip took him across eighteen states, allowing for major addresses in five key cities and more than three-score off-the-cuff rear platform talks. He not only got an early start, but also tested a new informal stump delivery instead of the stiff and dreary monotone that had been his trademark. Also, he could pass the bill for all of this to the federal treasury, instead of the impecunious Democratic Party.

Truman had begun this election year talking about civil rights and his legislative proposals, and the Southern reaction had made that issue a dominant feature of the political landscape. However, one revealing aspect of his first campaign trip, unofficial as it was, was how little he now had to say on that subject. On his June cross-country journey, he touched on civil rights only once, at the start of the trip and then only indirectly, touting its importance as a weapon against the spread of communism at home. The context was the alarm being spread about the need for the government to battle the Red menace in the cities and countryside of America. Truman told a Swedish American heritage group that the way to prevent communism from gaining a foothold was not by restricting political activity, but "rather by providing more and better democracy." Slum housing, substandard wages, denial of the right to vote, inadequate health care, widespread unemployment—each of these hardships amounted to "an invitation to communism," the president said. Calling for the nation to remedy such inequities, Truman declared, "We believe in human freedom and human equality and it is that belief which makes us strong today." Though Truman did not mention race or even use the term civil rights, at least one respected black journalist was eager to interpret the speech to make the point blacks wanted the president to be making. "If apprehensive Negroes feared, or Southern revolt Democrats hoped that the man would back track from civil rights advocacy, their fears of the former were needless, and the hopes of the latter have gone with the wind," wrote Stanley Roberts of the *Pittsburgh Courier*, who cited significant numbers of blacks in Truman's audience.

But Truman had a broader agenda for this trip, and for the rest of his campaign. He was laying out a blueprint for his election, and as it would turn out, with a few notable exceptions, civil rights would be little more than a footnote on his agenda. He did not retreat from his positions; in fact, he would launch new initiatives from the Oval Office. However, out on the hustings, he apparently concluded that bringing up the subject would benefit neither his candidacy nor the cause itself. If blacks and other civil rights supporters wanted evidence of Truman's continued good intentions, they would have to read between the lines and take the rest on faith. They could, for example, conclude that Truman considered the battle to improve the lot of black Americans as embodied in the underdog theme, which, it became clear, would undergird his candidacy. "There is just one big issue," he declared in a home state talk in Jefferson City, and elsewhere along his route. "It is the special interests against the people. And the president being elected by all the people represents the people."

Who represented the special interests? Why, the Republican Party, of course, most particularly the Republican-controlled Eightieth Congress. Truman was especially blunt about whose fault that was. "You have that special interest congress because only one-third of you voted in 1946 and you are getting just what you deserve," he said time and again. "I have no sympathy for you. And if you do that again you will get what you deserve."

The spectacle of the president of the United States rampaging across the land, spewing hellfire and brimstone at the Grand Old Party, was more than Republican Senate leader and presidential hopeful Bob Taft could stand. "The president," the Ohio senator protested, "is blackguarding the Congress at every whistle station in the country." Delighted Democrats seized upon the statement as evidence of Republican scorn for small- and medium-size towns across America, and the term whistle stop, a catchier variation of Taft's exact words, entered the political lexicon as a synonym for Truman's against-the-odds campaign.

Along with blasting the Republicans, Truman used his trip to solidify his position within his own party, where he was harried not only on the right, by Southerners grumbling about civil rights, but also on the left. As to the Southerners, that point had been covered in an unsolicited memo on political strategy originally written by former FDR aide Jim Rowe but revised and submitted by Clark Clifford under Clifford's name. In a platitudinous treatise that mostly recycled conventional wisdom, Clifford did stick his neck out on one point: how Dixie would respond to Truman's civil rights offensive. The gist was that Truman had nothing to fear. "It is inconceivable that any policies initiated by the Truman Administration no matter how 'liberal' could so alienate the South in the next year that it would revolt," Clifford wrote.

But no harm was done. Clifford's advice on strategy was so strewn with iterations of the obvious that, the author's later claims to the contrary, there is nothing to suggest that Truman took much stock in the forecast or the rest of the memo. Having run for office half a dozen times before, he followed a similar pattern. As in his underdog 1940 Senate campaign, he seemed tireless exhorting any crowd that could be assembled, no matter how small the size. Truman did not need a strategy memo to tell him that the South aside, he had other problems among the Democrats. For one thing, there was Henry Wallace, who was relying on the newly created Progressive Party to serve as a vehicle for his campaign. The main basis of Wallace's challenge was his contention that Truman's tough line with the Soviet Union would only worsen relations with the world's other superpower. In addition, by claiming that Truman's civil rights rhetoric lacked conviction, Wallace was competing for black votes.

But a fair number of liberal Democrats, while determined to remain within their party, badly wanted someone besides Harry Truman as their leader. This alienation was not entirely new. From the beginning of his presidency, liberals had difficulty mustering enthusiasm for Truman for a variety of reasons. For some, this had as much to do with style and personality as with substance. They lamented that the prairie-bred president lacked the sophistication and élan admired by the Eastern elite. Even many who did not share Henry Wallace's foreign policy views still resented Truman for replacing Wallace on the ticket in 1944. Eleanor Roosevelt sometimes criticized his policies in her newspaper column, "My Day," and others complained because he invited Herbert Hoover to the White House.

As the 1948 campaign ripened and Truman's prospects dimmed, the liberal attitude of being "just mild about Harry" turned to outright opposition. In April of election year, the national board of Americans for Democratic Action, probably the best-known and most influential of the nation's liberal groups, repudiated Truman's candidacy. As alternatives, the ADA urged instead the nomination of either Dwight Eisenhower or Supreme Court justice William O. Douglas. Adding its prestige to the clamor, the *New Republic,* in a front-page editorial in its April issue, called on Truman to retire and give way to Eisenhower.

The enthusiasm for Eisenhower, who had announced plans to become president of Columbia University on leaving the Army in June 1948, demonstrated how little the dump Truman movement was grounded in ideology—or, for that matter, in reality. No one in either party had a clear idea of what Eisenhower's political beliefs were. Moreover, he had ruled himself out as candidate early in the year. Nevertheless, two of FDR's sons, Franklin and Elliott, publicly supported Eisenhower for the Democratic nomination and a third, James, the California Democratic chairman, worked behind the scenes to organize an Eisenhower draft.

Though Truman may not have regarded the liberals' crush on Eisenhower to be a serious danger, he could not help being annoyed. He thus took advantage of his visit to Los Angeles on his cross-country tour to let the air out of the Ike boomlet. After basking in the tumultuous reception from a crowd of roughly one million that he had received in Los Angeles and then getting his honorary degree, Truman summoned to his suite at the Ambassador Hotel James Roosevelt, FDR's eldest son, who was trying to use the dump Truman movement to aid his political ambitions. "Your father asked me to take this job," Truman told Roosevelt as Truman's Secret Service agent, Henry Nicholson, later recalled. "I didn't want it but your father asked me to take it, and I took it. And if your father knew what you are doing to me he would turn over in his grave. But get this straight: whether you like it or not, I am going to be the next president of the United States." Whereupon Truman turned and walked out on the erstwhile insurgent, who had no time to think of a rejoinder.

Before Truman could nail down his party's nomination, he had to wait for the Republicans to choose their standard-bearer. Both parties had agreed to meet in the same city, Philadelphia, to ease the logistical and economic burdens on the television networks, which for the first time would cover the national conventions. Ultimately, of course, television would later alter the tone and shape of American politics, for better or for worse. But 1948 seemed like an inauspicious time to start. Interest in the campaign that summer was at a low ebb because most journalists, and most Americans to the extent they thought about it at all, were convinced that the Republicans would oust Truman. Nevertheless, the idea of getting involved in the making of the president was a potent lure for the infant medium. As for the parties, they were drawn to the chance to be immortalized in living black and white. It was true that there were fewer than a million TV sets in the country, only eighteen cities with television stations, and only half of those on the cable stretching from Boston to Richmond and thus able to transmit live coverage. But the networks pledged gavel-to-gavel coverage and to show kinescopes, made by filming broadcasts off the TV screen, to cities not on the cable.

At first glance, the Republican convention offered the networks the potential of at least a modicum of suspense. The question to be answered was whether the front-runner, New York governor Thomas E. Dewey, could overcome the onus of his defeat by FDR in 1944 and hold onto his lead over Ohio senator Robert Taft and former Minnesota governor Harold Stassen. Dewey took charge from the start, then steamrollered his way to a third ballot nomination. The New Yorker had started on this path when still in his thirties; he had earned a national reputation as a racket-busting prosecutor in New York City and won the governorship of the state in 1942. He had bounced back quickly from his presidential defeat in 1944, winning reelection to the New York governorship in 1946 by the largest margin in the state's history. True, Dewey had his flaws, particularly in the new age of television. At five feet eight inches tall, he was, in modern idiom, vertically challenged. He sometimes felt obliged to stand on an unabridged dictionary or a stack of phone books while giving a speech. He sported a thin mustache, which gave him a fussy look. For all his rapid rise, he seemed particularly vulnerable to ridicule. When he first took aim at the White House in 1940 at the tender age of thirty-eight, resident New Deal wit Harold Ickes gibed that he had thrown his diaper in the ring. Alice Roosevelt Longworth, the tart-tongued daughter of former president Theodore Roosevelt, had famously likened Dewey's appearance to that of "the little man on the wedding cake." His robotic style did not help the impression he made on voters.

Such misgivings were swept away when Dewey embellished his convention triumph by persuading Earl Warren, then governor of California and a famous vote getter in the Golden State, to be his running mate. The coast-to-coast reach of the Republican candidate gave the GOP what national chairman Senator Hugh Scott of Pennsylvania called "a dreamboat ticket" that darkened the already bleak outlook for the Democrats when they assembled in the same city three weeks later.

Liberal Democrats may have taken heart that the Republican civil rights plank was watered down from their 1944 statement. Instead of specifically pledging to enact a permanent Fair Employment Practices

Committee (FEPC), as in 1944, a promise the GOP Congress did nothing to keep, the 1948 convention settled for a vaguer endorsement of "the right of equal opportunity to work." But there was little else from which Democrats could take comfort. Nevertheless, expectations that the Democrats would have a dull and dreary convention were shattered in what turned out be a year filled with failed predictions. Underlying the surprising injection of drama into the convention was civil rights, the result of the determination by party liberals that Truman would run on a strong civil rights plank, whether he wanted to or not.

Truman had instructed Chairman McGrath to make clear to the Southerners that spring that he would not back off his civil rights proposals, no matter what threats the Southerners issued. A few weeks later, when a group of Southern Democrats privately pledged that Dixie would back his candidacy if he would only soften his stand on race relations, Truman took the trouble to reply in writing:

> My forebears were Confederates. I come from a part of the country where Jim Crowism is as prevalent as it is in New York or Washington. Every factor and influence in my background—and my wife's for that matter—would foster the personal belief that you are right. But my very stomach turned over when I learned that Negro soldiers, just back from overseas were being dumped out of army trucks in Mississippi and beaten. Whatever my inclinations as a native of Missouri might have been, as president I know this is bad. I shall fight to end evils like this.

His attitude toward the civil rights plank of the party platform was much less clear. He had initially supported strong language that tracked his own legislative proposals. However, just before the Democratic convention was to open, Truman softened his stance, on the advice of Clark Clifford, "to keep peace in Philadelphia." To be sure, Clifford had assured Truman in his political strategy memo that a Southern revolt was "inconceivable." But that was November 1947, and now it was July 1948. Clifford saw things differently. The result was that, at the behest of Clifford and the president, the platform committee drafted a statement offering little more than mushy backing for constitutional rights, much in the vein of the Republican position.

As Clifford should have known, that would not satisfy blacks or their white liberal allies. Walter White had made the black position clear in his own testimony to the platform committee. "The day of reckoning has come when the Democratic Party must decide whether it is going to permit bigots to dictate its philosophy," he declared. But as the *Baltimore*

Afro-American pointed out, White's comments and similar rhetoric from other civil rights leaders was met with "a strange silence" and no questions from Southern members of the platform committee. They merely sat back and smiled. "From here it looks like a deal has already been made," the paper asserted.

The paper was right, of course. Except that the deal fell apart because of the determined protest from liberals, spearheaded by leaders of the Americans for Democratic Action, notably Andrew Biemiller, a former Wisconsin congressman teamed with the young mayor of Minneapolis and Democratic candidate for the U.S. Senate, Hubert Humphrey. They introduced an amendment to the White House–approved platform language calling upon Congress to support four specific proposals made by Truman, guaranteeing full political participation, equal employment opportunity, and equal treatment in the armed services, as well as banning lynching. The platform committee voted the amendment down. Humphrey, after pondering the damage he might cause to his own Senate candidacy, agreed to force a floor fight on the issue. All this came to a head on Wednesday, July 14, 1948, which happened to be the day that the convention was scheduled to nominate its presidential candidate.

The debate over the platform was complicated when delegates from Texas, Tennessee, and Mississippi introduced three different versions of a proposed plank affirming the party's dedication to the principle of states' rights, which in effect would have voided any civil rights plank the convention adopted. In making their case, the Southerners studiously avoided any reference to discrimination, segregation, or anything else having to do with race. Instead, they couched their arguments purely in the dialectic of states' rights and constitutional theory. But as it turned out, this camouflage did the South little good once Humphrey offered his plea for the muscular civil rights plan. Hubert Humphrey would win his Senate race that year and go on to be a defining force in national politics for three decades, serve as vice president of the United States, and run for president three times. But that afternoon in Philadelphia, he gave the speech of his life.

"There are those who say to you we are rushing this issue of civil rights," Humphrey acknowledged. "But I say we are 172 years late." He took note of the South's platform proposals. "There are those who say this issue of civil rights is an infringement on states rights." He countered in a line that would be long remembered: "The time has arrived for the Democratic Party to get out of the shadow of state's rights and walk forthrightly into the bright sunshine of human rights." That touched off a ten-minute demonstration and set the stage for the vote.

The balloting on the Texas proposal came first. It lost on a roll call vote of 925 to 309. Then the Mississippi and Tennessee proposals were defeated by voice votes. Humphrey's amendment was next. Back in Washington, while he awaited the time for him to go to the convention, the president of the United States was monitoring the proceedings via television and his various agents on the scene. In his diary, he kept a running commentary. "Platform fight in dead earnest," the president commented. "Crackpot Biemiller from Wisconsin offers a minority report on civil rights. [Former governor Dan] Moody from Texas offers states rights amendments."

While Truman watched on the tiny screen at 1600 Pennsylvania Avenue, the convention called the roll on the Humphrey amendment. Few had thought the civil rights forces had the numbers to win, but Humphrey had gained important support from an unexpected quarter. The Democratic Party's big-city bosses had rallied behind his cause, not because of his stirring rhetoric but because of pragmatic politics. Fearful that their own local candidates would be demolished in the anticipated landslide against Truman, they saw the strong civil rights language, with its appeal to black voters, as offering a chance for survival.

Before Humphrey gave his speech, Ed Flynn, the Democratic leader of the Bronx, had asked Humphrey to see his minority report. "Young man, that's just what this party needs," he told the stunned Humphrey, who had feared the very opposite reaction. Then Flynn sent runners to the floor to spread the word to three other urban titans—Jacob Arvey of Chicago, David Lawrence of Pittsburgh, and Frank Hague of Jersey City. They gave the orders, and their minions on the floor obeyed. The minority civil rights plank carried by a vote of 651½ to 582½.

Back in Washington, Truman noted, "The convention votes down States Rights and votes for the crackpot amendment to the Civil Rights plank," adding, "The crackpots hope the South will bolt." Even as Truman jotted that in his diary, in Philadelphia, the Alabama delegation sought recognition. But convention chair and House Speaker Sam Rayburn of Texas, realizing what Alabama intended, ignored the vigorous waving of the state's standard and gaveled the convention into recess.

"I am sure they want to bolt," Truman wrote about Alabama.

He was right about that. No sooner did the convention resume proceedings that evening than Handy Ellis, chairman of the Alabama delegation, got the floor. Alabama's presidential electors had been instructed, he explained, never to cast their vote for a Republican, never to cast their vote for Harry Truman, and never to cast their vote for any candidate with a civil rights platform such as that adopted by this convention. Half of the Alabama delegation, a total of thirteen, therefore considered themselves pledged to walk out. "I am also authorized to tell you that the Mississippi delegation is joining us," he added. "We bid you goodbye," he cried to a chorus of boos.

The two Southern contingents, Mississippi in the lead, marched straight down the center aisle into the Philadelphia streets, then being drenched by a summer rainstorm. The rest of the Alabama delegation and the contingents from the eleven other Southern states remained in their seats, most of them signaling their protest by refusing to join in the landslide vote for Truman's nomination. Instead, they supported Senator Richard Russell of Georgia, who got 263 votes to 947 for Truman. Of the 278 Southern votes cast, Truman got only 13.

Truman's course on the civil rights plank in the platform is not easy to track, given his bobbing and weaving, but it is not hard to understand. He started off supporting a strong statement, but then, persuaded by Clifford that party platforms have little real meaning anyway, he switched back to the bland approach. In the end, he could hardly have had much substantive quarrel with the Humphrey plank since it closely resembled his own legislative program, only in less specific language. While Truman's proposals had asked for a permanent FEPC in so many words, the platform sought only "equality of treatment" in employment. To cap it all off, in his memoirs, Truman claimed credit for the plank, saying he had "incorporated" his legislative goals into the plank. That was obviously not what happened, but a case could be made that without Truman's prior recommendations, no such plank as the Democrats adopted would have passed. His use of the adjective "crackpot" in his diary to refer to the ADA insurgency reflected Truman's tendency to lose patience with situations that did not develop as he had planned.

Just as Truman accepted the tough civil rights plank without complaint, he went along with the recommendation of party leaders that he select Kentucky senator Alben Barkley as his running mate. Barkley had earned the post with a stem winder of a keynote speech. He began by noting that the Republicans had promised "to clean the cobwebs" from government. "I am not an expert on cobwebs," he conceded. "But if my memory does not betray me, when the Democratic Party took over sixteen years ago, even the spiders were so weak from starvation they could not weave a cobweb in any department of the government in Washington." That brought the delegates to their feet cheering, which they kept up for most of Barkley's hour-long effusion of partisanship.

At any rate, the platform seemed like nothing more than a distraction to Truman, who had a bold plan to use his speech accepting the nomination to reverse the defeatist mood that prevailed among most leaders and followers of his party. His opening salvo set the tone for the next three months. "Senator Barkley and I will win this election and make those

Republicans like it," he said. "And don't you forget that." There were no halfway judgments in the president's outlook on the campaign, only wrongs and rights. The Democrats would win "because they are wrong and we are right. The Democratic Party is the people's party and the Republican Party is the party of special interests and it always has been and always will be." Then he ticked off a series of failures of the Republican Congress on issues vital to the citizenry: rising prices, housing, labor reform, education, social security, and finally civil rights.

Here was a chance for the president to separate himself from the platform plank his allies had fought so hard against on the floor of the convention. However, he did no such thing. Everyone knew he had proposed a civil rights program to Congress, he pointed out. "Some members of my own party disagree with me violently on this matter but they stand up and do so openly." The Republicans, on the other hand, "all professed to be for all these measures but the Eightieth Congress didn't act." Then Truman sprang his big surprise. He would use his power as president to call the Congress back into session to do the good things they claimed to favor but had failed to enact.

This would take place on July 26, which he added, Missourians call Turnip Day. Actually Turnip Day was observed on July 25, which in 1948 fell on a Sunday. So Congress could not meet until the following day, July 26. According to Missouri folklore, a half-pound of seed planted on Turnip Day would yield a couple of acres of turnips, or, as might be inferred from Truman's challenge to Congress, a bountiful Democratic harvest on Election Day. Truman pledged to set as priorities for the special session remedies for the housing crisis and for rising prices. He also dared the GOP lawmakers to act on other matters they claimed to support—and high on the list, along with extending social security benefits and expanding public power, were the civil rights proposals he had submitted six months earlier. "They could do this job in fifteen days if they wanted to do it," he said. "They'll still have time to go out and run for office."

But before Congress could take on the job Truman had assigned, this extraordinary political year would see two more presidential nominating conventions staged by two parties who could not be further apart on the ideological spectrum. First up was the States Rights Party, as the Southerners who rebelled against Truman and the civil rights platform plank decided to call themselves. They wasted no time. The defecting Alabama and Mississippi delegates were hardly out the door of Philadelphia's convention hall when Alabama governor Frank M. Dixon announced plans for the rebels to meet that very weekend in Alabama's capital, Birmingham, "to register their protests and adopt plans for the future."

The motivation to some was clear. The North, declared Governor

Dixon, "has put a knife in the heart of the South." The truth was, some Southerners were finding it hard to accept the changes in race being pushed upon them—not just by Truman and the Democratic Party, but by the federal courts. The year before the platform tempest in Philadelphia, in Columbia, South Carolina, federal district judge J. Waties Waring, echoing the 1944 Supreme Court decision in the Texas Democratic primary case, had outlawed Louisiana's white primary, adding, "It is time for South Carolina to rejoin the union." Defiant, the state's Democratic Party had sought to circumvent the rule in the spring of 1948 by requiring all voters to take a loyalty oath swearing to accept racial segregation. However, blacks appealed, and while Democrats debated civil rights in Philadelphia, in South Carolina, Judge Waring threw out the loyalty oath and commanded the Democrats to open their primary election to everyone, regardless of race.

That just added to the indignation of the 6,000 delegates crammed into Birmingham's municipal auditorium on Saturday, July 17, for the opening session of their one-day conclave. Among those present was South Carolina's Strom Thurmond, who had not been there long before he was importuned by fellow governors to be the new party's presidential candidate. They gave him an hour to make up his mind. He really did not need that much time. True, Thurmond had to consider that if the States Righters contributed to Truman's defeat, he would bear part of the onus for returning the Executive Mansion to the Republicans, whom many Southerners still could not forgive for the perceived injustices of Reconstruction. On the other hand, there was a chance he could emerge a hero. Few among the ardent States Righters, or Dixiecrats as they came to be called, believed in the possibility of winning outright. However, a strong showing in the electoral college could conceivably force the election into the House of Representatives and assure the Southern cause of influence in the choice of the ultimate winner. Anyhow, unless he made a total fool of himself, Thurmond would probably emerge as a national figure, and perhaps the most significant Southern politician in the land. And this was, after all, the destiny he had sought for himself when he first took a leading role in the challenge to Truman's civil rights program.

In contrast to the restrained tone the Southerners had established for themselves in Philadelphia, the States Rights Party convention was considerably more open in expressing their fundamental discontents. The convention managers displayed only the Stars and Stripes and state flags in the hall, but handheld Confederate banners were ubiquitous among the delegates, and the strains of "Dixie" and "Carry Me Back to Old Virginny" filled the air. When presidential candidate Thurmond and his running mate, Mississippi governor Fielding Wright, having both been nominated by acclamation, were escorted to the platform, one of the escorts carried a picture of Robert E. Lee.

Striding the corridors, along with such established Southern leaders as Mississippi senator James Eastland, were some fringe figures, such as former Oklahoma governor "Alfalfa" Bill Murray, a racist icon and Oklahoma delegate, as well as notorious Nazi admirer and anti-Semite Gerald L. K. Smith. Unlike the circumspect language of the platform proposals made by Southerners at Philadelphia, those at this convention did not beat around the bush. "We stand for segregation of the races and the racial integrity of each race," the party's declaration of principles announced. Thurmond was nearly as blunt in his acceptance speech. "If the South should vote for Truman this year we should petition the national government for colonial status," he declared. As to ending segregation, Thurmond thundered his defiance. "There's not enough troops in the Army to force the Southern people to admit the Negro race into our theaters, into our swimming pools, into our homes, and into our churches," he declared while the delegates roared their approval.

After the cheering had died down and the crowds had departed, Thurmond evidently had some second thoughts about his unbuttoned rhetoric. In a hastily organized telephone press conference with reporters from several Northern papers, he tried to separate himself from believers in white supremacy. Instead, he wanted to be regarded as a "progressive Southerner" interested in bettering conditions for blacks and defending states' rights. He pointed to his role in the Willie Earle lynching case, claiming that at "all times I have advocated better facilities for the Negroes." Along the same lines, he rejected an offer of support from Gerald L. K. Smith, declaring, "We do not invite and we do not need the support of rabble rousers who use race prejudice and class hatred to inflame the emotions of the people."

Thurmond's efforts to appeal to Southern resentment of pro–civil rights efforts without being branded a rabble-rouser himself was only one of the dilemmas he faced. He also had to contend with the reluctance of Southern politicians, however much they might sympathize with his cause, to break away from the Democratic Party and face all the risks such a breach entailed. Significantly, Arkansas governor Ben Laney, who was widely reported to be the first choice of the convention for president, did not even attend the session. Instead, Laney issued a statement that urged a cautious and inhibiting course of action for the new party: "Whatever is done must be done through and by the official Democratic organization in each respective state." But for the prospects of the new party taking over the Democratic ticket in key Southern states, the list of absentees from the convention was a discouraging omen. Boss Edward Crump of Tennessee,

Virginia senator Harry Byrd, and governors Herman Tallmadge of Georgia and Earl K. Long of Louisiana were among those who did not show up. Their nonappearance made it seem that they, and others with similar standing, would be as likely to oppose the efforts of the Dixiecrats as help them. They were among a significant number of Southern Democrats reluctant to plunge into the states' rights rebellion, in large part because they regarded it as a lost cause. In addition, many thought a wiser course would be to stay within the Democracy and continue to fight for their beliefs there while retaining their status in Congress.

If the Democratic platform stance on civil rights helped energize the States Rights Party, it threatened to have the opposite effect on Henry Wallace's new party by undermining its hopes for getting black votes. The 1944 Democratic convention's rejection of Wallace in favor of Truman had been a major reason, along with the new vice president's border-state origins, for black resentment of Truman. That seemed to provide Wallace with a ready-made constituency. Wallace supporters who made that calculation had not reckoned with Truman's newfound militancy on civil rights, notably his recommendation for legislation based on the report of his Committee on Civil Rights, all of which had ultimately led to the dramatic battle over the issue at the convention.

Indeed, on July 24, 1948, the day after the Progressive Party began its deliberations in Philadelphia, the same city the Democrats had just departed, the *Chicago Defender*, one of the nation's largest and most influential black newspapers, in an editorial headlined "We March FORWARD—With Truman," called for Wallace to quit the race. "There can be no doubt in anyone's mind about the SINCERITY of President Truman," the *Defender* declared. Wallace, the paper added, "should LEAD THE PARADE" of those who wanted to elect a liberal president. Arguing that the campaign really came down to a choice between Truman and Dewey, whose party offered only a "MAYBE" on rights, the *Defender* concluded that for a black voter to support anyone but Truman "is a vote against HIMSELF."

Faced with this and similar comments from other black leaders, C. B. Baldwin, the former New Deal farm agency official who had become Wallace's campaign manager, derisively dismissed such talk, describing the Democrats as having nominated "the man nobody wanted and adopted a program nobody wanted." However, the Wallace party's bid for black votes did not rest solely on scorning the opposition. Blacks played a far more prominent role in their convention than in the Democratic conclave—or the Republican meeting, for that matter. Charles P. Howard, a black lawyer from Des Moines and former Republican, was the keynote speaker, after W. E. B. Du Bois turned down that honor, though he did attend. Larkin Marshall, the Progressive Party's black senatorial candidate from Georgia, nominated Idaho Democratic senator Glen Taylor for the vice presidency. Paul Robeson spoke and sang. Reflecting the passion many in attendance shared on civil rights, Edgar Brown, a black leader from Washington, told the platform committee that the convention should move to Washington on its opening day to pressure the special session of Congress for enactment of a broad civil rights program. He demanded that, if necessary, Truman should use federal troops to enforce the rights of blacks to vote in the South.

Meanwhile, the Progressive platform laid out civil rights proposals that went beyond the language that had caused so much dissension at the Democratic convention. Condemning "segregation and discrimination in all its forms and in all places," the Progressives called for a presidential order ending segregation in the armed forces, in federal civilian employment, in the nation's capital, and, for good measure, in the Canal Zone. In his acceptance speech, in unusually harsh language, Wallace called lawmakers who opposed civil rights measures "murderers." Their votes, he charged, "stifle legislation and appropriations which would eliminate segregation and provide health and education facilities to bridge the gap of ten years life expectancy between a Negro child and a white child born this day."

Despite the stress on civil rights and the conspicuous minority presence at this convention, a good many prominent journalists, when they looked at the Progressive Party gathering, saw mainly one color. This was not black but Red—or a subtler shade that *Time* used to headline its coverage of the convention: "The Pink Facade." However, there was nothing subtle about the story itself, which branded Wallace as "the center piece of U.S. Communism's most authentic looking facade." Similarly, the *Baltimore Sun* headlined its story on the Progressive Party's platform "Marxist Line Followed by Third Party." On foreign policy, it demanded repudiation of the Marshall Plan and the Truman Doctrine, and called for disarmament talks leading to outlawing nuclear weapons, the *Sun* pointed out. On domestic policy, besides its sweeping civil rights proposals, the platform called for nationalization of banks and railroads. All this, the *Sun* pointed out, matched, point for point, the platform demands of the U.S. Communist Party set forth the previous May.

This treatment reflected in part the press's eagerness to tap into growing public anxiety about the danger of subversion at home and the threat of Soviet aggression abroad. Given the intensity of the cold war at the time, this coverage was clearly damaging to Wallace's cause. Wallace, his advisers, and his followers had themselves to blame for the rough press treatment their enterprise received. Few of even the party's harshest critics contended that Wallace himself or his advisers were communists, but what the party's leaders did seem guilty of was gullibility about communist aims and tactics, naïveté in allowing themselves to be manipulated by communists and their allies, and excessive self-absorption that blinded them to the reactions of most Americans to their rhetoric.

Wallace himself set the tone for his party's vulnerability. Confronted with the resemblance between his party's platform and the Communist Party platform, he said, "Then I'd say that they have a good platform." Months earlier, in March 1948, when the Soviets engineered a takeover of the Czechoslovakian government, Wallace called it "evidence that a 'get tough' policy only provokes a 'get tougher policy.'" Though that response was widely judged a major gaffe, three months later, when the Russians clamped a blockade on West Berlin and Truman ordered a dramatic airlift of supplies, Wallace once again blamed the militant stance of the United States, adding in his acceptance speech, "If I were president today there would be no crisis in Berlin."

Wallace's self-inflicted damage was not limited to foreign policy. When reporters at the convention tried to question him about letters he wrote years before to his White Russian mystic friend, Wallace branded them as stooges and refused to answer their questions. Respected journalist Howard K. Smith, an otherwise sympathetic observer, suggested that this episode should be made "into a handbook on how not to handle press conferences."

Few, if any, Wallace supporters came away from that gathering with much hope that their candidate could actually win the presidency, but given the weaknesses they saw in Harry Truman's candidacy, they still believed they could make a strong mark on history by raiding his liberal base and ensuring his defeat. But whether they could succeed would depend not only on their own energy and faith, but on the response of the president they were trying to bring down.

9

THE UPSET

In every election involving a sitting president, his record inevitably defines the contest. During the campaign the record grows, creating challenges and offering opportunities both at home and abroad. In 1948, Harry Truman confronted a major foreign policy challenge and turned it into an historic opportunity in civil rights.

The flash point, in February 1948, was the Soviet-inspired communist takeover of the government of Czechoslovakia, a coup that had special resonance for Americans. Many recalled that it was this same tiny central European nation that a decade earlier had been victimized by the infamous Munich agreement, which opened the gates for World War II and Hitler's conquest of Europe. In 1948, with Washington under a full-fledged war scare triggered by the Czech crisis, Truman appealed to Congress to gird for conflict. He renewed his earlier proposal for universal military training and asked also for a revival of the military draft that had expired with V-J Day.

Led by the ever-militant and ever-vigilant A. Philip Randolph, blacks immediately began to agitate for a ban against discrimination in the new selective service system. Blacks would refuse to serve in a segregated military, Randolph told the Senate Armed Services Committee. He himself would do all he could to aid them "to quarantine any Jim Crow conscription system." Pressed by Republican senator Wayne Morse of Oregon, Randolph said he would stick to that position, even if the United States was at war. That would amount to treason, Morse contended. "I would be willing to face that," Randolph responded, "on the theory that we are serving a higher law than the law which applies to the act of treason."

Southern lawmakers opposing any change in the military's long-standing racial policies were just as impassioned. They threatened to filibuster the restoration of selective service unless Truman promised to stick with the segregated status quo. Their rhetoric underlined the depth of their opposition to racial mixing in the services. Senator Allen Ellender of Louisiana put the matter simply: Negroes were inherently inferior, especially when it came to physical courage, and this was why they had done so poorly in combat. Southerners made a point of quoting Dwight Eisenhower's testimony earlier that year, when, as Army chief of staff, he appeared before the Senate Committee on Armed Services. "In general the Negro is less well educated," Eisenhower said, would get only minor jobs, and would have trouble gaining promotion "because the competition is too tough." Eisenhower added, "I do believe that if we attempt merely by passing a lot of laws to force someone to like someone else we are just going to get into trouble."

In the face of this opposition, Truman refused to promise to maintain military segregation, a pledge that would have been hard for him to make. It would have contradicted the recommendations of his civil rights committee and the implications of his own response. Still, Randolph and his allies were not satisfied. They wanted a specific ban on discrimination in the new draft law and explicit support from the president by an executive order. Otherwise, Randolph wrote the president, "Negro youth will have no alternative but to resist a law the inevitable consequences of which would be to expose them to un-American brutality so familiar during the last war."

Given this pressure as well as his own previously stated intention, Truman's action was inevitable. On July 26, just as the Turnip Day special session of Congress was convening, Truman issued two executive orders: 9980 proclaimed a policy of employment without discrimination throughout the federal government's civilian agencies, and 9981 called for "equality of treatment and opportunity" for all persons serving in the armed forces, regardless of race or religion. However, Truman was not naive enough to count on automatic obedience from admirals and generals. As part of his order, he announced he would establish an advisory committee to monitor the process he had set in motion.

Reaction was understandably confused. One reason was a statement by Army chief of staff and World War II hero Omar Bradley saying that the Army was "not out to make any social reforms" and would change its policies only when the nation as a whole had changed. Bradley, it turned out, had not read the executive order and did not realize that reporters were present when he spoke. However, the more fundamental reason for confusion was that the president's order, while calling for an end to discrimination, did not specifically require an end to segregation. This appears to have been the result of simple sloppiness in drafting. Whatever the reason, Truman was obliged to clear that up in a press conference a few days after he had issued the order. Asked whether his order was aimed at eventually ending segregation, Truman's response was a flat "yes." A few days later, Democratic Party chairman McGrath, at a meeting with Randolph and his allies, announced that the committee created by the president to monitor enforcement of his order would be committed to doing what Truman had decreed: ending military segregation.

The early reaction on this issue from both sides, the outrage of Southern solons and the suspicions of black leaders, provided Truman with evidence, if he needed any, of how difficult the task to which he had committed himself and the country would be. However, this was a challenge he could not truly undertake unless he could maintain his grip on the presidency. His next step in that direction had to be to deal with an inevitable confrontation with the Republican Congress.

Truman surely realized that, given the open hostility between himself and the GOP lawmakers, the possibilities for constructive agreement were minuscule, but on the chance that this special session might turn out to be something more than partisan theater, Truman was determined to play his part to the fullest. At the start of the session, fulfilling the promise he had made in his acceptance speech, Truman offered an eleven-point program, including approval of the civil rights proposals he had submitted the previous February. However, the Republicans had a civil rights card to play themselves. They introduced a specific ban on the poll tax, which Truman had sought in his civil rights message the previous February. As the Republicans expected—correctly, it turned out—this stratagem would result in a Senate filibuster by Southerners, which would keep that body tied up for the duration of the session.

When the special session adjourned in twelve days with nothing of consequence having been accomplished, the result was a substantive stalemate. Still, there was a potential tactical advantage for Truman in that he had gained more ammunition against his designated opponent, the Eightieth Congress. If Congress took no action on civil rights, Truman himself pursued the subject with a longtime friend named Ed Reynolds, who had been a World War I comrade years ago in Battery D. Reynolds had appealed to his old buddy, as a Southerner, to "go easy" on the civil rights issue.

"I am going to send you a copy of the report of my Commission on Civil Rights, and then, if you still have that antebellum pro-slavery outlook, I'll be very disappointed in you," Truman wrote his old pal, now a successful Kansas City businessman. "The main difficulty with the South is that they are living eighty years behind the times," he added. As he had often done before, he stressed that he was not seeking social equality, adding elliptically, "because no such thing exists," but stressing, "I am asking for equality of opportunity." Once again, as often in the past, he referred to the brutal treatment of black veterans, adverting to the blinding of Isaac Woodward by a South Carolina police chief.

Truman also brought up the working situation on the Louisiana and Arkansas Railroad, where, when the trains ran on coal, blacks had been used as firemen "because it was a backbreaking job and a dirty one." When the railroad switched to oil to fuel its engines, attitudes changed, and some black firemen were murdered "because it was thought this was now a white-collar job and should go to a white man. I can't approve of such goings on and I never shall," he told Roberts. In a handwritten postscript, Truman added, "This is a personal and confidential communication and I hope you'll regard it as that—at least until I've made a public statement on the subject—as I expect to do *in the South*," underlining the last three words.

As strong and as forthright as the letter was, Truman never got around to his predicted "public statement in the South." The closest he came was in Waco, Texas, on a late September campaign trip, when he shook hands with a black woman, prominent in a local interracial group. This gesture drew some faint boos from the crowd that were quickly drowned out by cheers. On the same trip, when Dallas authorities did away with segregation for the occasion, blacks mingled with whites in the crowd of 20,000 that cheered the president in the city's Rebel Stadium. Texas governor Beauford Jester, who had been among the Southern leaders who cried out that the president's civil rights program had stabbed Dixie in the back, now seemed of a far different mind, publicly predicting that Truman would carry the Lone Star State in November.

Also enjoying the presidential visit was a young Texas congressman, Lyndon Johnson, who rode along on the presidential train and was singled out by Truman as first on the list of Texans who had helped his administration in its pursuit of peace and prosperity. "Send Lyndon Johnson to the Senate," Truman urged the crowd while Congressman Johnson beamed. This might have seemed more than passing strange, because in May, Johnson had called Truman's civil rights program a "farce and a sham—an effort to set up a police state in the guise of liberty." But now it was September, and Harry Truman needed the backing of bona fide Texans like Lyndon Johnson to keep Texas from straying into the Dixiecrat column. Johnson had just edged out former Texas governor Coke

Stevenson by eighty-seven votes to win the Democratic Senate primary, a margin that had earned him the sobriquet Landslide Lyndon. Facing charges of fraud by Stevenson that threatened to overturn his victory, Johnson was eager for the approbation of the Democratic president.

In avoiding the issue of civil rights as he campaigned in both the North and South, Truman may have been influenced by the typically cautious advice of his sometime speechwriter, Sam Rosenman, who had returned to presidential service on an unofficial basis. Rosenman, according to columnist Drew Pearson, had advised the president to steer away from civil rights because the issue "had already done enough damage to the party." In fact, Rosenman's counsel had so irritated Clark Clifford, who was writing most of Truman's speeches, that, according to Pearson, he had arranged for Rosenman to miss a campaign trip Truman had expected him to come on. Giving further reason for anxiety was the announcement by Ed Crump, the boss of the Tennessee Democratic Party, who, though he had passed up the Dixiecrat convention in Birmingham, decided in October to endorse the Thurmond–Wright ticket in his state.

Despite the absence of any civil rights rhetoric, the mere appearance of Truman at a racially mixed rally was enough to discombobulate Henry Wallace. Arriving in Dallas on the heels of Truman's appearance in that city, Wallace had been prepared to denounce Truman for speaking to segregated audiences. When he learned that this had not been the case in Dallas, Wallace felt obliged to praise the integrated rally as "a very splendid thing" and was forced to settle for chiding Truman for not speaking out directly on racial issues.

Not that Truman entirely abandoned the effort to win black support. He frequently held informal meetings with black supporters along the way, asking their help in raising money and collecting votes, producing such headlines as "Pres. Truman Gives Definite Reassurance of Rights Program" in the *Atlanta World*. And at the outset of the campaign, Democratic chairman McGrath announced the disbanding of the National Committee's Negro division and the distribution of its members throughout the staff, with nearly a score of blacks working at national campaign headquarters in New York.

Just as Truman's own voice was not heard on the civil rights issue in the first weeks of the campaign, neither was that of his chief challenger, Thomas E. Dewey. The Republican National Committee spent freely on advertising in black newspapers to boast about Dewey's relatively enlightened civil rights record in New York. However, the candidate himself, in keeping with the complacency based on his front-runner status that suffused his entire campaign, avoided specifics on this issue, as on other issues.

The mood in the Dewey camp can be judged from an exchange of letters between the candidate and his mother, Annie. She had written in early August asking where she and Dewey's father could stay for their son's inauguration. Dewey replied that he did not know whether there would be sufficient accommodations at the White House, but added, "You of course would stay there with us if we moved in after the Inauguration but I doubt there would be much room for any others." Not until October 16, 1948, about two weeks before Election Day on November 2, did Dewey take what the *Baltimore Afro-American,* which had endorsed him, called a "firm stand" on civil rights. But Dewey's stance in a talk at New Castle, Pennsylvania, did not get any firmer than a promise "to press forward in solving the problems of race relations and discrimination in the great American tradition of freedom and equality." A week later in New York City, he was still expanding platitudes: "We should deal with the problem of social injustice where it is to be found in America and solve that problem in American terms."

Paradoxically, Dewey's mealy-mouthed utterances did not discourage most of the major black newspapers from reverting to their pre-FDR Republicanism and endorsing the GOP's national ticket. Truman also had the support of some important black papers, including the *Chicago Defender* and the *Atlanta Daily World.* However, the majority were on the GOP side, among them the *Baltimore Afro-American,* the *Kansas City Call,* and New York's *Amsterdam News.* "IS TRUMAN THE EQUAL OF DEWEY ON THE CIVIL RIGHTS QUESTION?" an *Afro-American* editorial asked on October 9. "We think not." The paper conceded that Truman had made progress on civil rights but attributed this to crass politics. Truman, the paper charged, was "more expert on deals than ideals." Dewey, on the other hand, was no "Johnny-come-lately." Rather, his civil rights convictions were as "simple to him as his belief in truth or honor or in God."

But if Truman and Dewey could afford to personally bypass the civil rights issue most of the time, this was not the case with the two maverick candidates, Thurmond and Wallace. For Thurmond, the issue of race—or states' rights, the euphemism he preferred—was the lifeblood of his candidacy, and for Wallace, it was an issue nearly equal in importance to staving off the threat of nuclear war. Whatever the ideological gulf between them, Thurmond and Wallace shared the obstacles the political system placed in the path of so-called third or fourth parties. In addition to the winner-take-all rule for allocating the electoral votes of each state, there is the difficulty of ballot access as a result of the labyrinth of rules and regulations that new parties had to negotiate in order to get their candidates on the ballot. To ease that burden, Dixiecrat strategists sought to capture the machinery of the regular Democratic Party wherever they could. They started off with Wright's Mississippi, Thurmond's South Carolina, and Alabama, where the state's Democratic presidential electors had been committed by the party primary to vote against Truman. Not coincidentally, these states were among the first to secede from the Union in 1861, and they were also among the Southern states with the heaviest proportion of black voters. In early September, these three were joined by Louisiana, which also had a large black population. In addition, party leaders there hostile to Governor Earl Long took advantage of his absence from their meeting to embarrass him by putting Thurmond–Wright at the head of the Democratic ticket.

Efforts to gain that advantage elsewhere failed. In Virginia and North Carolina, local Democrats feared that defecting would open the path to power to a Republican Party that was already showing signs of life in their states. Elsewhere, the black population was not so large as to make civil rights such a threatening cause. Unable to expand the four-state base where they held the Democratic Party line, Thurmond's party eventually got on the ballot as an independent party in eleven other states, all in the South except for Maryland, California, and North Dakota. The restricted ballot access inevitably limited Thurmond's strategy and message. If he had won all the states where he was on the ballot, he could have gotten a maximum of 167 electoral votes, nearly 100 short of a majority in the electoral college. And even this figure was misleadingly high because his strength in California and the three other Northern states was negligible.

With no chance to win the election outright, and with only a remote possibility of gaining enough electoral votes to have any influence at all on the outcome, Thurmond's candidacy was in effect reduced to a protest campaign. That limited the willingness of other Southern leaders to back him. As Virginia governor William Tuck, who stayed with the Democratic Party despite sharing many of Thurmond's beliefs, explained, "What's the sense of jumping out of a fourth story window if it isn't going to save somebody's life?"

On the stump, Thurmond had to weave a message impassioned enough to get Southern voters to desert their lifelong Democratic allegiance, but not so rabid that he came across as a racist demagogue. At times he took refuge in ominous warnings couched in abstract terms. In Asheville, North Carolina, he called for Southerners to "stop the misnamed civil rights proposals of Dewey, Truman and Wallace and prevent the invasion of local self government which they would cause." Other times his rhetoric was more visceral. At a rally in Texas, he raised the bugaboo of what Truman might have described as social equality. Imagine, he asked, what life at the workplace would become under the dreaded Fair Employment Practices Committee, "when the annual office party is held or the union sponsors a dance. There the races must also be mingled or else the sponsors face fines or jail sentences."

"States rights is the issue only insofar as it concerns the right of states to solve—or refuse to solve—their race problems," as veteran journalist John Ed Pearce described Thurmond's plight in the *Louisville Courier Journal.* "The real issue is one word, and that word is never spoken. The issue is Nigger." Thurmond "never says the word, he's not the type. It's like an old fashioned father trying to explain sex to his son without saying the words."

Trying to make a case for states' rights north of the Mason–Dixon Line, Thurmond refined his argument. New York City had suffered more gangland murders in five years than the South had experienced lynchings in thirty years, he told the Overseas Press Club. "If we need a federal law for murder by lynching we need a Federal law for murder by gangsters," he argued. Without realizing it or intending to, Thurmond had anticipated the day when the national government he resented so much would indeed make murder and other misdeeds by organized criminals a federal offense.

Striving for a broader forum, Thurmond several times challenged Truman to debate "face to face" his "so-called civil rights program," suggesting Virginia, Texas, or Missouri as possible locales. "You name the place," he said. Truman, who had no intention of talking about civil rights in the South, least of all on the same podium with Thurmond, ignored the challenge. Not surprisingly, Thurmond disregarded his independent party rival, Henry Wallace. He did also challenge Dewey to debate, but Dewey, like Truman, did not take the bait. Desperate as he was for attention, Thurmond made no attempt to speak to black audiences in the South or anywhere else, though that certainly would have made page one news almost everywhere. He turned down an invitation from black businessmen to address an "orderly meeting" in Harlem, explaining that his name was not on the ballot in the state, though that had not kept him from speaking to the Overseas Press Club about lynching and gangland murder.

In contrast with Thurmond, who determinedly avoided blacks every step of the way, Henry Wallace in late summer suddenly made reaching out to black voters, particularly in Thurmond's own Southland, a campaign priority. Wallace was partly acting out of desperation, to save his candidacy from disappearing behind the fog of indifference that traditionally obscured independent party ventures. Wallace had been doing far better than Thurmond so far as ballot access was concerned. He got off to a head start in New York thanks to the already established American Labor Party. The ALP, which had endorsed Roosevelt in 1944, switched its allegiance to the Progressive Party's presidential candidate in 1948. Elsewhere, the Progressives demonstrated support that was far-reaching if not always deep. With the help of an informal network of labor organizers, college teachers and students, leftist lawyers, and other similarly minded activists, Wallace found a place on the ballot in every state but two, Illinois and Oklahoma.

Nevertheless, enthusiasm among his followers fueled by their convention had faded quickly, cooled by the generally critical press coverage of their gathering. And the taint of communism, which had dogged Wallace at his convention, took on an extra edge early in August with a widely publicized spy scare. This was touched off by the testimony before the House Un-American Activities Committee of two confessed former communists, an FBI counterspy named Elizabeth Bentley and former *Time* editor Whitaker Chambers. Between them, they named several score former New Deal officials whom they swore had been card-carrying communists, and in some cases had shared classified information with the party and therefore with Moscow. Among them were a former top treasury official whom Truman had named to head the International Monetary Fund, Harry Dexter White, and most prominent of all, Alger Hiss, a prominent diplomat. Truman dismissed the charges as a "red herring," a statement he would have reason to regret two years later when a federal court jury convicted Hiss of perjury for denying Chambers's accusations. For the time being, the brunt of the furor fell more heavily on Wallace. He had worked closely with some of the accused when he was agriculture secretary, and some were involved in his current campaign. There were also demands on Capitol Hill to subpoena Wallace and make him part of the spy hunt.

With the peace issue blunted by the spy scare, not to mention the Soviet siege of West Berlin, and with the economy humming along in high gear, the inequities of race seemed to offer the best target for a presidential challenger. Though Truman had dominated the issue early on, he had barely mentioned it since the Philadelphia convention, nor had Dewey. Setting out on a weeklong four-state Southern trip, Wallace planned to strengthen his case by doing the unprecedented. He would include blacks in his traveling party and refuse to speak in segregated halls or stay in segregated hotels.

He got off to a relatively peaceful start with talks before racially mixed audiences in Virginia. But in Durham, North Carolina, where he proposed a $4 billion version of the Marshall Plan to aid the South's economy, a melee broke out on the floor of the city's armory, delaying his arrival. The candidate finally appeared only after a National Guardsman preceded him brandishing a pistol. Next day in Burlington, about forty miles to the west, a shouting crowd of several hundred kept Wallace from speaking, hurling eggs and tomatoes at the candidate. After an egg hit the back of his head, splattering his hair, the angry Wallace shouted back at the crowd, "I would like to see some indication that I am in the United States." The next day, at a little town called Hickory, boos drowned out much of what he tried to say amid the hurling of more eggs, most of which were rotten, leaving a foul stench over the area. Though angry and frustrated much of the time, Wallace did not entirely lose his sense of humor. The famed agricultural researcher remarked that once the campaign ended, he would turn his attention to developing a nonsplattering egg.

The ugliness of these episodes was enough to provoke the disapproval of the president. White House press secretary Charles G. Ross let it be known that Truman "thought the throwing of eggs and other missiles was certainly a highly un-American business and contrary to the American spirit of fair play." He then added, "Mr. Wallace was entitled to say his piece the same as any other American." Truman's comments, relayed through Ross, suggested a sense of responsibility on his part, and arguably a measure of courage, since he was sticking up for someone who was attacking the South's treasured racial customs and laws. Outside the South, it was probably politically beneficial because he appeared to be on the side of the better angels of the American spirit, defending free speech for an adversary.

Wallace pushed deeper south from North Carolina into Alabama, where farmers and factory workers in rural areas received him politely but where he was stalemated by segregation laws in the cities. In Birmingham, police chief Bull Connor saw to it that some 200 blacks who flocked to the courthouse square to hear Wallace were separated from some 2,000 whites who came mostly to boo and throw eggs at the candidate.

The press coverage of the rowdyism and Truman's statement appeared to have had some effect at Wallace's next stops, in Mississippi, Louisiana, and Arkansas, where large state police contingents kept the heckling and the egg throwing in check. In Nashville, Tennessee, where he concluded his trip, Wallace got one of his most favorable receptions in the South from a crowd of 2,000. He even drew cheers when he said his tour had renewed his faith in "the great and God-fearing people of the South."

Even the fortitude he had displayed did not change the tone of some of his critics. "He acted more like an agitator than a presidential candidate," *Time* complained. Yet the magazine conceded that Wallace "had thrown a harsh light on the problem of racial segregation—a problem which the U.S. as a whole cannot continue to shrug off." Similarly, *The Nation*, most of whose leftward-leaning editors were supporting socialist candidate Norman Thomas in preference to Wallace or Truman, predicted that the Southern trip "would turn out to be the redeeming effort of an otherwise ill advised candidacy." The magazine contended that while Wallace's trip may have been designed as a gambit to win votes in the North, it had served to dramatize the growing struggle of Southern Negroes to attain political rights denied them since Reconstruction days. *The Nation* suggested that Wallace's trip was bound to influence the behavior of the two major party nominees. However, there was no evidence of that on the Republican side. Despite talk from his campaign that the candidate would make a determined bid for votes in Dixie, Dewey did not shake off his complacency enough to venture into the region. Nor did he even bother to follow the example of Truman in condemning the Southern abuse of Wallace.

As for Truman, he seemed to be biding his time on civil rights. Seeking to exploit that silence, Wallace went south again in late September, this time for a three-day swing through Texas, where he sniped at Truman for lack of fealty to the civil rights cause. Arriving in Dallas on September 28, hard on the heels of Truman's appearance there, Wallace charged that the president "indirectly said he doesn't believe in civil rights at all." This was a fair inference to draw, Wallace contended, from the hope Truman expressed while stopping in Speaker Sam Rayburn's hometown of Bonham, Texas, "that the Democratic Party would be a party in the image of Sam Rayburn." Rayburn, Wallace said, had consistently boasted of his opposition to anti–poll tax and antilynching measures. At his next stop, Houston, Wallace again was showered with eggs and tomatoes, but he spoke to a racially mixed audience of 4,000, the largest integrated political rally the city had ever seen, and probably one of the largest in any Southern state. There Wallace drew a similarly negative inference about Truman. This time it was Truman's visit with another Texas icon, former vice president John Nance Garner. "In many ways an estimable gentleman," Wallace said of Garner. This about a man whom the fiery labor leader John L. Lewis, in testifying before a congressional committee, had described as "a labor baiting, poker playing, whisky drinking, evil old man." Wallace, respecting Texans' pride in their prominent son, rather mildly said only that "Cactus Jack," as some called him, "was never noted for his support of civil rights." Wallace was much blunter after he left Texas and moved on to Truman's hometown of Kansas City, where he charged that while "discrimination is and has been rampant" in Missouri, "Truman isn't doing anything to eliminate it." In the harshest attack he had made on the president yet, Wallace accused him of "engaging in remarkable political acrobatics and becoming a verbal liberal of the noisiest sort for election purposes."

As the presidential campaign careened toward its resolution, Truman not only had to endure the brickbats of his foes, with Wallace on the left and Dewey on the right, but also found doubts and defeatism within his own camp. "There is much confusion and taut nerves due to the political campaign and the belief that the president is going to be defeated," press aide Eban Ayers noted less than a month before the election. "There are few optimists in the place. There are jealousies and undercurrents all through the staff. There is a general feeling that the president is making some progress in his campaign, but few believe he can overcome the lead which his opponent has."

For anyone to feel differently would have required ignoring the supposed wisdom of the public opinion survey and the press. From start to finish, all the major polls predicted a solid Dewey victory. Indeed, one prominent pollster, Elmo Roper, stopped polling in early September because he was already convinced that "Mr. Dewey is just as good as elected." In October, *Newsweek* published a poll of fifty top political reporters around the country who unanimously forecast a Dewey victory.

The underdog status helped define Truman's candidacy. It combined well with the blend of Bryanite populism and New Deal progressivism that shaped his thinking. He reveled in his long-shot role. At one of his early campaign stops in Omaha, the crowd was so dismal that Truman's aides urged him to cancel to avoid embarrassment. "I don't give a damn whether there's nobody there but you and me," Truman snapped at the former AEF comrade, whose misfortune was to have arranged the rally. "This is one of the best things that's happened to me in this campaign. It will make a martyr out of me."

For most of the fall, Truman had heaped abuse on the Republican Congress for letting down farmers, union workers, and ordinary taxpayers. Now, as if to put the finishing touches on his candidacy, he devoted the last week before Election Day reaching out to the religious and racial cohorts that FDR had assembled into the New Deal coalition, and that still remained the base of the Democratic Party. In Chicago, in the same hall where he was nominated for the vice presidency in 1944, Truman warned various segments of that base that a Republican victory would heighten the threat of fascism in the United States. Apparently suspending any restrictions on hyperbole, he condemned "an evil force" working within the Republican Party to foment racial and religious prejudice. "Dangerous men," he said, "who are trying to win followers for their war on democracy are attacking Catholics and Jews and other racial religious minorities."

Two nights later, addressing a largely Catholic audience in Boston, in an ambitious analogy, he likened the whispering campaign based on religious prejudice that Republicans had used against Al Smith in 1928, to current GOP slurs that his administration was soft on communism. "Don't think the elephant has changed his habits in the last twenty years," Truman said. The next night in New York's Madison Square Garden, he appealed to American Jews not as a foe of bigotry but as a friend of the Jewish state, still less than a year old and besieged by Arab nations on all sides. Truman reminded his audience that he had only a few months before made the United States the first nation to recognize Israel. Now he offered the sweeping pledge that he would make certain that Israel would be "large enough, free enough and strong enough to make its people self supporting and secure."

The climax and in some ways the most dramatic in this series of talks came outdoors on a sunny Saturday afternoon in Harlem on October 29, four days before the election. "It was clear from the beginning of the campaign that there would have to be a major speech on civil rights before the end," Philleo Nash, who had helped create the President's Committee on Civil Rights, recalled later. It was Nash's suggestion that the president should save this utterance for the end, purportedly to heighten its dramatic impact. The forum was a meeting of the local Council of Negro Clergymen, who planned to honor Truman with the Franklin D. Roosevelt Memorial Award for his record on civil rights.

The site was Dorrence Brook Square, across from the College of the City of New York, named after a black doughboy and son of a Civil War veteran who died in combat in France shortly before the end of the Great War. On the night before Truman was to speak, Nash received a last-minute summons to come to New York, where he arrived about 5 A.M. on speech day. A few hours later, he handed his draft of the speech to the president, who was bracing himself for the day's full schedule. "Well I've been waiting for a long time to get this taken care of," Truman told him. After reading the entire fifteen-minute speech aloud, he declared, "Well, anybody who isn't for this ought to have his head examined."

However, he asked for a change. Referring to the President's Committee on Civil Rights, Nash had written that its main contribution had been to show Americans how to create unity. Truman objected. "Unity is basically a weak concept," he said. "We should be doing what's right even if we can't be united about it. And this speech is about what is right." After some discussion among other aides, the word "freedom" was substituted.

"That's fine," Truman said. "That's a good word."

Nash and press secretary Charles Ross rushed out to get the manuscript retyped and stencils made for the mimeograph machine.

The president's introduction included a lengthy prayer, which seemed to help shape the mood of the crowd of more than 60,000. As the president rose to speak, students from nearby City College began to shout, "Pour it on, Harry. Give 'em hell, Harry," echoing a familiar refrain from the campaign trial. However, no one in the Dorrence Brook Square crowd picked up the chant, and the students fell quiet. To Nash, who had his back to the scene while he looked over the speech text, that seemed ominous. But when he turned to view the crowd, he saw the reason for the silence. "Almost everybody in the crowd was praying, either with his head down, or actually kneeling," Nash recalled. "They were praying for the president and they were praying for their own civil rights. And they thought it was a religious occasion."

Truman's delivery was deliberate and solemn, making clear he was recommitting himself to the cause of civil rights, and specifically to the legislative program he had proposed to Congress. Adding significance to the occasion, it was, as Truman pointed out, the first anniversary of the submission of what he called the "momentous report" of his Committee on Civil Rights. "The job the Civil Rights Committee did was to tell the American people how to create the kind of freedom the American People need," he said, using the word "freedom" where Nash had originally written "unity." Truman repeated the word "freedom" in the next five paragraphs in explaining the full significance of the committee's report. Referring to the proposals based on the committee's report, which he had submitted to Congress, Truman added wryly, "You know what they did about that." Then he added, "I went ahead and did what the president can do, unaided by Congress." He spoke of his executive orders, one desegregating the armed forces and the other ordering an end to discrimination among the government's civilian workers. He also reminded the crowd that the justice department had gone to court to help win a Supreme Court ruling striking down housing bias. "Our determination to attain the goal of equal rights and equal opportunity must be resolute and unwavering," Truman said. "For my part I intend to keep moving toward this goal with every ounce of strength and determination I have."

The Harlem talk was devoted entirely to civil rights and was free of Truman's usual stump speech invective. He did not even use the word "Republican," and the closest he came to referring to the opposition was his brief allusion to Congress's failure to act on his program. Truman gave one more campaign speech in New York and several others of no great consequence on his way back to Independence to hear the returns. The last Gallup poll, completed a week before, showed him losing to Dewey by four points. The margin in the Crossley poll was three points. No poll showed Truman winning.

Though he was outwardly confident, Truman felt enough tension to slip away to a nearby resort hotel in Excelsior Springs on election night. After hearing the early returns, he fell sound asleep. A Secret Service agent, Henry Nicholson, woke him at midnight to tell him he was carrying Massachusetts. "Nick, stop worrying," Truman told him. "You all go to sleep and we'll get up early in the morning."

At 4 A.M., he woke again to find out that he was leading the popular vote by two million. He told his bodyguards that it was time to get back to campaign headquarters, Kansas City, "because it looked very much like we were in trouble for four more years." On the way back to Washington, when the train stopped in St. Louis, someone handed him a copy of the *Chicago Tribune*, probably the most steadfastly Republican paper of its time, with the headline, written for an early edition on Election Day: "DEWEY DEFEATS TRUMAN." The president held it aloft for a photograph that for many years to come would provide a cautionary reminder for those who consider forecasting election outcomes.

Though Truman won the electoral college with 303 votes to 189 for Dewey and 39 for Thurmond, with Wallace getting zero, the election was actually much closer than the numbers suggest because several big states were closely contested. The popular vote totals better reflect the narrowness of the president's advantage. He got 49.5 percent to Dewey's 45.21 percent, with Thurmond and Wallace each winning slightly better than 2 percent. Though it was commonly asserted during the campaign that Truman's civil rights efforts were motivated mainly by the hopes of winning black votes, the electoral calculus of civil rights is not so easy to compute because of the variables built into any campaign. Truman's speech in Dorrence Brook Square may have impressed his Harlem audience, but it was not enough to win New York State from Dewey, any more than was his support for Israel, largely because Henry Wallace got nearly 10 percent of the vote. On the negative side, the 39 electoral votes won by the Dixiecrats, rebelling against Truman's civil rights proposals, would almost certainly have gone to Truman if he had fired blanks on civil rights because he won every other Southern state. As for the miscalculations of the pollsters, a study committee appointed by the Social Science Research Council concluded that the pollsters, like candidate Dewey, had been overconfident, "led by false assumptions into believing their methods were much more accurate than in fact they are."

After his ignominious defeat, Dewey reacted with a grace and humor that would have served him well on the campaign stump. He told supporters that he was reminded of the man who, having participated too enthusiastically in a "very successful" wake, woke up in a coffin with a lily in his hand and wondered, "If I am alive what am I doing here? And if I am dead, why do I have to go to the bathroom?"

In their own postmortem in victory, black leaders claimed credit for delivering California, Illinois, and Ohio, with their seventy-eight electoral votes, to Truman, since his margins in those states were wide and the black vote for him was substantial. However, it was by no means certain that Truman would have gotten significantly fewer black votes if he had taken no more risks for civil rights than Franklin Roosevelt, whose modest contributions to the cause were honored when Truman spoke in Harlem. In the face of all the other factors that shaped the election—the general prosperity, the ineptitude of his Republican opponent, the dip in some farm prices, his own strong response to the Soviets on Berlin—it is hard to sustain an argument that civil rights carried the day for Harry Truman.

In fact it is reasonable to conclude that Truman did more for the civil rights cause than it did for him. To be sure, those fundamentally responsible for any progress were black Americans and their mounting impatience with what they seemed to be getting from most white Americans—indifference at best and violence at worst. However, it was Truman who responded to this black anger more strenuously than any other president since Lincoln ended slavery. In the process, for the first time in history, Truman put the cause of black Americans on the agenda of a presidential campaign. It was Truman's burst of activity that led to the Democratic platform plank, to the Dixiecrat defection, and to Wallace's challenge to the segregated South.

Nevertheless, no one could tell what this promised to civil rights in the new term Truman had just implausibly won. He had helped carry congressional Democrats back to majority status on Capitol Hill, but there was little reason to believe that Southern Democrats would be so grateful for having their committee chairmanships restored that they would forbear to filibuster Truman's ten points of civil rights.

Perhaps the soundest guidance for black Americans came from the politically astute Roy Wilkins of the NAACP. "If any of us are now mad at the rest of us, let us forget it, come Nov. 3," he advised a week before the election. "Let us realize that the continuing job of American Negroes is to win their rights as citizens, no matter who is in office."

10

★ ★ ★ ★ ★

FREEDOM TO SERVE

Nearly overwhelmed by the surprise German offensive in the Ardennes in December 1944, Allied commander Dwight Eisenhower found himself desperately short of infantry. At first he sought help from the thousands of GIs inside Army stockades, offering a full pardon for anyone who would fight. Faced with the dangers of combat, only a few accepted, generally those serving fifteen years or more at hard labor. Finally Eisenhower turned to the black soldiers in his command, sending out a call for volunteers to get infantry training before front-line assignment. "It is planned to assign you without regard to color or race to the units where assistance is most needed, and give you the opportunity of fighting shoulder to shoulder to bring about victory. Your relatives and friends everywhere have been urging that you be granted this privilege." In other words, though Eisenhower did not quite say it, the volunteers would be agents of racial integration.

That offer got only as far as the desk of Eisenhower's chief of staff, Lieutenant General Walter Bedell Smith, whose overbearing manner Eisenhower attributed to his Prussian lineage. In a blunt note to Ike, Smith pointed out that the offer to blacks violated Army regulations, which required that black soldiers serve only in segregated units. Smith also suggested that civil rights advocates in the United States might seize on this instance of racial mixing to demand wider integration in the Army. Eisenhower, who described Smith's relationship to him as like "a crutch to a one-legged man," was not about to dispense with his crutch. He hastily revised his offer to black troops, leaving out the provision for integration. Still, so many blacks answered the call that more than half had to be turned down to avoid hindering the units in which they served. Because there were no black infantry units then in combat, the 2,500 volunteers who completed training were organized into all-black platoons, typically of about forty men each, and then assigned to white units on the front line.

The Nazi surrender ended this experiment in quasi-integration. Someone in Eisenhower's command was imaginative enough to order interviews of 250 officers and noncoms who had commanded the black troops, nearly all of whom acknowledged that the camaraderie between the races was far better than they had expected. The impact of the survey conducted by trained interviewers was limited because the Army suppressed it. General Brehon B. Somerville, commanding general of the Army service forces, contended that it would alienate members of Congress who were "vigorously opposed" to integration under any conditions. If Eisenhower saw the survey results, they apparently did not make much impression, given his later Senate testimony against military integration.

Despite the patriotism and bravery of black soldiers in the Eisenhower experiment and in other battles against the Axis powers, the Army emerged from World War II as firmly committed to segregation as before. The episode illustrated the depth of the resistance Truman would face in trying to implement what would become the standout success of his civil rights program: the integration of America's armed services.

Not that Truman intended for the gains against military Jim Crow to be an outlier. His hopes and plans were more ambitious than that. Meeting with the indefatigable Walter White in the days after his election triumph, Truman scotched talk he might compromise with the South on his agenda for racial justice. Instead, according to White, Truman said "he planned to carry out each one of his campaign promises." Indeed, in his State of the Union address on January 5, 1949, the winner of the 1948 election called on Congress to enact the civil rights proposals he had made the previous February.

Later that month the president signed a proclamation harking back nearly a century in the struggle for racial justice. The document, authorized by both houses of Congress, established February 1 as National Freedom Day. Among the black leaders looking on was Mary McCleod Bethune, who had established her credentials as a civil rights gadfly in FDR's White House. On that same date in 1865 President Lincoln had signed the joint congressional resolution proposing the 13th Amendment to the Constitution abolishing slavery. Lincoln, fearful that the impact of his Emancipation Proclamation would be eroded, had fought hard to win congressional approval of the 1865 resolution, which was ultimately ratified by the states.

In this regard he had better luck than Truman would have with his 1949 civil rights proposals. Despite his urging in the State of the Union, it soon became clear that the president's chances for success were no better than in the past. The tip-off came in March, when the Senate, by a vote of 46 to 41, turned down a maneuver to make it easier to invoke cloture to cut off debates. The majority included twenty Republicans and twenty-three Democrats, nearly all from the South.

This sounded the death knell for any civil rights measure of consequence—not only in the Eighty-first Congress but also in its successor, which served till the end of Truman's tenure. The administration and civil rights advocates kept striving on key issues, notably creating a permanent Fair Employment Practices Committee and banning the poll tax, but any apparent gains, such as House approval of an anti–poll tax bill in July 1949, proved temporary and illusory in the face of the stone wall of Southern opposition in the Senate.

Disappointed civil rights advocates took aim not only at Southerners and conservative Republicans in Congress, but also at the president. He failed to make civil rights a clear priority, it was said; others contended that he could have used his patronage power more effectively or appealed to the public over the heads of Congress. It was true that in 1865 with the impending Union victory over the Confederacy at his back Lincoln managed to nudge Congress into approving the 13th Amendment. However, there was little evidence in Truman's time or in any subsequent administrations that, barring such extraordinary circumstances, a president could have much luck making Congress do something most of its members did not want to do. Whatever other flaws had developed in the Constitution since the founding of the Republic, James Madison's device of pitting ambition against ambition was still working all too well for Harry Truman, who complained, "I sit here all day trying to persuade people to do the things they ought to do without my persuading them. That's all the powers of the president amount to." As Lyndon Johnson would put it years later to his White House lobbying team, when he stood in Truman's shoes: "I have watched the Congress from either the inside or the outside, man and boy for more than forty years and I've never yet seen a Congress that didn't take the measure of the president it was dealing with."

Faced with these circumstances in the Eighty-first Congress, Truman, as he said in his talk at Harlem's Dorrence Brook Square, had gone ahead and done "what the president can do, unaided by Congress," notably ordering an end to racial barriers among the nation's warriors. That would prove a formidable enough challenge. Indeed, racial prejudice had been a major obstacle to black acceptance in the armed services for most of American history, though it was sometimes offset by the practical need for manpower. Thus, a good many of the 5,000 blacks who served in the often outnumbered Continental Army and Navy fought in integrated units. That situation did not last much beyond the end of the Revolution itself. From the time of the War of 1812, when Louisiana's Free Men of Color were recruited by Andrew Jackson to bolster his makeshift Army in the Battle of New Orleans, and for more than a century afterward, segregation prevailed in the Army. In the Civil War, the 186,000 blacks in the Union Army were assigned to sixteen segregated combat regiments and the labor units. After the war, federal laws establishing four black Regular Army regiments in effect gave the government's imprimatur to a system that was racially separate, though in theory equal. That made for totally segregated armed forces since the Navy, which had originally been integrated, adopted Jim Crow policies after the turn of the nineteenth century. In the years afterward, black sailors almost vanished from the fleet, amounting to little more than 1 percent in World War I and limited chiefly to mess duty.

The prejudice that blacks faced in all walks of American life was reinforced in the military by the widespread conviction by whites that blacks were too cowardly to make good soldiers. The story of Private First Class Dorrence Brook, in whose honor the Harlem square where Truman gave his campaign talk on civil rights was named, was a case in point. Brook's segregated unit, assigned to support the battle-thinned ranks of the French army in the bloody summer of 1918, suffered such heavy casualties that Brook himself, though only a private first class, took command and led a charge that cost him his life. When New York mayor John Hyland announced plans to honor Brook, the *New York Herald Tribune,* a relentless critic of Hyland, ran a series of articles deriding black soldiers as worthless cowards. Speaking at the ceremony dedicating the square, seven years after Brook died in battle, Mayor Hyland denounced the paper and declared that Brook and his comrades had demonstrated the capacity of blacks to fight "valorously and heroically."

Nevertheless, the allegations that blacks lacked courage and patriotism helped sustain the Army's racism. Despite continuing pressure and complaints from blacks and other civil rights advocates, not until the end of World War II did the military seriously consider changing its treatment of blacks. One reason was the mounting pressure from civil rights groups. Another was the enlarged postwar military responsibilities of the United States. Technically the nation was at peace. Yet for the first time in its history, the United States would be forced to maintain a large standing army, navy, and air force. With blacks badly needed to fill out the ranks, the services had to finally find an efficient way to use that 10 percent of the population made up of Americans of color. A board of senior Army officers headed by Lieutenant General Alvan C. Gillem Jr., after studying the other services, concluded that the system of partial integration adopted by the Navy worked better than the strict segregation practiced by the Marine Corps. However, its report, issued in November 1945, was cloaked in ambiguity and stopped short of recommending full-scale integration. Instead, it called for flexible use of black manpower without spelling out how to reach that goal. Its most specific recommendation was to establish a quota based on the proportion of blacks in the civilian population, which meant that the Army would strive to make blacks 10 percent of its total strength, no more and no less. As the *Pittsburgh Courier* observed, the new policy meant that the Army command had undergone "no real change of heart."

Remarkably, the Navy, which had been far more backward on racial policy than the Army, seemed more receptive to change. Blacks who had been restricted to mess stewards now could be assigned to the rest of the Navy—the general service, in naval nomenclature. However, there was nothing said about assigning blacks as officers or whites as mess stewards. The Air Force adopted the Army's postwar racial policy as its own. The Marine Corps maintained that separate but equal service was not discriminatory. When equal opportunity often proved unattainable, the Marines stuck with segregation. The services contended that while their racial policies fell short of the demands of blacks, they represented an improvement over practices in most institutions in civilian society. But even if this were true, it missed the point. Blacks in uniform were serving their country and putting their lives at risk, and that reality should have reinforced their claim to their full rights as citizens. As the President's Committee on Civil Rights had concluded: "The injustice of calling men to fight for freedom while subjecting them to humiliating discrimination within the fighting forces is at once apparent."

The services' record of slipping and sliding on race, combined with the challenge of what increasingly loomed as a perpetual international emergency, left Truman with no choice except to command integration by executive order. But it was evident from the onset that the effectiveness of the order would depend greatly on the committee the president had prudently decided to establish to oversee the response of the services.

The service chiefs themselves were fully aware of the importance of the committee, as was evidenced by Army secretary Kenneth Royall, who protested to Truman and to defense secretary James Forrestal that some men under consideration for the committee had publicly supported the end of military segregation. Royall specifically mentioned Lester Granger, a black and the head of the Urban League who had worked closely with Forrestal on integration efforts when the latter had been secretary of the Navy. This might seem a tendentious argument because the purpose of the executive order was to end segregation, the very idea to which Royall objected. However, the fifty-four-year-old Royall was a man of strong beliefs who did not easily yield on them. A native of North Carolina and a product of the University of North Carolina and Harvard Law School, he had served in the Army in both world wars. In 1942, when the United States captured eight would-be Nazi saboteurs who had been landed by submarine on a Long Island beach, President Roosevelt ordered them tried by a secret military tribunal. Royall, then a colonel with the Army's Judge Advocate General Corps, was named as co–defense counsel. He promptly wrote Roosevelt, contending that he did not think civilians could be tried by a military court. When that did not change FDR's mind, Royall appealed to the Supreme Court, which upheld Roosevelt in this case, but which also held that no presidential order could supersede the authority of the Supreme Court.

Royall's stance in the saboteur case did not seem to hurt his career. The Army promoted him to brigadier general; Truman made him undersecretary of war, then in 1947 moved him up to secretary of war, in which post he never stopped resisting Truman's integration order. Royall lost the first round, when Granger was named to the committee. The other appointees could hardly have given Royall much comfort: Dwight Palmer, a businessman active in the Urban League and a foe of job discrimination; John Sengstacke, publisher of the *Chicago Defender*, one of the handful of big black papers to have supported Truman in the 1948 campaign; and Oberlin College president William Stevenson, strongly recommended by Urban League officials. Two other appointees did not take a significant part in the committee's work, Alphonse Donahue, a prominent Catholic layman, because of illness, and Lever Brothers president Charles Luckman, because of lack of interest.

But the appointment that mattered most was the chairman, fifty-six-year-old Charles H. Fahy, a soft-spoken Georgian and veteran of New Deal legal service. By all accounts, Fahy, who combined evenhandedness with fervent commitment, would be the man principally responsible for making the committee work and turning integration from a fuzzy objective into an ultimate reality. Fahy's name was put forward by David Niles, who described him as a "reconstructed southern liberal on race" and someone who could handle sensitive problems with "quiet authority and the punch of a mule." Clearly Fahy was no provincial Southerner. He had graduated from the University of Notre Dame and then Georgetown

University Law School and had been admitted to the District of Columbia bar in 1914. He won the Navy Cross as a naval aviator in World War I, after which he spent more than a decade in private practice. He then signed on with the New Deal, serving on the legal staff of several agencies, and became FDR's solicitor general in 1941.

Of the many cases Fahy argued before the Supreme Court, probably the most memorable for its historic significance and the odium later associated with it was his successful defense of the World War II internment of 100,000 Japanese Americans, most of them American citizens. Ultimately most Americans would regret this episode, and many officials would share the blame and the shame. But Fahy, it was later learned, bore particular responsibility. Years after the war, Peter Irons, a legal researcher, turned up evidence, most notably a report from the office of naval intelligence, that concluded Japanese Americans did not pose a threat to the nation's security. Fahy knew of this report when the case was before the High Court. But he kept it to himself and told the justices that the government and the military agreed that the internment was a matter of "military necessity."

Partly because of the new evidence turned up by Irons, the federal court of appeals in the 1980s granted a measure of vindication to the victims of internment by setting aside the criminal convictions of two Japanese who had defied the internment order. Congress later voted a national apology for the internment and agreed to pay $20,000 in compensation to surviving internees or to their descendants. As solicitor general, Fahy had an obligation to defend the government's action, unless doing so would violate his conscience. But he also had a responsibility to turn over relevant evidence to the Supreme Court. His failure to do so is a reminder, along with the entire episode, of how much war blurs the judgment even of decent men and their governments.

Fahy had left his post as solicitor general in 1945 because he preferred not to work with Tom Clark, the Texas lawyer and justice department official whom Truman had appointed to replace FDR's last attorney general, Francis Biddle, and whom many in Washington viewed as a political hack. Fahy had returned to private practice before Truman called him back to the government to head the oversight committee. As he had with the Committee on Civil Rights, the president made it clear to Fahy's committee at the start that theirs was no mere ceremonial function. "I want concrete results, not publicity on it," Truman told the panel in January 1949. "I want the job done and I want to get it done in a way so everybody will be happy to cooperate to get it done. Unless it's necessary to knock somebody's ears down, I don't want to have to do that, but if it becomes necessary it can be done."

It soon became apparent to Fahy and his committee and staff that their biggest stumbling block would be the U.S. Army. This was in part because of its size, but also because of the attitude of Secretary Royall and many other Army leaders. This is not to say that the other branches of the service did not offer resistance to the president's ultimate goal. However, each of them had made some progress toward equal treatment, and each of them seemed far more willing to acknowledge the need for more change than the Army.

Perhaps the most cooperative was the Air Force, which, as the youngest of the services, had the most flexibility and had, in its secretary, Stuart Symington, the most enthusiastic proponent of integration in the armed forces. "Our plan is to completely eliminate segregation in the Air Force," Symington told the president at the Fahy committee's opening session. "For example we have a fine group of colored boys," he said. "Our plan is to take these boys, break up that fine group, and put them with the other units themselves and go right down the line one hundred percent." Symington's choice of words left room for refinement, and his optimism proved unrealistic, but for Truman and Fahy, his enthusiasm contrasted favorably with the attitude of the other service chiefs, which ranged from the dour reluctance of the Marines and the Navy to the downright rejection by the Army's Royall.

"The Army entered objections every step of the way," recalled E. W. "Ned" Kenworthy, the journalist who signed on as the Fahy committee's executive secretary. "They were impossible. You had to cram it down their throat."

The Army's resistance reflected Secretary Royall's professed belief that segregation was not in itself discrimination. It was a view bolstered by the widely shared opinion of his officer corps that in open competition with white soldiers, few blacks would ever achieve a proportionate share of promotions and better military jobs—in other words, the same judgment Eisenhower had given at the Senate. Besides, as Royall testified at Fahy committee hearings held in the first months of 1949, two world wars had shown blacks to be unfit for combat but "particularly qualified for manual labor." Because segregation was the rule in civilian life, particularly in the South, which produced a substantial share of Army volunteers and where a disproportionate number of Army bases were located, the Army's leaders argued that an attempt to integrate the Army would cause disruption and inefficiency.

For their part, Navy officials initially defended their policy, even though two-thirds of black seamen were consigned to service as stewards. However, the top sailors did concede in their testimony the need for more change. As an indication of the backwardness of the Navy's racial policies, the Naval Academy at Annapolis did not graduate its first black midshipmen until 1949. By contrast, West Point graduated its first black cadet, an ex-slave, in 1879, though in the following years through World War II no more than a handful of blacks attended at any one time.

Contributing to the service's persistent foot-dragging, along with bureaucratic inertia and a legacy of racial bias, was the reluctance of the first boss of the newly unified armed services, James V. Forrestal, to use the sweeping powers granted to him. To be sure, his background as a World War Navy flyer, head of the Dillon Read investment banking firm, and World War II Navy secretary, where he had championed efforts to change the Navy's racial practices, made him seem the logical man for the job. Yet he himself questioned, as he told Truman early on, whether any one man "was good enough to run the combined Army, Navy, and Air Departments." His misgivings about imposing his will on the separate services was particularly evident in his approach to racial integration. Though he professed to be opposed to discrimination, he believed that "progress must be made administratively and should not be put into effect by fiat." In other words, don't rush into things on race.

Even as Forrestal grappled with racial problems, he became involved in continuing disputes with Truman over the president's proposals to reduce military spending. In the midst of this, the Pentagon chief was apparently undergoing a siege of psychological turmoil stemming from his mentally and physically exhausting workload. All this led to Forrestal's resignation in March 1949 and his replacement by Louis Johnson. Soon after he left his post, weary and distraught, Forrestal sought psychiatric help and was diagnosed with severe depression. In May, a few weeks after admission to Bethesda Naval Hospital, he died in a fall from his sixteenth-floor room. Found in his room were some scribbled lines from a Sophocles tragedy, construed by many as a suicide note.

His successor, Louis A. Johnson, the fifty-eight-year-old onetime assistant secretary of war for FDR, spectacularly successful corporate lawyer, and leading fund-raiser for Harry Truman's 1948 campaign, provided a dramatic contrast in personality and management style. In place of the introverted, ascetic Forrestal, the new boss at the Pentagon was a free-wheeling and often heavy-handed boss. Unlike his predecessor, Johnson had no compunctions about bullying the services into conforming with the new order of the day: unification, according to the letter of the new law. Or else.

The difference between Forrestal's soft-pedaling style and Johnson's vigor soon became apparent in the Pentagon's response to Truman's executive order on race relations. The shift had its genesis in the closing days of Forrestal's regime. Despite his reluctance to impose his will on the services, Forrestall was eager to steal a march on the Fahy committee, so he ordered his personnel chief, Thomas R. Reid, to establish a general policy on integration for the services before the committee told him what to do. Reid's proposal, which was modeled after the Air Force's approach calling for a fast start on integration, ran into immediate opposition from the Army brass. They complained that it did too much too soon. By this time, Johnson had taken the helm at the Pentagon, and Reid shrewdly took his proposal to his new boss, mentioning that "this is a matter that has the president's direct interest."

Johnson got the message, and on April 6, 1949, he promptly issued the statement Reid had drafted as a directive to the service secretaries. Under the new regimen, enlistment, promotion, assignment, and admission to advanced training schools would all be decided on the basis of individual merit and ability. Some segregated units would be retained, but "qualified" Negroes would be assigned without regard to race. Each of the services was ordered to submit detailed plans for carrying out this directive by May 1.

By this time, Louis Johnson's political instincts, honed in the West Virginia house of delegates, where he became speaker, and in the American Legion, where he rose to national commander, were in high gear. He made public his directive, with emphasis on the sections that spoke of the need for change, and saw to it that it got wide attention.

Though at first glance this seemed like progress, Fahy committee staffers were skeptical. Johnson's major goal, they suspected, was really not full-scale integration but rather full-scale command for Louis Johnson while shunting the Fahy committee into the background. But for Johnson's strategy to succeed, he would need to show genuine progress, and here he ran into the same roadblock that had frustrated the Fahy committee: the resistance of the Army. While the Air Force submitted a plan that won Johnson's approval and objections to the Navy plan were readily solved, the Army remained a tough nut to crack. The president's order now produced a sustained, grinding struggle, with first Louis Johnson, then the Fahy committee, and ultimately Truman himself bearing down against the military, but mostly the Army.

Negotiations between the Army and the Fahy committee dragged on through the spring and into the summer. In the meantime, Kenneth Royall's steadfast opposition to desegregation had led to his forced resignation in April. His replacement by Gordon Gray was made possible by a breakthrough in the impasse over Army integration. Even then, progress was slow. It came only after the Army, employing a favorite tactic of the military, sought to outflank the committee. It sent its latest proposal, which differed only slightly from its predecessors, directly to defense secretary Johnson, circumventing the committee. Johnson endorsed the plan without consulting the Fahy committee, which he sought to have disbanded.

Furious, Fahy protested to Truman. Faced with that objection as well as a storm of protest in the black press and from civil rights organizations, Truman declared that the report approved by Johnson was just a progress report, and that the job "isn't finished yet." His goal, he made clear, was still complete integration. Truman sent word to the Army and the Fahy committee that no Army policy would be accepted without the approval of the Fahy committee.

Even so, tensions between the Army and the committee were so high that Ned Kenworthy, Fahy's executive secretary, set what amounted to a trap for the Army. Kenworthy deliberately left his Pentagon office door and his desk unlocked. He was counting on the likelihood that blacks working in the Army's message center elsewhere in the oversized build- ing and sympathetic to the work of the committee would keep him in- formed of any behind-the- scenes efforts to undercut the committee. Sure enough, one morning Kenworthy discovered in his drawer a copy of an order that effectively countermanded an order of the acting secretary, Gordon Gray. This had represented an apparent major concession by the Army: opening up all educational courses to blacks.

Kenworthy took the new order reversing the concession to the *Wash- ington Post*, which reported the turnabout. In a tart editorial under the heading "Army Runaround," the paper urged Gray to "assert himself." The new order, the *Post* contended, amounted to "an attempt to sabotage the declared policies of the president and Defense Secretary Johnson." Em- barrassed, Gray issued a statement countermanding the countermanding order, stating that it violated Army policy. Now Gray realized that thanks to Kenworthy's leak and the support of Truman, the Fahy committee was in the driver's seat.

In its prolonged negotiations with the Army, a combination of ca- joling and arm-twisting, the Fahy committee was aided by the examples provided by the relative gains against segregation made by the Air Force and the Navy. By August 1949, the Air Force, with minimal conflict, had more than doubled its integrated units, to 797 from 273. In June, *Ebony* called this the "most amazing upset of racial policy in the history of the U.S. military." Equally amazing in its own way was the turnabout at the Navy, which had decreed that all assignments and promotions would be handled without regard to race, and which launched a program to trans- fer qualified blacks from the stewards branch to the general services. The

Navy announced that change had even come to the Marines, with the abolition of racially separate training. As it turned out, the Marine Corps refused to comply and would remain a problem for some time to come. Even so, the Navy seemed justified in its claim that "racial tolerance" was spreading in ships and in shore installations alike.

Against this background, the Fahy committee worked out a compromise with the Army on a key issue: integration of assignments. The committee agreed in January 1950 that this process could take place gradually, starting with skilled blacks and working down to the less qualified.

One problem remained, and it was a substantial one: the Army's 10 percent quota for blacks. Gray fought hard against change, but with Truman in favor of ending quotas, the secretary had little choice. He did manage to wring from Truman the assurance that the quota could be reinstated, "if, as a result of a fair trial of this new system, there ensues a disproportionate balance of racial strengths," an arrangement that never came into play. At Truman's request, Gray outlined a program for open recruitment, fixing April 1950 as the date when all vacancies would be open to all qualified individuals. From his vacation quarters in Key West, Truman added a final encouraging word: "I am sure that everything will work out as it should."

Well, maybe. Whatever Gordon Gray had agreed to and President Truman had approved, there were still plenty of voices in the Army saying nay. Fahy committee members worried whether they could count on the Army to live up to the commitments Gordon Gray had made and wanted some form of oversight group to be retained after they had concluded their work. But Secretary Johnson had made clear to Truman that he "felt very strongly about having a watchdog group over him." Truman realized that if he kept the committee, he would probably need to get a new defense secretary. Persuading himself that the services were headed in the right direction, Truman told Fahy that the armed forces should have the opportunity to put into effect the new racial policies. But he added that he would leave his executive order in effect, just in case.

Would integration have gone faster if the Fahy committee had been kept in place? Hard to say. Foot-dragging by the Army would have continued in any event, and the outbreak of the Korean war on June 25, 1950, would have provided Johnson with another argument for calling off the watchdog.

Meanwhile, in May, the Fahy committee had issued its final report, a forty-three-page document titled "Freedom to Serve." "It is the Committee's conviction that the present programs of the three services are designed to accomplish the objectives of the president," the report declared.

"As the programs are carried out, there will be, within the reasonably near future, equality of treatment and opportunity for all persons in the armed forces with a consequent improvement in military efficiency." The report won rave reviews from, among other publications, *Time*, which pronounced the Fahy committee's handiwork the "greatest change in service custom since the abandonment of the cat-o'-nine tails." Summing up the committee's case in pithy fashion, *Time* reported, "There were bright Negroes and there were dumb ones, just like white men. To refuse a job to an intelligent or skilled Negro was simply a waste of manpower. Concentration of unskilled Negroes in segregated units just multiplied their inefficiency." It was just this stress on efficiency that helped win the report widespread approval. Nevertheless, Fahy and his colleagues refused to ignore the profound moral issues also involved. "The integrity of the individual, his equal worth in the sight of God, his equal protection under law, his equal rights and obligations of citizenship and his equal opportunity to make just and constructive use of his endowment these are the very foundation of the American system of values," the report said in its peroration. "The President's Committee throughout its deliberations shaped its course consistently with these principles."

Despite the blend of common sense and idealism that the report offered, many in the Army remained as resistant to integration as ever. As it turned out, the major impetus for overcoming this opposition came from a totally unanticipated event—what President Truman dubbed the Korean Police Action. One change that made this trend possible was that the Army's goal, at least on paper, was no longer to preserve segregation but rather to achieve integration. The consequences of this shift became evident even before the outbreak of fighting in Korea with the new draft law, which went into effect in 1949. When Fort Ord, California, was reactivated to handle the flood of new recruits, officers there found that the simplest way to deal with them was to assign blacks and whites to the same unit. There was now no rule protecting segregation to gainsay them; indeed, the rule went the other way.

Just as important in expediting segregation was the abolition of the racial quotas. Under the old 10 percent rule, the Army could control and predict how many black soldiers it would have to fit into its long-established segregated table of organization and make any necessary adjustments. But with the end of quotas, the Army had no way to forecast or limit the flow of black recruits. Driven either by patriotism or the belief they had a better chance to make a living in uniform, blacks now signed up in growing numbers. Within five months of the outbreak of the conflict in Korea, the Army had doubled its size to 1.6 million, with more than 200,000 serving in Korea with the Eighth Army. The percentage of black enlisted men, which had been 10.2 percent of total strength when quotas were lifted in April 1950, climbed to 11.4 percent in five months; it reached 11.7 percent by the end of the 1951 and 13.2 percent by December 1952.

The impact of these numbers was soon felt in Korea. Many of the black units sent there from Japan or the United States were assigned to service jobs mostly behind the lines. Accordingly, they suffered few casualties while the white combat units took heavy losses. At the same time, because of the heavy influx of black draftees and volunteers in the quotaless system, there were more blacks among replacements sent to Korea than there was room for them in the segregated black units. Korean commanders did the only thing that made sense to an Army fighting desperately to avoid being driven into the Sea of Japan. They began assigning individual black soldiers to understrength units, just as Eisenhower had proposed to do in 1945. This time, there was no pro-segregation policy to stop them.

By December 1950, six months after the start of hostilities, blacks made up 11 percent of the strength of the Ninth Infantry regiment of the Second Division, which saw heavy action during the costly retreat from the Yalu River, when a horde of Chinese "volunteers" threatened to engulf U.S. forces. Brigadier General S. L. A. Marshall, a respected military historian serving as an analyst for the Second Division, called "C" Company, an integrated unit with a black commander, as "'possibly the bravest' unit in that action." Indeed, Marshall thought the integrated units as a whole fought brilliantly, and he told Lieutenant General Walton H. Walker, Eighth Army commander, later killed in a jeep action, that integration had proven itself. When Marshall, at Walker's suggestion, repeated this assessment at a press briefing, he got word from Tokyo that the headquarters of General Douglas MacArthur, supreme U.S. commander in the Far East, disapproved of racial mixing.

Despite MacArthur, the local commanders in Korea continued with their own integration programs assigning individual blacks to white units as replacements. By May 1951, eleven months into the conflict, more than 60 percent of the Eighth Army's infantry companies were integrated. By this time, MacArthur was gone, dismissed by Truman for striving to expand the war beyond the limits the president set. His replacement, General Matthew B. Ridgway, had been commanding the largely integrated Eighth Army, and the experience convinced him that segregation was "wholly inefficient, not to say improper." In his memoir of the Korean war, Ridgway declared, "It has always seemed to me both Un-American and Un-Christian for free citizens to be taught to downgrade themselves this way as if they were unfit to associate with their fellows or to accept leadership themselves."

Ridgway's idealistic view gained support from Army research into the racial policies at work in Korea. One study, called Project Clear, based on interviews with officers in integrated units, found that blacks soldiers performed better in racially mixed units. As for white soldiers, they generally accepted blacks when they were part of their own unit, while viewing them more negatively when they were seen as part of a separate group. Key conclusions of Project Clear were that "racial segregation limits the effectiveness of the Army." Contrariwise, "integration enhances the effectiveness of the Army." With these judgments to back him, Ridgway in May 1951 sought and gained permission to completely integrate Eighth Army, the largest combat unit in the U.S. Army. The results of the test of combat in Korea undermined the most powerful argument in support of segregation, that blacks would let their comrades down in battle, and thus created a watershed moment for Truman's executive order.

Integration now gained momentum. In December 1951, seven months after Ridgway decided to integrate the Eighth Army, all Army units in the United States and Alaska were ordered to proceed with integration. There was no specific timetable except to meet the goal of new Army secretary Frank Pace to complete the process within "the next few years." The next big target was the European command, where for some reason resistance was strong. Indeed, a manpower consultant sent there to advise on the preparation of a plan to integrate ran into a stone wall. Senior officers refused to believe that the Army intended to integrate, and they also did not accept the news of successful integration in Korea. It took a visit from Army chief of staff Lawton J. Collins and sustained follow-up pressure to get integration started by April 1952. It went ahead faster than expected, and by October 1953, the Army announced that 95 percent of its black troops in Europe were now integrated, with the rest to be assigned on that basis by June 1954.

Not surprisingly, given its fast start and Secretary Symington's enthusiasm, segregation collapsed more swiftly in the Air Force. By the end of 1950, 95 percent of black airmen were serving in integrated units.

In some ways, integration in the Navy had a slower path because it had been the most segregated of the services at the end of World War II. By 1949, most blacks were still assigned to the steward's branch. The entire Navy had only nineteen black officers. The Navy's efforts to make progress were hurt by the understandably bad reputation it had in the black community, thus discouraging the black enlistments it needed to gain ground against segregation. Prodded by the Fahy committee, the Navy slowly but steadily increased the number of blacks serving in the general service branch. The overall race problem took years to work out. Not until 1961 was the Navy able to announce that it had put a black officer in command of a warship, a destroyer escort. The Navy's experience demonstrated, as critics of racial change argued, that legal and formal reforms do indeed take a long time to alter deeply ingrained custom and culture. But the Navy also showed that such reforms set a different direction that fosters change.

The Marine Corps operated under the Navy's stated policy of racial quality but had been even slower than the Navy to change. One reason was the small number of black Marines, only 1,500 in 1949 when the Fahy committee started its work, most of them in a few segregated units as stewards. Once again, as with the Army, it was the Korean war and the consequent boost in manpower that opened the door to change. By 1952, the Marines could count thousands of black Marines, accounting for 5 percent of their total strength. To make up for the casualties of battle against the North Koreans and the Chinese, the Marine Corps, like the Army, sent blacks in as replacements wherever they were needed. This inevitably changed the culture of the corps, as it did of the Army. The net result was that by 1951, when the Marine Corps canceled its last all-black unit designated as such, its ranks included 17,000 blacks, nearly 10 percent of the corps' total strength, with only 500 of them serving in separate steward duty.

The story of Marine integration made up the closing pages in probably the most paradoxical chapter in the history of the Truman presidency. The Korean war ruined the final years of Truman's tenure in the White House. But that war also made possible his greatest domestic policy triumph: the integration of the armed forces of the United States. It was a long struggle that dragged on into the Eisenhower administration, and to some degree even afterward. But by time Truman left the White House, integration had become a reality in the war zone itself and in nearly all training programs. The rest of the services were on a course that made the final result inevitable. It was the literally life-and-death demands of the bloody three-year struggle in Korea that compelled the services, particularly the Army and the Marine Corps, to abandon their traditions and their-deep seated prejudices to assign black fighting men without regard to their race and solely on the basis of need. Even absent the Korean war, the exigencies of other cold war tensions and the continuous threat of conflict would have ultimately led the services down the same path to integration that they followed from 1950 to 1953. But it seems certain that the process would have dragged on for much longer.

If an unforeseen event in the shape of the Korean war provided the wind behind the back of executive order 9981, Truman made it possible for that circumstance to work to his advantage. Not only did he issue the executive order that started the process by creating the Fahy committee and giving it his full support, but he also he got the armed forces to integrate by setting the services on a course from which there was no turning back.

Fahy later told his top aide, Ned Kenworthy, that his role on the committee gave him more satisfaction that anything else he had done in public life. Truman had a right to feel much the same way. As sociologist Charles Moskos pointed out a nearly two decades after the military's integration, the military's "apartness" from the rest of American society, along with its hierarchical power structure, meant that the experience with racial mixing could not be easily translated in the civilian world. Yet it had important symbolic and pragmatic implications. This policy took on extra significance in the new world of the cold war. The armed services, once a lesser component of American society, had become a huge component not only in numbers but also in terms of its significance as the bulwark of the United States in what seemed a struggle for its very existence. Moreover, it provided for black Americans a powerful engine to improve themselves economically and in the eyes of their fellow citizens, to say nothing of what it did for their patriotism. For black and white Americans alike, it served as a powerful example of what both races could achieve to benefit each other and the common good. "The advent of the integrated society in this country is yet to occur," Moskos wrote nearly half a century ago. He added presciently, "The desegregation of the armed forces has served to bring that day closer."

11

★ ★ ★ ★ ★

FRIENDS OF THE COURT

Throughout his presidency, Harry Truman's efforts to advance civil rights were blocked by congressional resistance to any change to the Jim Crow status quo. This opposition combined the desperation of Southerners who saw their political lives imperiled and the timidity of Northerners unwilling to risk the goodwill of white Americans by taking on the cause of black America.

It was one of Truman's most significant achievements in the struggle for racial justice that he found ways to get around Congress by using his own authority as chief executive. In addition to commanding the integration of the armed forces, he used the United States justice department, working through the courts, to reverse a half-century trend of rulings denying the rights of black Americans and to open the way to unprecedented advances. In dealing with the courts instead of depending on executive orders, Truman's justice department wielded a more subtle, but as it turned out equally potent, weapon: the amicus curiae, or friend of the court brief. This is a legal device by which interested parties, with court permission, can participate in a case they are not directly involved in as litigants.

In five years, the justice department would file a series of such briefs that would have a profound impact on the jurisprudence of civil rights. But this tactic was not initially part of anyone's master plan. Instead, it stemmed from the uneasy relationship at the start of Truman's civil rights crusade between the justice department and civil rights advocates. This tension was evidenced in the spring of 1947, as the president's recently created Committee on Civil Rights wrote to the attorney general of the United States, Tom Clark, seeking his guidance on recommendations for the report. Underlying these recommendations was strong dissatisfaction among some committee members and many black Americans with what they considered the justice department's lack of vigor in pursuing the struggle for racial justice.

Clark was well aware of this unhappiness, but he chose to put the blame on the absence of direct federal authority to act on behalf of black victims of violence and other abuses. In a statement to the President's Committee on Civil Rights at one of its early meetings, he had suggested at least a partial remedy—broadening existing federal statutes against mob violence. In the meanwhile, Clark would try to find a case that would lead to a court ruling extending his department's reach under existing law.

Clark was striving to alter a bleak legal landscape. This was the result of a notorious chapter in American judicial history, written in the post-Reconstruction nineteenth century. During those years, the Supreme Court had eviscerated most of the federal statutes enacted after the Civil War to protect the rights supposedly granted to the newly freed slaves. What was left Clark himself viewed as "a very thin thread of law," making him hesitant to seek judicial backing. This, he feared, could lead to rulings that would demolish what little legal redress was available to blacks. Not everyone accepted this rationale. The NAACP's Walter White, for example, wired Truman that Truman's justice department, instead of taking advantage of what authority it did have under the law, had instead decided to "collapse" in the face of Southern opposition.

Rather than pursue this controversy, which had to do mostly with criminal law, the civil rights committee in its letter to Clark raised an issue under civil law. Specifically, the committee asked whether the government should not intervene more often in suits brought by private parties by filing an amicus curiae brief.

Clark was not enthusiastic. That tactic should be resorted to only rarely, he said in responding to the committee in July 1947. His reasoning was not convincing. Sometimes the objectives of private suits don't match the government's goals, he said. Sometimes private suits don't raise issues in a way that would help the government reach its broad purpose of advancing the cause of civil rights, he added. Clark's arguments were so unpersuasive, even to himself, that he told Robert Carr, executive secretary of the committee, he would not entirely rule out using the amicus brief weapon. Indeed, he promised Carr that his department would continue to actively monitor private civil rights cases, adding that "it may well be that we should resort to the amicus brief more frequently."

If Clark seemed to be hemming and hawing, his uncertainty probably in part reflected the reality that working with a committee charged with advancing the cause of civil rights was a long way from his roots in the heart of Texas. That he found himself in this situation was in large part due to his relationship with President Truman, beginning in Truman's Senate years. "Tom Clark has always tried to do what the president wanted," was the conventional wisdom about the attorney general among Washington insiders. Whatever those efforts by Clark amounted to, they were amply rewarded, for it was Truman who, despite the Texan's lack of imposing credentials, had made him the highest law enforcement officer in the land.

Clark came by his profession naturally enough, since it was his father's calling. However, the young man did not take after his parent in at least one respect: extreme bigotry. His father was raised in Mississippi, graduated from the University of Mississippi, and was said by his grandson, Ramsey, who succeeded *his* father, Tom, as attorney general, that the old man could "out-Bilbo Bilbo." After graduating from the University of Texas law school, five years of practice in the family firm, and another stint as civil district attorney of Dallas County, Tom Clark, with the help of the state's influential senator, Tom Connally, got a job in the justice department in 1937. There, after Pearl Harbor, he served as civilian coordinator of the Japanese American internment before moving to the fraud unit of the antitrust division.

It was in that post that he came to know and work with Truman, whose Senate committee was then leading the charge against the misdeeds of military contractors. Clark was eager for the prosecutions that resulted from Truman's probing and was prudent enough "not to try to get them to let me take charge for the committee. We worked pretty well together," Clark said later, "and I guess that's why he appointed me attorney general."

For many in the department, that was not a red-letter day, as evidenced by the departure of Charles Fahy as solicitor general. Among the disheartened was Paul Freund, a brilliant New Deal lawyer, who told a colleague that he now knew how justice department lawyers must have felt when Warren Harding named as his attorney general his campaign manager, Harry Daugherty, later indicted on corruption charges.

Unlike Daugherty, Clark's reputation was not tainted by allegations of shady dealings. His critics simply viewed him as limited in background and overly conservative. That judgment was strengthened by his first major assignment, as Truman's Red-hunter-in-chief. It was a task that many, including ultimately Truman himself, came to feel he went about with excessive enthusiasm. At Truman's direction, Clark created and then guided the loyalty program, which became one of the least savory and most irresponsible chapters in the Truman presidency. After he left the White House, Truman would complain that Clark would always come up with a "secret police proposition," contravening Truman's concern with protecting individual rights. He described him as the "dumbest man I've ever run across." But these deficiencies did not reveal themselves to the president at the time.

Clark seemed to genuinely believe drastic steps were needed to protect against the threat of Communist subversion and, not incidentally, shield Truman from political damage on the issue. So far as civil rights was concerned, though he had escaped the blatant racism of his father, he had some blind spots of his own. In April 1947, asked what the civil rights committee and the justice department could do to combat discrimination among federal civilian workers, he said, "I don't know of any discrimination in the federal government." In reality, although discrimination among civil servants was more subtle than in the military, its pervasiveness would be acknowledged in 1948 by the executive order Truman issued to eliminate it. In his 1947 statement denying discrimination anywhere in the civil service, Clark made a point of bragging of the record of his own justice department, which he said had attorneys, clerks, and stenographers "of all races."

Using a vocabulary more appropriate to informal conversation in his Texas youth than to official discussion in 1947 Washington, Clark remarked, "Some of our best attorneys happen to be colored men." In particular, he cited one lawyer in the claims division, who, though he had served as a World War II captain, Clark described as "a boy named Ballinger."

Whatever his personal attitudes, Clark recognized that the president he served had made civil rights a high priority, and therefore an important political issue with a presidential election soon to come. This factor was underlined in *To Secure These Rights*, the civil rights committee's provocative report, issued in October 1947. The report's suggestions for improvements did not skip over Clark's justice department, devoting nearly 1,000 words to a dozen or so recommendations. Some of the proposals, such as raising the existing civil rights section to a full-fledged vision and increasing appropriations, were subject to the will of Congress. Others, such as a sweeping reorganization of the department, including the establishment of regional offices, Clark had already rejected in his appearance before the committee. Hard-pressed to find a recommendation within his purview that was not downright objectionable to him for one reason or another, Clark decided to reconsider a tactic mentioned by the committee's report that he had previously frowned on: the use of amicus curiae briefs.

The committee report had mentioned as likely candidates two housing suits that the Supreme Court had already agreed to hear. One, *Shelley v. Kramer*, stemming from cases in Detroit and St. Louis, challenged private agreements called restrictive covenants that barred blacks from buying homes in certain neighborhoods in the various states. The other, *Hurd v. Hodge*, involving two cases in the District of Columbia, attacked the same practice in the capital.

As the President's Committee on Civil Rights explained it, with Supreme Court rulings making it legally impossible to segregate housing by zoning ordinances, restrictive covenants had emerged as the most effective way to accomplish the same purpose. These agreements were written into deeds of sale by which property owners bound themselves not to sell or lease to an "undesirable," sometimes defined as one minority and sometimes a slew of them. The beauty of the arrangement, from the viewpoint of the property owner, was that state courts, and in the case of the national capital, federal courts too, had enforced them. These restrictions were widespread in the North and the West, and by one estimate, they covered about 80 percent of all property in the city of Chicago.

Even before the committee published its recommendations Clark had been urged to intervene in the two housing cases cited in the report by Philip Elman of the solicitor general's staff. A native of New York City, Elman graduated from the City College of New York in the 1930s, when intellectual energy and political activism were both at fever pitch. His record at CCNY earned him a scholarship to Harvard Law School, where he matriculated with the intention of becoming a labor lawyer and working for "social justice and economic change." Instead, on graduation, he made a detour that took him first to the Federal Communications Commission, then to the Supreme Court, where he clerked for Justice Frankfurter, and then to the justice department, where he worked for then–solicitor general Charles Fahy. When Tom Clark took over at justice and Fahy left to work for the Army in Germany, Elman went with him for a year, then returned to the solicitor general's office.

His interest in social justice remained, but he now shifted his focus from labor law to civil rights and the challenges to the restrictive covenants in housing. Together with a like-minded friend at the interior department, Elman persuaded interior secretary Oscar Chapman, one of the administration's committed liberals, to suggest to Clark that he enter the housing cases. Elman then got a state department official to write Clark telling him that racial problems were hurting the nation's image abroad. Finally, Elman wrote a formal recommendation to Clark urging him to file an amicus brief.

What clinched Clark's decision, though, was the recommendation to do just that in *To Secure These Rights*. After reading the report and getting approval from Truman, Clark then passed the word to Solicitor General Philip B. Perlman, who, not surprisingly, called in Elman. "We're going in," he told him, and Elman set about drafting the brief.

When Elman's draft brief was approved, he noticed that higher-ups had taken the unusual step of adding Attorney General Clark's name on the brief. That bothered Elman not at all because Elman realized it was intended to make the brief seem an authoritative statement of the position of the U.S. government. "If I could have, I'd have put Truman's name on it," he said later.

Clark's name was followed on the draft brief by Elman's, then the names of three other assistants in the solicitor's office, Hilbert Zarky, Oscar Davis, and Stanley Silverberg. But Arnold Raum, Perlman's chief assistant, deleted Elman's name and the names of the other assistants. Raum, as he told Elman, wanted to avoid having it seem "as if a bunch of Jewish lawyers in the Department of Justice put this out." So as Elman noted, the historic brief—the strongest condemnation of all forms of racial discrimination the U.S. government had ever made before the Supreme Court—itself involved an act of discrimination, one committed by Raum, who himself was Jewish.

In his brief, Elman wasted no time establishing the Truman administration's stake in the outcome of the case. "The Federal Government has a special responsibility for the protection of the fundamental civil rights guaranteed to the people by the Constitution and laws of the United States," he wrote. Then he quoted from Truman's speech to the NAACP in June 1947. "We must make the Federal Government a friendly and vigilant defender of the rights and equalities of all Americans."

Elman, whose literary skills had been honed by his City College English courses, took care to put flesh and blood on the bones of his argument. Contending that by fostering ghettos, restrictive covenants had denied life, liberty, and the pursuit of happiness, he wrote that for those trapped in the ghettos, "There is no life in the accepted sense of the word; liberty is a mockery, and the right to pursue happiness a phrase without meaning, empty of hope and reality." Determined to make use of every argument offered to him, Elman turned to foreign relations and told the High Court that racial segregation had caused "serious embarrassment to the United States," citing statements by state department officials, delegates to the United Nations General Assembly, and critical articles in Soviet periodicals.

In making the oral argument before the justices, which Elman drafted for him, Perlman underlined the significance of the case. He told the Court that the suit represented the first federal intervention in a case whose sole purpose was the vindication of rights guaranteed by the Fifth and Fourteenth Amendments.

While the justice department relied on the Constitution for its challenge, the NAACP, which had entered the case early, took a leaf from the casebook of Justice Louis Brandeis. As an advocate for various reformist causes, Brandeis had depended heavily on sociological and economic arguments. In its version of what had come to be known as the Brandeis brief, the NAACP relied on more than 150 articles, reports, and books, together with charts and maps to quantify the impact of segregation.

In addition to all this legal firepower, another factor brightened the prospects for the housing challenges. Three of the justices, Stanley Reed, Robert Jackson, and Wiley Rutledge, had recused themselves. Though they had offered no explanation, the general presumption was that they had been personally involved with property covered by restrictive covenants and were therefore the most likely to uphold such agreements.

Also giving grounds for optimism was that two of the remaining six justices, Chief Justice Fred Vinson and Associate Justice Harold Burton, were Truman appointees. Truman and Vinson, whom the president had selected in the second year of his presidency, had known each other since Truman's earliest days in Washington. Vinson had been part of the coterie of poker-playing pals whom Truman relied on for friendship and advice and had been his treasury secretary before going to the Court. Burton, a former Ohio senator and Truman's first appointment to the Court, though a Republican, had been on good terms with the president and had served on his war investigation committee. The justice department could hope that Truman's connection to the government's case might encourage a sympathetic reaction from his two old friends.

Whatever underlay the justices' reasoning, all six who participated supported the government's arguments on both *Shelley* and *Hurd* in the decision announced in May 1948. As Vinson, who wrote the opinion, declared, "We have concluded that in these cases the States have acted to deny petitioners the equal protection of the laws guaranteed by the Fourteenth Amendment."

Blacks cheered the decision. "In Michigan, Missouri and D.C. We Can LIVE ANYWHERE!" exulted the *Pittsburgh Courier* in a banner across the top of its front page, though the ruling of course applied everywhere in the country. In New York City and other cities with significant Jewish populations, there was also rejoicing when the justice department declared that the ruling banned religious as well as racial discrimination.

The case also had collateral benefits within the justice department itself, according to Elman, by reshaping the attitudes of Solicitor General Perlman, who made the oral argument for the government. A native of Baltimore, conditioned by the racial mores of that quasi-Southern city, Perlman was "very moved" by the experience and by the congratulations he received from Walter White and other civil rights leaders. "He couldn't wait to get back to the Supreme Court again and again, arguing for equality," Elman recalled.

Perlman had to wait little more than a year for opportunities not only to argue for equality, but also to overturn the "separate but equal" doctrine of *Plessy v. Ferguson,* which had been a bone in the throat of civil rights advocates since 1896. The circumstances of the first case, *Henderson v. United States,* which involved segregated rail transportation, were unusual because when it got to the Supreme Court, the justice department was pitted against another federal agency, the Interstate Commerce Commission. The plaintiff, Elmer Henderson, had been denied service in a Southern Railway dining car because only seats in the white section of the car were open. He filed a complaint with the ICC, contending that he had been discriminated against, in violation of the Interstate Commerce Act. When the ICC rejected his claim, Henderson filed suit in federal district court, where he was opposed by lawyers for the ICC and the justice department. Defeated in the district court, Henderson appealed directly to the Supreme Court. As his lawyer, Belford Lawson of Washington, pointed out, Henderson's only option was to eat at one end of the dining car, behind a curtain. "It was as if you were a pig or some kind of animal," Lawson said. The ICC prepared to oppose him in the Supreme Court. But when the agency's brief got to the solicitor general's office, Elman read it, decided that the government had been on the wrong side, and convinced Perlman to enter the case in support of Henderson. The attorney general's approval was still needed, but this turned out not to be a problem. By this time, the fall of 1949, Clark had left the justice department to go to the Supreme Court, replacing Frank Murphy, who had died of a heart attack. As Clark's replacement, Truman named J. Howard McGrath, who, as party chairman, had stiff-armed the rebellious Southerners in the wake of Truman's civil rights message. McGrath was all for battling the ICC in the Henderson case, so much so that he wanted to argue it himself. He yielded to Perlman, who once again turned to Elman for the brief, which in this case would be a litigant's brief, not an amicus brief. In Elman's brief, signed by Perlman, he argued that the ICC's regulations permitting

169

compulsory segregation denied black passengers the equality of treatment promised by the Constitution and the Interstate Commerce Act.

Because the segregation violated the Interstate Commerce Act, the case was not governed by the *Plessy v. Ferguson* precedent, Elman argued. But he added that if the Court felt it could not decide Henderson's case without referring to the "separate but equal" doctrine, it could and should overrule *Plessy v. Ferguson*. Making this occasion particularly tempting for such an historic challenge was that *Plessy*, like *Henderson*, was a railroad case in which the High Court had upheld a Louisiana law segregating passenger train travel. "The notion that separate but equal facilities satisfy constitutional and statutory prohibitions against discrimination is obsolete," Elman wrote. "The phrase 'equal rights' means the same rights."

Even in the midst of the preparations for *Henderson*, the justice department plunged into two other civil rights lawsuits against two universities in the Southwest, the University of Texas law school and the University of Oklahoma. These would represent the U.S. justice department's first involvement in education, the area most critical to the hopes of black Americans for overcoming the burden imposed on them by American history. Blacks and their supporters could readily see the potential that good schooling offered. In addition, the deficiencies in the education of many blacks was one of the prime rationales offered by white Americans for perpetuating segregation. Notably, for example, in explaining his opposition to integrating the Army, Dwight Eisenhower, then the chief of staff, had contended in U.S. Senate hearings that because "the Negro is less well educated," he would therefore find in an integrated Army that the "competition is too tough." These cases touched the rarified ground of higher education, not the elementary and secondary schools that reached most blacks—and whites. Still, a challenge to segregation at a high level would open the door to a broader confrontation.

The plaintiff in the Texas case *Sweatt v. Painter*, was a black mailman named Herman Marion Sweatt. In 1946, Sweatt had asked a federal court to order his admission to the University of Texas's prestigious law school, which had turned him down. The judge commanded the state of Texas to provide a comparable facility for Sweatt to get his legal education or admit him to the university. Rather than do that, Texas created a new three-room law school in downtown Houston, far from the University of Texas's law school in Austin, Texas, which Sweatt was urged to attend. Instead, he went back to court, where his attorney, the NAACP's Thurgood Marshall, contended that the three-room school designed exclusively for Sweatt was in no way equal to the University of Texas law school. When the ruling went against Sweatt, he and Marshall appealed to the Supreme Court.

In *McLaurin v. University of Oklahoma State Regents*, the plaintiff was George W. McLaurin, who already had a master's degree but in 1948 was denied admission when he sought to enter the graduate school of the University of Oklahoma to earn a PhD in education. In his appeal to the federal courts, he too was represented by Marshall. McLaurin was chosen from other potential plaintiffs in part because he was sixty-eight years old, an age that Marshall thought would defuse the standard allegation that integration of graduate schools would inevitably result in racial intermarriage. Under order from a three-judge federal court to provide McLaurin "with the education he seeks," the Oklahoma Board of Regents agreed to admit him to the University of Oklahoma. But if Oklahoma surrendered on the admission, the state stuck to its guns on segregation. When McLaurin showed up for class, he was made to sit at a desk in a room outside the regular classroom. Similar separation followed him to the library and the cafeteria. But when Marshall appealed to a three-judge federal court contending that the circumstances stamped McLaurin with "a badge of inferiority," the court backed Oklahoma. Once again, Marshall turned to the Supreme Court.

The justice department's decision to enter the two school cases as amicus was approved first by the new attorney general, McGrath, who in turn got Truman's backing. In the briefs, Elman once again assaulted *Plessy v. Ferguson,* as he had in *Henderson.* "The fact of racial segregation is itself a manifestation of inequality and discrimination," Elman wrote. "The United States in these cases again urges the Court to repudiate the 'separate but equal' doctrine as an unwarranted deviation from the principle of equality under the law." Once again, Elman used a quote from Truman's 1947 civil rights message, in which the president said that "if we wish to fulfill the promise that is ours we must correct the remaining imperfections in our practice of democracy."

The 1948 decisions in *Shelley* and *Hurd* gave the justice department and the NAACP reason for optimism in *Henderson* and the education cases. But the normal uncertainties surrounding an impending High Court decision had been magnified by the changes in the Court in the past two years. In addition to Clark, whom liberals suspected of deep-dyed conservatism, Truman had appointed another new justice, former Indiana senator Sherman Minton. Minton's opinions on the court of appeals, where he had previously served, had shown little concern for civil rights.

As it turned out, Justice Clark made himself an advocate for the plaintiffs in the education cases inside the Court. In a memo to the other justices based on his familiarity with the Southwest region, Texan Clark dismissed the notion that ruling against the states would result in what he called "horribles," referring to sexual liaisons between the races. "There would no 'incidents' in my opinion if the cases are limited to the graduate schools," he wrote, though he added that he would be opposed to similar judgments in elementary and secondary schools.

In unanimous decisions handed down on the same day, June 5, 1950, the Court ruled for the plaintiffs in *Henderson* and in the two education cases. The justices held that the ICC had violated its governing statute by discriminating against Henderson. They also said that by forcing Sweatt to go to a separate law school and denying McLaurin a seat in the regular classroom, the two universities had violated the rights of the two students. But having dealt with these specific circumstances, the justices said they saw no need to ponder the merits of *Plessy v. Ferguson* and so denied the NAACP and the justice department the goal of their grand strategy, to overturn the ruling doctrine of "separate but equal."

Many believed that the combined impact of the cases the justice department had entered—*Shelly, Henderson, Sweatt,* and *McLaurin*—had battered the underpinnings of *Plessy* so much that this landmark would ultimately collapse. Among those who felt that way apparently was one of the High Court's new justices, Tom Clark. In urging his colleagues to rule that segregation of graduate schools denies equal protection of the law, Clark added, "If some say this undermines *Plessy* then let it fall, as have many nineteenth century oracles."

If anyone doubted the president's connection to this historic series of cases, he made matters clear in a campaign speech for 1952 Democratic nominee Adlai Stevenson. "At my request the Solicitor General of the United States went before the Supreme Court to argue that Negro citizens have the right to enter state colleges and universities," he declared, referring to the *Sweatt* and *McLaurin* cases. "At my request, the Solicitor General again went before the Supreme Court and argued against the vicious restrictive covenants that had prevented homes in many places from being sold to Negroes," he added, referring to the *Shelley* and *Hurd* cases.

As it turned out, Truman's justice department was not through yet. Following the election of Dwight Eisenhower to succeed Truman but before Truman's term ran out, he approved his justice department taking one more shot at *Plessy v. Ferguson.* After the favorable decisions in the higher education cases left that troublesome precedent shaky but still more or less in force, it seemed likely that the next major test would come from a series of suits the NAACP was bringing against segregation in the public elementary schools. As civil rights advocates well knew, this was much more difficult terrain than the graduate schools. One reason was the scope of the target—hundreds of thousands of students in thousands of schools across more than a dozen states. Another concern was the age of the students and its link of age to the specter of sexual fears that haunted

Southerners whenever they were forced to confront the issue of race. Those in the South who had been troubled by miscegenation at graduate schools, as Thurgood Marshall had noted, would be that much more appalled at the prospect of racial mixing among students just approaching puberty.

The intensity of feeling was driven home to Elman in 1952 when he urged Perlman to file an amicus brief in one of the first NAACP cases challenging segregation in elementary school education, *Briggs v. Elliott,* which, when they came before the Supreme Court, would be bundled under the rubric of *Brown v. Board of Education.* Perlman's enthusiasm for the civil rights cause, kindled by his role in the housing cases, was now extinguished by the prospect of integrating schoolchildren at a tender age. "No, it's much too early to end segregation in public schools," Elman remembered Perlman telling him. "You can't have little black boys sitting next to little white girls." This was pretty much the same point Eisenhower had made to Chief Justice Warren at the White House stag dinner. "The country isn't ready for that. This would lead to miscegenation and mongrelization of the races."

That's where matters stood as the clock ticked away the last months of Truman's presidency, with the High Court set to hear arguments on *Brown* in December. Then an unexpected event in a seemingly unrelated sphere, the sort of thing that makes history difficult to forecast, caused a dramatic change. Ensnared in the web of corruption charges that darkened the close of Truman's White House tenure, Attorney General McGrath was forced to resign in the spring of 1952. He was replaced by James McGranery, a federal judge who had served in Congress with Truman and had become a good friend of the then senator.

McGranery struck Elman, as he later put it, "as a kind of a nut," unstable and given to emotional outbursts. For the sober, stiff-necked Perlman, this erratic behavior was more than he could bear. He resigned, a development that Elman viewed as an "act of god." Robert L. Stern, who had been Perlman's deputy, became acting solicitor general, and he and Elman promptly met with the new attorney general and urged him to approve a justice department brief in the school desegregation cases, consistent with the department's previous attacks on the "separate but equal" doctrine. "You're right boys," McGranery told them. "Go ahead and write a brief."

McGranery, for all his reputed volatility, was not without a sense of political prudence. Before giving the final and official green light to Elman and Stern, he visited his old friend at the White House. Details of the conversation are unknown. But it seems likely that McGranery reminded Truman of the justice department's previous amicus briefs in civil rights cases and pointed to the profound significance of a challenge to Jim Crow at the educational level, where young Americans' minds and values were shaped. One thing is clear. With the presidential election a month in the past and with his own tenure coming to an end, there was no political pressure on the president one way or another. What is known is that Truman gave his new attorney general permission to join the assault on elementary school segregation.

So Elman once again set to work on an amicus brief in a civil rights case, which would turn out to be his most important. To understand Elman's work product in this case, it helps to appreciate the thirty-four-year-old lawyer's relationship with seventy-year-old Justice Felix Frankfurter, who had become a major influence on his professional life. It is easy to see why. Frankfurter had a powerful intellect and a domineering personality. He had advised FDR before and during his presidency, and he had turned down the new chief executive's offer to be solicitor general because he believed he could be more influential if he stayed on at his faculty post at Harvard while advising Roosevelt on an informal basis.

He was probably right about that. In addition to the counsel on a wide range of policy matters he offered FDR directly on his weekly visits to Washington, he became recruiter-in-chief for the New Deal. Not surprisingly, he drew on the pool of talent generated by Harvard Law School, many his own promising students, who became known as "Frankfurter's little hot dogs." As a result of these activities and his closeness to FDR, one high-ranking early New Dealer, General Hugh Johnson, would pronounce Frankfurter "the most influential single individual in the United States," a judgment he did not offer as a compliment. Frankfurter, Johnson contended, had "insinuated" his "boys" into "obscure but key positions in every vital department" of the New Deal.

In his younger days, Frankfurter had been known as an inveterate crusader for nearly every left-wing crusade of note. His major involvement was in the defense of Sacco and Vanzetti, the anarchists whose murder conviction became one of the great causes célèbres of the 1920s. In his years on the Court, Frankfurter became more reluctant to defy the establishment and more eager to seek compromise. His influence on the young people he worked with remained great, as evidenced by the title in Elman's memoirs of his chapter on his two years clerking for Frankfurter, "The Towering Justice Frankfurter."

By looking up to Frankfurter, as the chapter title suggests, Elman was fulfilling Frankfurter's own expectations for how others should regard him, and not only his clerks. He had considered himself a child prodigy, likening his precocious absorption with world events to the childhood achievements of Mozart and John Stuart Mill. Apparently he wanted to be treated as a sort of adult prodigy. "He regarded himself as the intellectual leader of the Court," Elman wrote. He expected, Elman believed, from the other justices not only respect but "perhaps a little more, a deference and acceptance of his views." But Elman added, "Of course that did not come."

Fortunately for Elman, Frankfurter had a high regard not only for his own abilities, but also for Elman's gifts. While most law clerks at the Court spent their time working on requests for the Court to grant writs of certiorari, an agreement to review a lower court's judgment, Frankfurter thought Elman's time too valuable to be wasted on such routine chores. Instead, Elman was able to focus on the loftier task of helping to draft Frankfurter's opinions.

Elman's relationship to Frankfurter did not change markedly when his clerkship ended. The justice considered the clerkships he awarded to be lifetime jobs. "He regarded law clerks, present and past, and no matter where they were, as still his law clerks, " Elman wrote. "We were his boys, his family." Even after Elman went to work for the solicitor general from Frankfurter's office, Frankfurter continued to discuss colleagues and issues at the Court with him. "When he was talking to me, he was talking to his law clerk, his intimate, his confidante," Elman wrote. "He wasn't talking to me as assistant to the solicitor general." But the reality was that Elman *was* assistant to the solicitor general. Though Elman respected Frankfurter's confidence "as if I were a priest," what Elman seemed to ignore was the opportunity this relationship gave Frankfurter to influence the government's filings to the Court, an arrangement many jurists would regard as problematic at best.

However, Frankfurter was not one to be stifled by conventional standards of propriety. His attitude reflected the conduct of his mentor, the widely revered Justice Louis Brandeis, whom FDR referred to as Old Isaiah. For most of the more than twenty years Brandeis served on the High Court, and before he became a justice himself, Frankfurter served as Brandeis's all-expenses-paid conduit to the outside world of politics and government.

For his part, unwilling to give up his role as privileged adviser to Franklin Roosevelt after FDR named him to the Supreme Court, Frankfurter at one time or another contributed phrases for Roosevelt's speeches, recommended candidates for appointment to federal office, including the Supreme Court, and proposed tax policies for the treasury department. He probably eased any twinge of conscience by avoiding, so far as is known, any counsel on cases before the Court. But the areas in which he offered advice were so broad and contentious that it was inevitable that litigation of some sort would arise.

Elman comforted himself with the fact that the many conversations he had with Frankfurter about *Brown* took place before December 1952, when the government filed its amicus brief. But this seems disingenuous because all during the time he and Frankfurter were talking, the possibility was always open that the government would enter the case, as indeed it did. Then there was no way Elman could scrub his mind clear of what Frankfurter told him, nor did he try.

What Frankfurter passed on to Elman was not a set of facts as much as it was a depiction of the moods and inclinations of his colleagues on the bench toward the school cases as perceived by Frankfurter. All of this was made that much more convincing by Frankfurter's characteristic self-assurance and theatrical flair. The picture he painted was a worrisome one for the cause of civil rights. It was of a badly divided Court, and Frankfurter believed that the more divided the Court was in issuing its opinion, the more difficult it would be to get compliance with a desegregation order. He was not alone in that view, or so he told Elman. Justice Hugo Black, an Alabama native and an erstwhile Klan member, wanted to overturn *Plessy v. Ferguson*, but, according to Frankfurter, "he was scared to death, and scared everybody on the court." When he talked to Elman in the fall of 1952, Frankfurter was not sure he could count on even five votes, a bare majority, for overruling *Plessy*. Frankfurter's strategy was to delay a ruling until he believed a united Court would overturn school segregation and assure compliance.

It was with Frankfurter's ominous words in mind that Elman laid out his brief. He started out on familiar ground. Once again, as in the other civil rights cases, he emphasized the federal government's new sense of responsibility for civil rights, using a Truman quote from his civil rights message to Congress to make that point: "We shall not finally achieve the ideals for which this nation was founded so long as any American suffers discrimination as a result of his race, or religion or color."

Then he suggested to the justices an easy way to strike down segregation. The cases grouped together under *Brown* involved five school districts in four states, South Carolina, Virginia, Delaware, and Kansas, as well as the District of Columbia. In the four states, the lower federal courts had already found inequalities in the black schools, thus allowing the Supreme Court to order that their students be assigned to white schools without upsetting *Plessy*. So far as the case in the capital, *Bolling v. Sharpe*, was concerned, the justices need not decide that immediately because no testimony had been taken in the district court hearing. But if the Court found that it could not ignore the "separate but equal" doctrine, then, Elman argued as bluntly as he had in the previous amicus briefs, it must overturn *Plessy*. "'Separate but equal' is a contradiction in terms," Elman wrote. There can be no enjoyment of equality "for children who know that because of their color the law sets them apart from and requires them to attend separate schools especially established for members of their race."

Finally Elman came to the crucial section of his brief (point four, as it was styled), the part most influenced by Frankfurter. If the Court did decide to strike down school segregation, he told the justices, "the government would suggest that in shaping the relief the Court should take into account the need, not only for prompt vindication of the constitutional rights violated but also for orderly and reasonable solution of the vexing problems which may arise in eliminating such segregation. The public interest plainly would be served by avoidance of needless dislocation and confusion in the administration of the school system."

It was this section that made this brief "the one thing I'm proudest of in my whole career," Elman said later. "It offered the court a way out of its dilemma, a way to end racial segregation without inviting massive disobedience."

Still, when Elman's amicus brief in the *Brown* cases was filed on December 3, 1952, not everyone cheered. After all, as Elman later conceded, what the brief was saying to the black schoolchildren was "you're right, your constitutional rights are being violated. But we're not going to do a damn thing for you. We'll take care of your children perhaps."

Elman's old allies in the civil rights movement were outraged by his argument for delay. "I had been a great hero of the NAACP and all those other people who were fighting to end racial segregation but after that brief was filed, I wasn't a hero anymore," Elman wrote later. "They thought point four was gradualism, and to them gradualism meant never. Unlike Frankfurter and me, they couldn't or didn't count the votes on the court."

Frankfurter was not infallible as a vote counter, or anything else, for that matter. He might have misjudged Vinson, who despite his reputation as a conservative had voted with the NAACP and the justice department on the housing cases, the railway case, and the higher education cases. He seems to have ignored Tom Clark's memo in the higher education cases in which Clark, despite being leery about the desegregation of elementary school children, seemed prepared to accept the end of *Plessy v. Ferguson.* Moreover, Vinson and Clark were said to vote as one. The point is, no one could predict how these justices would vote in cases that had not yet been argued. Frankfurter was entitled to his opinion. But he was not entitled to Elman's opinion too.

Elman insisted in his memoir that he had no discussions with Frankfurter about the crucial gradualism section of his brief. However, he gave the game away in an earlier interview with Richard Kluger, author of

Simple Justice, a magisterial study of the school desegregation cases. Marshall and his NAACP staff, in complaining about his brief, Elman said, "failed to grasp that our brief had been done the Frankfurter way, bearing in mind the key problem and how it vexed the court."

So far as Truman was concerned, though he knew nothing of the thinking and parleying that went into Elman's brief, the episode illustrates the hindrances he faced as president even when he tried to circumvent Congress by using his executive power. Though the NAACP's attack on segregated schools was of a piece with Truman's civil rights program, his most important domestic priority, he was prevented at first from entering the case by a balky justice department official, his solicitor general, Philip Perlman. Even when Perlman resigned for unrelated reasons, opening the way to an amicus brief, the attorney who wrote it, Philip Elman, was under the spell of Justice Frankfurter. As a result, he presented an argument for gradualism, which, as he later acknowledged, "as a matter of constitutional principle was simply indefensible." Not only that, but this gradualism, as interpreted by the High Court when it finally decided the *Brown* cases, opened the way for years of litigation and controversy.

Truman's decision to approve the justice department amicus brief was the crowning triumph in the department's effort to use the courts to make the country live up to its constitution. Enhancing its importance was the impact it would have on his reluctant Republican successor in the White House.

12

★ ★ ★ ★ ★

LEGACY

In November 1952, ten days after his party had lost the White House to Republican Dwight Eisenhower and two weeks before his justice department asked the Supreme Court to overturn segregation in the nation's schools, Harry Truman met briefly with a group of black leaders. They were directors of the National Newspaper Publishers Association representing every black newspaper of note, and they had come to present the president with a plaque inscribed: "To Harry S. Truman, 33rd President of the United States who has awakened the conscience of America and given new strength to our democracy by his courageous efforts on behalf of freedom and equality of citizens."

Truman thanked the group for their praise and added: "I hope I will always deserve it."

After he left office, Truman was not always the avatar of racial justice the inscription depicted. Inside his heart and mind, he still clung to the sometimes self-contradictory view that while blacks were fully entitled to protection of their constitutional rights, they should also know their place. Also, as a former farmer and shopkeeper, he believed strongly in property rights, an attitude he expressed in unbending fashion when he declared that if anyone staged such a sit-in in a store he ran, "I'd throw him out." When Martin Luther King, who had emerged as the leader of the burgeoning civil rights movement, and others deplored this comment, Truman acknowledged that he believed businesses should serve all comers. The former president added his opinion that the sit-ins had been organized by communists, just like the sit-down strikes of the 1930s, which he had also opposed at the time. This brought a gently chiding note from his former secretary of state and close friend, Dean Acheson, urging him to hold his fire and pointing out that his remarks were "totally out of keeping with your public record." Truman thanked Acheson for his advice, and took it.

Whatever fuss he stirred as a postincumbent, while serving in his country's highest office, Truman earned the plaudits showered on him by the black publishers and by countless other Americans, black and white. He did so in numerous ways: by ordering the integration of the armed forces, by throwing the weight of the federal government behind the long struggle in the courts to end segregation in the nation's schools and housing, and more broadly, by a flood of public utterances and proclamations putting the prestige of the highest office in the land on the side of the least-favored Americans. To compare Truman's civil rights record to that of any of his predecessors in the White House is like comparing Gulliver to the Lilliputians. He was the first to make the struggle for racial justice part of the national agenda, to define bias against Americans of color as an evil that violated the Constitution, and ultimately, though it took him a while to do it, to define segregation, as distinguished from discrimination, as inherently a component of that evil. In fact, in the closing months of his presidency, as he campaigned valiantly but vainly for Adlai Stevenson, instead of merely denouncing discrimination, he spoke more frequently of "integration" and "integrating" than ever before.

Just as striking as the comparison of Truman to previous presidents is the contrast between his actual record and the earlier expectations of his performance based on his heritage in border-state Missouri. "Poison to the Negro citizen" is the way one prominent black group branded Truman's choice as FDR's running mate in 1944. It was a condemnation echoed with varying words and to varying degrees by critics, black and white. A range of complex and interrelated circumstances helped Truman disprove such forecasts and turn himself into the president who was honored by the black publishers. For one thing, a look at his early years makes clear that he personally did not share the impassioned hatred of blacks attributed to his state and region. Beyond that, on the positive side, at the core of his pursuit of politics was his commitment to government as a force for good, particularly in the lives of citizens who had endured more than their share of the slings and arrows of existence. This attitude was rooted in his childhood. The severe eye problems that limited his boyhood fun gave him an awareness of the unfairness of life. So did the collapse of his father's finances as a result of grain market speculation and the dreary years he spent as a young man tilling the family farm. Added to that was the disappointment brought by nearly all his various business ventures, climaxed by the bankruptcy of his haberdashery.

All this might have led to bitterness except for the uplifting influence of the values that reflected his Middle Border upbringing of that period, inculcated in him mostly by Martha Truman. Young Harry was taught to be honest, to do his duty, and to adhere to the Victorian moral code and the admonitions of the Good Book. But the harsh edges to his life made him receptive to the populism that was endemic in the prairies in Truman's youth, particularly embodied by William Jennings Bryan, his first political hero. Truman later combined Bryan's fiery gospel with the progressivism of Woodrow Wilson and the interest group politics of FDR's New Deal, all leading him in the same direction: becoming champion of the underdog. This theme was infused with pragmatism stemming from his alliance with boss Pendergast. Their collaboration was of particular tactical importance in teaching him to respect the value of black voters and the insights of black leaders.

Then there was his sense of history, which made him conscious of the potential of leadership. From his childhood, Truman read history, concentrating on the lives of men who had risen to greatness and focusing on models and patterns of behavior that he would later try to follow. The job description that he absorbed of a leader as "a man who has the ability to get other people to do what they don't want to do" sometimes exceeded his capacities. But he remained faithful to it, as he demonstrated each time he thrust a new round of civil rights proposals against the obduracy of Capitol Hill.

His sense of history, along with his two years of law school and the three decades he spent in elective office and seeking it, made Truman keenly aware of constitutional principles. It was this cornerstone that he relied on most often in his early utterances on civil rights. Apart from all that, his two years as Captain Truman of Battery D gave his response to racial injustice a special urgency. It was the brutal treatment of black veterans, who had worn the same uniform as he, that, as he told the Southerners who wanted him to back down on civil rights, "made my stomach turn over." He came to realize, drawing on the full meaning of his childhood teachings, that racism was not only unjust but immoral. In a speech to the Howard University graduating class of 1952, he said that in 1947, many people had advised him that by raising the issue of civil rights, he would make things worse. "But you can't cure a moral problem or a social problem by ignoring it," Truman said. "Now instead of making things worse our efforts in the field of civil rights have made things better—better in all aspects of our national life, and in all parts of our country." It was the first time he had described civil rights as a moral problem, a concept later adopted by his first Democratic successor in the presidency, John Kennedy.

The singular nature of Truman's leadership in civil rights is underlined by the contrast between his performance in office and the laggardly record of the two politicians who immediately succeeded him in the White House. The actions of Dwight Eisenhower and John F. Kennedy bear out one of the lessons from Truman's performance, underlining how a president's personal background and inclinations often override supposedly empirical political decisions. Dwight David Eisenhower had assumed the leadership of the Republican Party at a time and with the credentials to undertake a sea change in national politics. His personal prestige uniquely positioned him to gain the confidence of blacks and also to reassure whites, while at the same time making clear to them that they had little choice but to accept change. But as soon as he was nominated, Eisenhower was counseled that any effort to win the support of black Americans would cost him the support of Southern whites.

Eisenhower evidently found this advice persuasive, not surprising, because it fit in well with his beliefs on race, which had been shaped by his background, before and during his military service. In his hometown of Abilene, Kansas, there were scarcely any blacks, and there were none at all at West Point when Eisenhower attended. Indeed, from the Civil War to World War II, only thirteen blacks had been admitted to the military academy, and only three of these graduated. His military career was especially limiting on racial issues because of the predominance of military posts in the South, and of Southerners in the officer corps. All this helped account for Eisenhower's mind-set in 1948, after he had left the Army for the presidency of Columbia, when he testified at a congressional hearing against integrating the military. Eisenhower later told E. Frederick Morrow, a black member of his White House staff, that his views on integration were based on the opinions of his field commanders. It only occurred to him later, he said, that nearly all of the field commanders were from the South.

Early in his presidency, Eisenhower proclaimed his personal commitment to the principles of equality and fair play and apparently considered himself to be a supporter of civil rights. "I believe with all my heart that our vigilant guarding of these [civil] rights is a sacred obligation binding upon every citizen," he declared in his State of the Union speech in February 1953. He lamented the existence of discrimination but placed the burden of combating this evil on "each individual in every station of life in his every deed." As this admonition suggested, he was averse to using the power of the federal government to deal with problems he considered to be rooted in men's hearts and minds, which was his view of racial problems. In a revealing letter to his friend, segregationist leader Governor James Byrnes of South Carolina, Eisenhower wrote, somewhat echoing his Senate testimony against military integration, "I do not believe that prejudice, even palpably unjustified prejudices, will succumb to compulsion. I believe that federal law imposed upon our states in such a way as to bring about a conflict of the police power of the states and of the nation would set back the cause of progress in race relations for a long, long time."

As strongly as he clung to his passive approach to civil rights, Eisenhower resented criticism on that count. Indeed, in the 1952 campaign, stung by Truman referring to his Senate testimony against military segregation, Eisenhower accused Truman and FDR of "systematic exploitation" of a minority by promising more than they could deliver. He particularly lashed out at Truman on racial discrimination in the District of Columbia, which he said was a national humiliation. This was an aspect of discrimination, unlike Jim Crow in the states, that Eisenhower felt comfortable attacking because the nation's capital was clearly under federal jurisdiction.

Defending his record, Truman cited progress that had been made toward integrating parks and playgrounds and some schools in the capital. But he also acknowledged the difficulties, which, he charged, Eisenhower had ignored. "I ought to warn him that the president can't get things done in the District of Columbia by simply waving a wand."

Under the existing system, the capital was governed by a board of commissioners who were under the thumb of congressional committees dominated by Southerners dedicated to perpetuating Jim Crow. As Truman pointed out, he had sought to change the system by advocating home rule, but, as he added, "I can't get the Congress to agree."

In reality, Truman's problem was not just Congress but also the federal courts. In 1950, a local civil rights group had challenged the Jim Crow policy at a restaurant operated by a local chain, invoking the 1872 home rule law banning discrimination. They won support from the municipal court of appeals, which in 1951 declared the old Reconstruction-era law still valid. But the restaurant immediately appealed, and the district commissioners announced they would ignore the municipal court ruling until the case was finally decided. Thus, efforts by Truman and other local groups to end segregation in the district were effectively throttled pending the appeal.

Meanwhile, Philip Elman in the solicitor general's office once again filed an amicus brief, this time in support of the civil rights protestors and the 1872 law. However, in January 1953, just as Eisenhower was taking office, the U.S. circuit court ruled against the civil rights plaintiffs, holding that the old law was invalid. Elman immediately urged J. Lee Rankin, an assistant attorney general under Herbert Brownell, Eisenhower's attorney general, to tell the District of Columbia lawyers to appeal to the Supreme Court. Rankin agreed. Not only that, he asked Elman to write another amicus brief and argue the case before the Supreme Court. The result was a unanimous opinion by the Court upholding the 1872 law. It went a long way to driving Jim Crow from the capital.

In praising the decision, Eisenhower hailed the victory as one of a series of steps "designed to remove terrible injustices rather than to capture headlines," a none too subtle dig at his Democratic predecessor in the White House. In fairness, what Ike had done was follow a path blazed by Truman's justice department and to use a former Truman lawyer, Elman, to nail down the victory.

Another and broader area in which Eisenhower pursued Truman's policy was in the integration of the armed forces, which was officially completed by October 30, 1954, over a period of twenty-one months. Understandably, he took credit for finishing the job. Actually, complete integration would take years more, and the struggle, particularly against segregated facilities for military families, would last into the Kennedy and Johnson administrations. It needs to be remembered that thanks to Truman's order and the vigilance of the Fahy committee, by the time Eisenhower was inaugurated, most of the Army's Far East and European commands and its training facilities had been integrated, and most of the fundamental battles over race had been fought and won.

The integration of the District of Columbia and the armed forces was soon overshadowed by conflict on another civil rights front: school desegregation. This struggle would endure throughout the Eisenhower administration—and indeed carry over to the next century. And by his reluctant response to this challenge, Eisenhower clearly added to the burdens of the civil rights forces. From the very start, Eisenhower made plain that he wanted little to do with this legal controversy. The Supreme Court would not let him off the hook.

The justices had initially been scheduled to rule on the *Brown* cases during the 1952 term ending in June 1953, the time frame Elman had in mind when he filed his amicus brief in December 1952. But late in the spring of 1953, still divided on the issue, they agreed to set the case for reargument in the fall of 1953. At the same time, following its customary procedure, the Court asked all parties to the suit to submit briefs responding to questions on the scope of the Fourteenth Amendment. Also, if the court did decide to rule against segregated schools, the briefs were asked to explain how the desegregation process should take place.

From the outset, Eisenhower seemed to feel that the court was trying to drag him into this controversy. His distress was reinforced by a letter from Governor Allan Shivers of Texas, who called the "unusual" Supreme Court request "an attempt to embarrass you and your Attorney General." Although ostensibly a Democrat, Shivers felt he had every right to counsel the Republican president, because in the 1952 campaign, as the leader of the so-called Shivercrats, he had helped deliver Texas's electoral votes to Eisenhower. Shivers expressed his confidence that Attorney General Brownell "will see the implications involved and advise the court that this local problem should be decided on the local and state level."

Despite Eisenhower's resistance, the justice department, as Brownell realized, as a practical matter had little choice but to comply with the Court's request. To do otherwise could harm relations between the administration and the Court and cause public embarrassment for the administration. Once again, Elman was put in charge of writing the brief, but this time he was under strict constraints. The brief responded to the Court's specific questions, but unlike Elman's 1952 submission, which called for the overturn of *Plessy*, this new brief took no position on that issue or on the merits of the case itself. The most it told the High Court was that under the Fourteenth Amendment, it had the authority, if it wanted to use it, to overturn segregation in local schools. Elman did add one touch to the brief, the significance of which may have gone unnoticed by his superiors. He called it a "supplemental brief" for the United States, which meant that it did not alter the argument for overturning *Plessy* he had made in the 1952 brief, which was submitted when he was still working for Truman. In the oral arguments, J. Lee Rankin, speaking for the government on instructions from Brownell, specifically stated that the Eisenhower administration supported the 1952 brief's contention that segregation in public schools violated the Fourteenth Amendment.

While these preparations were going forward, an event occurred that would turn out to have a profound influence on the *Brown* case and on the ensuing struggle for civil rights. This was the death of Chief Justice Fred Vinson in September 1953 and his replacement by California governor Earl Warren. Vinson, a native of Kentucky, the home of Truman's slave-owning forebears, had been viewed by some as an obstacle to the court reaching a just and consistent decision on the segregation cases. His death prompted his former colleague, Felix Frankfurter, to remark to his former clerk, Philip Elman, "This is the first indication I have ever had that there is a God."

Over the next sixteen years, Chief Justice Warren would help transform race relations in the United States as well as profoundly tip the scales of the legal system in favor of the disadvantaged in criminal justice, civil liberties, and the political process. But no one guessed this at the time—certainly not Eisenhower, who by several accounts came to regard the appointment as one of his biggest mistakes. What the new president did know was that he had promised Warren the first vacancy on the Supreme Court to placate him after his own bid for the 1952 Republican nomination was undermined by fellow Californian Richard Nixon on his way to becoming vice president.

Eisenhower had little thought of Warren's views on civil rights when he appointed him in September 1953. A few months later, in February 1954, while the Court was in the midst of its deliberations over *Brown*, the president apparently tried to impress the new chief justice with the merits of the Southern side in the school case. As a resentful Warren told the story in his memoirs, at a White House stag dinner, Eisenhower seated him next to the chief lawyer for the segregationist cause, and the Democratic Party's 1924 presidential standard bearer, John W. Davis. At the White House dinner, Eisenhower spoke highly of Davis in Warren's presence. Moreover, as the guests filed out of the dining room after the meal, Eisenhower took Warren by the arm and put in a good word for the Southern side of the *Brown* litigation. "These are not bad people," he said of Southern foes of desegregation. "All they are concerned about is to see that their sweet little girls are not required to sit in school alongside some big overgrown Negroes." Soon after that, in May 1954, the Court handed down its unanimous decision, read out by Warren, that "in the field of public education 'separate but equal' has no place. Separate educational facilities are inherently unequal." And "with it," wrote Warren, "went our cordial relations."

But then the chief justice, with the acute political instinct that helped make him unbeatable as a candidate in California, offered the South a measure of solace. The Court would not decide how to implement its dramatic ruling for another year, until it heard further from all the parties involved. This decision would be crucial, as everyone involved understood, including Eisenhower. He was so concerned that he took the extraordinary step of helping to edit the government's amicus brief, which had been prepared mainly by Eisenhower's solicitor general, Simon Sobeloff. He had just been appointed to the post and was a wholehearted advocate of school desegregation. In his draft, Sobeloff had written that "the vindication of the constitutional rights should be as prompt as possible." At Eisenhower's insistence, the word "feasible" was substituted for "possible," a nuance that would allow for a broader range of excuses to delay, including the attitude of the community. In a less subtle change, Eisenhower had removed a section of Sobeloff's draft brief that cited the positive experience with speedy desegregation of the armed forces. This section had suggested that interracial contacts could improve race relations and implied that community resentments should not slow down the pace of desegregation.

Six months after that brief was submitted, the Court handed down its decision in what became known as *Brown II*, turning the implementation of its previous ruling over to the district courts, which were to negotiate with local schools. Desegregation should take place "with all deliberate speed," the Court held, a crucial phrase that would infuriate advocates of desegregation. As they feared, this wording provided a legal cover for Southern school districts to resist and delay for years the desegregation that the Court had apparently ordered in its initial decision.

It is impossible to judge how much the justice department's brief, with Eisenhower's emendations, influenced the Court's decision on implementing the 1954 ruling. The initial brief of the Truman administration filed by Elman had argued for gradualism. There was certainly similar sentiment among the justices themselves. By altering the thrust of Sobeloff's argument, Eisenhower deprived the Court of hearing a different voice, making an argument for urgency like that made by the black plaintiffs, but with the authority of the federal government behind it.

Eisenhower's revision of Sobeloff's work pointed the way to his defining response to the prolonged legal and political struggle over school desegregation, which reached a climax in Little Rock, Arkansas, in 1957. Well before his dramatic confrontation with Arkansas governor Orval Faubus, Eisenhower had been deeply troubled by the consequences of the Supreme Court ruling. The unanimous opinion offered Eisenhower an historic opportunity to rally the nation behind the decision. Instead, he sought to maintain a sort of neutrality between the Court and the opponents of the decision, a posture that inevitably fostered resistance to the ruling.

Asked for advice to the South in the first press conference after the *Brown* decision, Eisenhower said he had none to offer, adding, as if through gritted teeth, that he would obey his oath to "uphold the Constitutional process in this country." During his remaining six years in office, Eisenhower never went any further in backing this or later court decisions on civil rights. His views, cloaked in the shield of privacy, tended to bear out the impression given by his cryptic public stance. For example, in the summer of 1956, shortly before he accepted the nomination for a second term by the Republican convention in San Francisco, Eisenhower told his personal secretary, Ann Whitman, that "the troubles brought about by the Supreme Court decision were the most important domestic problem facing the government today." When Whitman asked him what other course the Supreme Court could have taken, he suggested a step-by-step process starting in graduate schools, and later moving on to colleges and high schools, as a way "of overcoming the passionate and inbred attitudes developed over generations." Eisenhower did not seem aware that the Supreme Court had struck down segregation in graduate schools two years before he became president. Nor did he seem to hold anyone but the Supreme Court responsible for the troubles over desegregation.

In his campaign for reelection in 1956, Eisenhower took pains to reassure Southerners that he believed racial disputes should be handled locally. Addressing campaign rallies in the North, candidate Eisenhower claimed credit for progress against desegregation in the military, in government employment, and in the nation's capital. The formula worked. Again running against Adlai Stevenson, Eisenhower won nearly 40 percent of the black vote, the biggest percentage for any Republican presidential candidate since the New Deal. He was helped by Stevenson's tepid campaigning on civil rights while he focused more on holding the South.

Despite Stevenson's efforts in Dixie, Eisenhower did well with white Southerners, carrying six southern states, adding Kentucky and Louisiana to Texas, Florida, Virginia, and Tennessee, which he had won in 1952. In other words, Eisenhower had managed to have it both ways, gaining ground among Southern whites and more dramatically among blacks in the North. Much of this had to do with his overall personal popularity and the outbreak of crises in the campaign's final days in the Middle East and Hungary, which tended to overshadow other issues. Beyond that, Eisenhower had plainly gotten across to Southern whites the notion that the Court decision was not his fault, and that he would not force that issue. Blacks, on the other hand, could not help being swayed by the overriding fact of the *Brown* decision handed down by a chief justice appointed by a Republican president who at least had stated his nominal willingness to support the ruling.

Eisenhower's second term saw no change of heart on civil rights. During a press conference in July 1957, more than three years after the *Brown* ruling, Eisenhower acknowledged that as president, he had authority going back to Reconstruction days to use military force to implement integration. But he went on: "I can't imagine any set of circumstances that would ever induce me to send federal troops into any area to enforce the orders of a federal court." To Southerners who believed that their die-hard resistance could turn back the tide of integration, these were encouraging words.

This was the outlook that the president brought to bear on the Little Rock crisis. The trouble had been brewing since May 1955, when the local school board adopted a plan for gradual integration to begin in September 1957 at Little Rock's Central High School. Governor Faubus tried to persuade the school board to drop the plan, and foes of desegregation sought court orders to block it. When all that failed, on September 3, 1957, Faubus deployed the Arkansas National Guard outside the school. Despite a decree by federal judge Roland Davies commanding the admission of nine black students, Faubus told the guard to keep them out.

Just as Eisenhower set the stage for the confrontation in Little Rock by his overall approach to civil rights and by his statement ruling out the use of troops once the struggle got under way, Eisenhower allowed it to drag on unnecessarily. First there was his decision to go ahead with a planned vacation in Newport, Rhode Island, which he began the day after Faubus ordered the guard to prevent black students from entering Central High School. Moreover, Eisenhower decided to stay in Newport in the midst of the showdown, resisting suggestions even from old friends such as General Alfred M. Gruenther that he return to the White House. "I do not want to exaggerate the significance of the admittedly serious situation in Arkansas," he wrote his old comrade in arms. "The great need is to act calmly, deliberately and give every offender opportunity to cease his defiance." Whatever impression Eisenhower was striving for, the perception he inevitably created was of temporizing. This was bound to provide aid and comfort to opponents of desegregation in Little Rock and elsewhere.

For his part, though, federal judge Davies stepped up the pressure on Faubus. With the National Guard still blocking the black students from entering Central High, Davies set a date for a hearing on the legality of Faubus's action. Faubus's response was to seek a meeting with Eisenhower. Attorney General Brownell argued against that. As he saw it, this was a simple case of "this is the law" and "it must be obeyed." But Eisenhower responded that the situation was not that simple and that he must take into consideration "the seething in the South." On September 14, the president and the governor met for twenty minutes at the Newport naval base. After Faubus told Eisenhower that he had "been one of Ike's boys" in World War II, serving under him as a major in the infantry, Eisenhower proposed to the governor a face-saving way out of his predicament. Instead of using the National Guard to prevent the black youngsters from entering the school, Eisenhower suggested that Faubus tell the guardsmen just to keep the peace while the students went to school. If Faubus would go along with that idea, Eisenhower would try to get the governor excused from the court hearing he faced.

When Faubus departed, he left Eisenhower with the impression that he was going to accept the proposition. Faubus had no such intention. He continued to use the National Guard to keep out the black students, and Eisenhower continued to delay action. Finally, on September 20, under pressure of an injunction from the federal court, Faubus pulled out the

Guard, but reiterated his opposition to desegregation and disclaimed any responsibility for preserving order.

This happened on a Friday. Over the weekend, with school closed, Little Rock was quiet. But on Monday morning, a racist mob surrounded the high school and beat up two black reporters. The black students managed to get in the school though a side door, but with the mob threatening to lynch them, Mayor Woodrow Wilson Mann ordered police to remove them. The next day, the mob, now grown larger, surrounded the school and swarmed through the streets. Mayor Mann wired Eisenhower for help. "The immediate need for federal troops is urgent. Situation is out of control and police cannot disperse the mob."

The president could delay no longer. He dispatched 500 men of the 101st Airborne Division and federalized the Arkansas National Guard. Then he flew back to Washington to address the nation. He was sending in the troops only to enforce the law, not because he favored desegregation, Eisenhower emphasized. "Personal opinions" on the Supreme Court's ruling had no relevance, he contended. He lamented that "our enemies," presumably the Soviet Union and its allies, "are gloating over this incident and using it everywhere to misrepresent our nation." But he made no mention of the indignities and the terror inflicted on the black schoolchildren in Little Rock, nor of their right to an equal education. The president clearly wanted to appeal to Southern whites. In trying to do this, he might have talked of shared American values of fair play and of the importance of a good education for all children. To raise these points in this context might have stirred some resentments and involved some risks—consequences that Eisenhower wanted to avoid.

His speech was an attempt to conciliate, but it was a bloodless and legalistic appeal. Little Rock's impact on the nation was enlarged because it dramatized and personalized the fierce conflicts involved in civil rights, with Eisenhower, Faubus, the black schoolchildren, and the white mob each playing out compelling roles. It was a transforming event because Eisenhower's example tended to discourage avenues for leadership by government officials and locked American politics and society on a divisive and sometimes violent course that shaped race relations into the next century.

Eisenhower's most evident deficiency in civil rights was his failure to speak out for the cause of racial justice. In a determined attempt to rebut critics of Eisenhower's civil rights record, historian David O. Nichols contends that "a myopic preoccupation with public statements produces a distorted picture of Eisenhower's leadership." But public statements are not a sideline for American presidents. They are a major part of how they define themselves and their stewardship. Eisenhower's neglect of this obligation is particularly striking because he often described the resistance to civil rights as based on deep-seated attitudes, which he felt laws alone could not change. But he ignored the opportunity he had as president to reshape public attitudes.

During the Eisenhower years, Truman's record was not forgotten by civil rights supporters, black and white. "It was not just his words but his deeds," recalled Harris Wofford, a Notre Dame law professor who became chief civil rights adviser to John Kennedy. "They were a beacon, the only light of hope in the dark years of Eisenhower."

With Kennedy's 1960 election, civil rights advocates had high hopes. Hailing from Massachusetts, a stronghold of urban democracy, Kennedy was expected to lead a march toward civil rights goals with "vigor" (that was one of his favorite catchwords), an expectation bolstered by his campaign rhetoric. Instead, his first two years in the White House were as passive on civil rights as Eisenhower's had been. Though more intellectual than Eisenhower, and with a better understanding of the political process, Kennedy's decisions were dominated by skepticism rather than ideology.

Though he was a member of a wealthy and powerful family, the circumstances of his life, notably his Irish Catholic heritage, made Kennedy think of himself as an outsider. The lofty causes that attracted liberal reformers in the Democratic Party, notably civil rights, were in some cases anathema to the Irish Catholic masses who made up Kennedy's initial base of support. As he sought the presidency, rather than commit himself to either the reform camp or Irish tradition, he tried to make a place for himself some distance from both. This stance led, as biographer James MacGregor Burns put it, to his being "committed only to non-commitment."

Kennedy had shown little interest in civil rights during his years as a congressman and senator. But when he became his party's 1960 presidential nominee, no one was more biting in criticism of Eisenhower's handling of civil rights than he. The president had the authority to abolish discrimination in federal housing simply, as Kennedy put it, with "a stroke of the pen," by issuing an executive order. However, for the first two years of his presidency, he once again distanced himself from the struggle for racial justice, offering no civil rights proposals and blaming anticipated resistance in Congress for his inaction. He held off for months that "stroke of the pen" to strike down the racial barriers in federal housing, which he had referred to so often in the campaign. Finally, after he was deluged with inkwells and pens mailed by frustrated civil rights supporters, he issued the much-anticipated executive order—on Thanksgiving Eve of 1962, when his action was likely to attract minimal attention.

By this time, Southern blacks had long since lost patience with the racism that ruled their existence and with the president's hesitation. They took to the streets, and their revolt went far beyond the symbolic protests that had been the rule in the past. Sit-ins, "freedom rides," bus boycotts, and mass marches led by the Reverend Martin Luther King Jr., who charged Kennedy with tokenism, inspired blacks and captured the imagination of millions of whites. Heightening the public response was the harsh retaliation of Southern authorities, notably Birmingham's Bull Connor, a principal figure in the 1946 violence against blacks. It was the impact of this new wave of brutality that finally provided the impetus for Kennedy to speak out.

Building on the rhetoric of Harry Truman, the previous Democratic president, Kennedy demanded action that went beyond what Truman had ventured. He asked for nothing less than the use of federal power to strike down the legal defenses of segregation everywhere of significance they existed—in hotels, lunch counters, schoolrooms, offices, and factories. Echoing Truman's trope of a decade earlier but not heard from a president since, Kennedy defined civil rights as a moral issue "as old as the Scriptures and as clear as the American Constitution."

For all the drama of his oratory, Southern opposition in Congress remained staunch. At the time of Kennedy's assassination, five months after his civil rights address, it was questionable how many, if any, of his proposals would be made real. That challenge, and the fulfillment of Harry Truman's civil rights legacy, was left to Kennedy's successor, Lyndon Baines Johnson of Texas. He seemed an even more unlikely champion of the civil rights cause than had been Truman. While Truman hailed from a border state whose loyalties had been divided between the Confederacy and the Union, Johnson was born and bred in a state that proudly remembered its allegiance to the Southern rebellion. Other portions of his past would also have seemed to put Johnson on the wrong side of the struggle for racial justice: his attack on Truman's 1948 civil rights proposals and his joining Southern colleagues in 1949 in voting down a proposed change in the Senate rules to restrict filibusters, thus effectively killing any chance of passage for civil rights measures.

Yet Truman and Johnson had early life experiences that made their commitment to civil rights easier to understand. Both men had seen hard times in their youths. Lyndon Johnson's father, Sam Ealy Johnson Jr., like Harry Truman's father, John Truman, had gone bust because of the gyrations of commodities. The grain market was John Truman's downfall; Sam Ealy was brought to ruin by the collapse of cotton prices. The harmful impact on their sons was much the same. They struggled to survive, but the struggles fostered a sense of compassion and understanding for the less advantaged, a feeling that Johnson demonstrated for the Mexican

American youngsters in his class when he was a twenty-year-old elementary school teacher back in Texas.

Another convergence in their early days was exposure to populism. Johnson's grandfather, Sam Ealy Johnson Sr., ran on the populist ticket for the state legislature, and populist candidates carried the Texas Hill Country, with its unyielding soil and arid climate, where Johnson grew up. This populist legacy was to serve Johnson well. It provided him with a political grammar for communicating first with his House constituents and then with broader interest groups. Like Truman, Johnson not only accepted but wholeheartedly embraced the use of government to aid people, most particularly in promoting the Great Society and in particular the advance of civil rights.

Both men also shared a keen understanding of power and a determination to use it when it served their own interest and what they perceived as the national interest. Both had stumbled into the White House by accident. Truman, after asking reporters to pray for him, still found the nerve and will to bomb Japan into submission, to face up to Stalin's siege of West Berlin, and to challenge the South's legacy of racism. As for Johnson, in the chaos that followed Kennedy's assassination, the new chief recalled: "I knew it was imperative that I grasp the reins of power and do so without delay."

Civil rights was the first test of his resolve. Dealing with the issue as Democratic Senate leader, Johnson had steered a cautious course. But as president, Texan Johnson saw the need for much bolder action to establish his bona fides with his party's liberal constituencies and leaders. The instrument to serve that need lay readily at hand: John Kennedy's civil rights program. The immediate impact of Kennedy's slaying was to unify the nation in a way not seen since Pearl Harbor, thus providing Johnson with an opportunity, as he later explained privately, to "take a dead man's program, and turn it into a martyr's cause." He transformed the slain president's controversial proposals into an issue that, despite fierce Southern resistance, won wide support in both parties. For Johnson, the Kennedy assassination served as the functional equivalent of the Great Depression in overwhelming the traditional resistance of Congress to presidential will. Thus Johnson signed the far-reaching civil rights bill that had germinated in the Kennedy White House into law on July 2, 1964, and went on to defeat the hapless Republican nominee, Senator Barry Goldwater of Arizona, in the 1964 election. Goldwater carried only five states beyond his own Arizona, all in the deep South. But those five Southern states, while of little practical importance in the midst of LBJ's landslide, were an ominous portent of things to come, as Johnson fully realized.

On the night Congress passed the voting rights bill, a few months before Election Day, his aide, Bill Moyers, found him in his bedroom, looking glum at the moment of his greatest victory. "I think we've just delivered the South to the Republican Party for a long time to come," the president explained. Even so, Johnson did not flinch when, after his election victory, the civil rights movement pressed for more. Johnson, like Truman, had a sense of history. He wanted to be known as the president who had done more for black Americans than any other white man. In 1965, he capped his achievements on the road to racial justice by pushing through a voting rights act, exhorting congressional support by adopting the civil rights movement's own battle cry: "We shall overcome."

Johnson's presidency would be wrecked by the Vietnam War. The tragedy in Southeast Asia did not diminish the scope of his civil rights achievements. This success had severe political consequences for his party, as Johnson himself understood, converting the once solidly Democratic South into a Dixie that was now solidly Republican. The impact of Johnson's voting rights act endured. In 2008, it opened the way for the election of the first black president, who, to make his victory even more meaningful, carried three Confederate states.

Barack Obama's election triggered a wave of euphoria among black and white Americans. For blacks, his election kindled hopes for even greater strides. Whites, even some who did not vote for him, felt a measure of pride that fellow citizens had overcome the distortions of bigotry sufficiently to turn the stewardship of their country over to a man of color. On top of Obama's success were signs of increasing social mobility for blacks, which seemed to contravene the early resistance of Harry Truman and many others to what was called social equality. More and more blacks were finding homes in previously all-white neighborhoods, and interracial marriage was on the rise.

But the celebratory mood also spawned an insidious delusion, the concept of a so-called postracial America, in which color no longer mattered. This idea has evident appeal for blacks and civil rights supporters in general because it would mean that they had won and their work was done. It is also attractive to people who are opposed to or just indifferent to the cause because it would mean they would not be bothered by it any more.

The fatuousness of this notion was apparent even before Obama was sworn in. One telltale clue was the exit poll results in the election that sent him to the White House, which showed the continued evidence of racially polarized attitudes confirmed by polling after Obama's re-election in 2012. Of far greater impact was the economic debacle that at the very start of his presidency undercut the tangible gains blacks hoped to reap from Obama's political success. The great recession, which damaged the lives of almost all Americans, and none more so than blacks, underlined a long-standing verity: the struggle for racial justice is inextricably tied to the battle for economic fairness. For all Americans, whatever their color, except for the privileged 1 percent at the peak of affluence, this is an up-hill fight. For more than a generation, the gap between rich and poor has steadily widened, and the economic and political power of the superrich has steadily grown. For blacks, neither racial pride nor special pleading offers an answer; their only realistic goal is to find political leaders who will work to reverse the economic tide, not just for blacks but for all their fellow citizens. The nineteenth-century aphorism of Frederick Douglass rings true today: "Find out what any people will quietly submit to, and you have found the exact measure of injustice and wrong which will be imposed upon them."

NOTES

ABBREVIATIONS USED IN NOTES

HST   Harry S. Truman
HSTL   Harry S. Truman Library, Independence, Missouri
PP   Public Papers of the Presidents of the United States, Harry Truman,
        http://www.trumanlibrary.org/

CHAPTER 1: THE PRESIDENT'S DILEMMA

Page
    1 Truman's dismal condition in 1948: McCullough, *Truman*, 518–524; Phillips,
Truman Presidency, 159–162; Donovan, *Presidency*, 231–235.
    2 "This war is crucial": Myrdall, *American Dilemma*, 2:997.
    2 "Senator Halfbright": Hamby, *Man of the People*, 386.
    2 "A simple formula": PP 1950, No. 250, November 11.
    2 "A wistful echo": *Time*, November 18, 1946.
    2 "Simple despair": *New York Times*, November 24, 1946.
    3 Negative view of Wallace: Phillips, *Truman Presidency*, 38–39.
    4 "His regard for the common people": Margaret Marshall, "Portrait of Tru-
man," *Nation*, April 21, 1945.
    4 Postwar anxieties: Donovan, *Presidency*, 107.
    4 Eight million unemployed predicted: Goulden, *Best Years*, 92.
    4 Actual job losses: Donovan, *Presidency*, 108.
    4 The demon inflation: McCoy and Ruetten, *Quest and Response*, 59.

5 "To err is Truman": Donovan, *Presidency*, 230.

5 Yielding to pressure: *New York Times*, October 31, 1945.

5 Labor strife: *New York Times*, September 12, 1945.

6 "Peace is hell": HST handwritten draft of speech to Gridiron Dinner, Washington, December 15, 1945, President's Secretary's File, Harry S. Truman Papers, HSTL.

6 Demobilization blues: Goulden, *Best Years*, 20.

6 Fear of "disintegration": PP 1946, No. 84, April 17.

6 Rail strike imbroglio: Ibid., No. 125 May 25; *New York Times*, May 24, 25, 26, 1946.

6 Labor bill veto: *New York Times*, June 12, 1945.

6 Dubinsky's threat: *New York Times*, June 5, 1946.

7 Truman Doctrine: PP 1947, No. 56, March 12; *New York Times*, March 13, 1947.

7 Wallace's departure: Gosnell, *Truman's Crises*, 288–292; Truman, *Memoirs*, 1:555–560.

7 Myrdall's work: Myrdall, *American Dilemma*, 21–22.

8 Black reaction to Wallace ouster: McCoy and Ruetten, *Quest and Response*, 99.

8 Wormley Hotel agreement: Poxpey, "Washington–DuBois Controversy."

8 Invitation to Booker T. Washington: Severn and Rogers, "Theodore Roosevelt."

8 Wilson's segregation edict: Smith, *FDR*, 98–99; Weiss, "Negro."

9 Harding raises hopes: Sherman, "Harding Administration."

9 Blacks' views of FDR: Weiss, *Farewell*, 20, 180.

10 Randolph's march and the FEPC: Foner and Garraty, *Reader's Companion*, 699–700.

10 "Negro militancy": Walter White in *Chicago Defender*, November 17, 1945.

10 Du Bois's view: Kwame Anthony Appiah, "Battling with Du Bois," *New York Review of Books*, December 22, 2011, citing W. E. B. Du Bois, *The Souls of Black Folk* (1903).

11 Dabney's warning: Dabney, "Nearer."

11 Attack on Isaac Woodward: *Baltimore Sun*, July 25, 1946, citing $1,000 reward offered by NAACP for information about assault.

11 Clark seeks anti-lynching law: *Pittsburgh Courier*, August, 24, 1946.

12 "Speak Mr. President!": *New York Times*, July 31, 1946.

12 White's background: White, *Man Called White*, 3–5. In 1922, White married Leah Gladys Powell, a black NAACP staffer. In 1949, he divorced her and married Poppy Cannon, a white woman who was well known as the food editor of *House Beautiful*. One NAACP official wanted him fired, but others reasoned that would seem to contravene the organization's advocacy of racial integration. White remained as the NAACP's official spokesman until his death in 1955, at which time he was still married to Poppy Cannon. African American Registry, http://www.aaregistry.org.

12 "We've got to do something": White, *Man Called White*, 331.

CHAPTER 2: FACING THE CENTURY

14 Kansas–Nebraska Act: Foner and Garraty, *Reader's Companion,* 690, 108–192.

15 Bloodshed in Kansas: Felman, *Inside War;* Leuchtenburg, "Conversion"; McCullough, *Truman,* 29.

15 Slave owners poured in: Missouri Digital Heritage, http://www.sos.mo.gov/md; Missouri Historical Society, St. Louis, http://www.mohistory.org.

15 Truman's forebears' ties to slavery: Leuchtenburg, "Conversion"; McCullough, *Truman,* 30–31.

16 Anderson Truman's slaves: Ethel Noland oral history, HSTL.

17 "Don't bring it here again": Hamby, *Man of the People,* 22.

17 I'll sleep on the floor": Leuchtenburg, "Conversion."

17 Political turmoil: Mitchell, *Embattled Democracy,* 2–6.

17 Truman's national pride: Leuchtenburg, "Conversion."

18 "Blind as a mole": McCullough, *Truman,* 41.

18 "They called me four eyes": Miller, *Plain Speaking,* 23.

18 "I was kind of a sissy": Ibid., 34–35.

18 Studying "great men": McCullough, *Truman,* 43.

19 Weak presidents: Miller, *Plain Speaking,* 351. This string of presidents includes James K. Polk, whom many historians count among strong presidents because of his seizure of territory from Mexico. However, some also consider him shortsighted for not dealing with the worsening of the divisions over slavery that his expansionism caused. That seems to be Truman's point here.

19 An outsize temper: Miller, *Plain Speaking,* 63.

19 Father favored Vivian: Hamby, *Man of the People,* 17.

19 "I was a dud": Ferrell, *Off the Record,* 388.

19 First political hero: McCullough, *Truman,* 67.

20 "I used to drive a hundred miles": Miller, *Plain Speaking,* 117.

20 Great joy to Truman home: Daniels, *Man,* 44.

20 "Some men are greedier": Miller, *Plain Speaking,* 116.

20 "Bryan was a great one": Ibid., 116–117.

21 Bryan's rise: Hofstadter, *American Political Tradition,* 186–196; Kazin, *Godly Hero,* 15–28.

21 Reenacting Calvary: Cherny, *Righteous Cause,* 86.

21 Bryan's vigorous stumping: Boller, *Presidential Campaigns,* 169.

21 Bryan at the Scopes Trial: Kazin, *Godly Hero,* 285–295.

22 "Shouldn't be held against him": Miller, *Plain Speaking,* 116.

22 Twists and turns: Kazin, *Godly Hero,* 88–93.

22 Populism and racism in Dixie: Weiss, "Negro."

22 "Too far ahead of his time": Miller, *Plain Speaking,* 117.

22 Bryan's impact on 1912 convention: Kazin, *Godly Hero,* 186–191.

23 Move to Independence: Daniels, *Man,* 46.

23 John Truman's downfall: Ibid., 59–60.

23 More bad luck for John Truman: McCullough, *Truman,* 73.

24 Farm life: Daniels, *Man,* 75–76.

24 The fight over the will: Hamby, *Man of the People,* 31.

24 Courting Bess: HST to Bess Wallace, June 22, 1911; July 10, 1911, Family, Business, Personal File, Harry S. Truman Papers, HSTL.

25 Target Montana: HST to Bess Wallace, October 29, 1913, Family, Business, Personal File, Harry S. Truman Papers, HSTL.

25 Early politics: Hamby, *Man of the People,* 40–45.

26 Varied ventures: McCullough, *Truman,* 96–100.

26 "I am going to keep guessing": HST to Bess Wallace, August 5, 1916, Family, Business, Personal File, Harry S. Truman Papers, HSTL.

26 Fears of being a "cripple": Hamby, *Man of the People,* 58.

26 "I felt we owed for Lafayette": Many details on Truman's Army experience are in HST, "The Military Career of a Missourian," n.d., Senatorial and Vice Presidential File, Harry S. Truman Papers, HSTL, cited in Hamby, *Man of the People,* 649.

27 Canteen enterprise: Truman, *Memoirs,* 1:128.

27 "I have a Jew in charge": HST to Bess Wallace, September 30, 1917, Family, Business, Personal File, Harry S. Truman Papers, HSTL.

27 "No one can be that good": Hillman, *Mr. President,* 171.

27 Dealing with roughnecks: Miller, *Plain Speaking,* 95–100; HST to Bess Wallace, July 22, 1918, HSTL.

27 First combat: Truman, *Memoirs,* 1:128.

27 Meeting the next challenge: Ibid., 1:130–131.

28 "Maybe a little politics": HST to Bess Wallace, December 14, 1918, Ferrell, *Dear Bess,* 285.

28 Haberdashery venture: Truman, *Memoirs,* 1:133–135.

29 In came Mike Pendergast: Ibid., 136.

29 Truman's Masonic link: Ibid., 125–126.

30 "It is race prejudice": HST to Bess Wallace, June 22, 1911, cited in Robert; Ferrell, *Dear Bess,* 39.

30 Reserved her hostility: M. Truman, *Harry S. Truman,* 49.

30 "A grand time": Truman, *Memoirs,* 1:115.

CHAPTER 3: THE BOSS'S APPRENTICE

32 Problems at home for the aged: *Kansas City Call,* December 2. 1927, cited in Grothaus, "Kansas City Blacks."

32 Home for troubled girls: Wilson, "Chester Franklin and Harry S.Truman," 55.

32 Praise for Big Jim: Ibid.

33 Recruiting the immigrants: Cornwell, "Bosses."

33 Senator Hoar's view: White, *Making of the President,* 429.

33 The Red scare: Murray, *Red Scare,* 219.

34 The second wave: Gregory, *Southern Diaspora,* 10–15; U.S. Census Bureau, Census of Population and Housing, 1940; Smith, "Redistribution."

34 Missouri getting its share: "Progress amidst Prejudice," Missouri State Archives, http://www.sos.mo.gov/archives.

35 Rural counties lost blacks: Mitchell, *Embattled Democracy*, 63–64.
35 Big Jim's rise: Reddig, *Tom's Town*, 21–23; Dorsett, *Pendergast*, 4–5.
35 "I've got friends": McCullough, *Truman*, 152.
35 "He stood by the city": Dorsett, *Pendergast*, 19.
35 Boss Tom's style: Reddig, *Tom's Town*, 32; Ferrell, *Truman and Pendergast*, 9.
36 Denouncing the police: *Kansas City Times*, March 29, April 2, 1920.
36 The Klan's revival: Chalmers, *Hooded Americanism*, 28–38.
37 "The real indictment": Newman, *Black*, 89.
37 "You are not wanted": Mitchell, *Embattled Democracy*, 65.
37 Hugo Black and the Klan: Newman, *Black*, 90–98.
37 Truman and the Klan: McCullough, *Truman*, 164; Edgar G. Hinde oral history, HSTL.
38 Klan links Truman to Pendergasts: Hamby, *Man of the People*, 114.
38 The Democrats' unruly convention: Murray, *103rd Ballot*, 143–161. Making matters more complicated, some states expanded the size of their delegations so that the votes of individual delegates were fractionalized.
38 Favorite son Reed: Ibid., 85–86; Mitchell, *Embattled Democracy*, 71–72.
38 Bryan loses his grip; the Klan vote and aftermath: Murray, *103rd Ballot*, 159–161.
40 Truman's losing fight: Hamby, *Man of the People*, 127–131; Mitchell, *Embattled Democracy*, 182.
41 "He'd get into something else": Ted Marks oral history, HSTL.
41 Kansas City School of Law: After Truman became president, the school awarded him an honorary degree.
41 Truman's big break: McCullough, *Truman*, 154.
41 Midwest Yankee Ethic: Hamby, "Insecurity."
42 Summoned by Pendergast: Truman, *Memoirs*, 1:141.
42 The private version: Pickwick memo, n.d., President's Secretary's File, Harry S. Truman Papers, HSTL, cited by Hamby, *Man of the People*, 152.
42 Plagued by self-doubt: various Pickwick memos, President's Secretary's File, Harry S. Truman Papers, HSTL, cited by Hamby, *Man of the People*, 160.
42 "Unimpeachable character": Daniels, *Man*, 172–173.
42 Broadening the platform: Mitchell, *Embattled Democracy*, 98.
43 A share of patronage: Wilson, "Chester Franklin and Harry S.Truman."
43 Franklin's complaint: Grothaus, "Kansas City Blacks."
43 "A ground hog dinner": Mitchell, *Embattled Democracy*, 65.
43 Harding's background: Russell, *Shadow of Blooming Grove*, 141–149; White House, "The Presidents," http://www.whitehouse.gov/history/presidents.
44 Blacks drawn to Harding: Sherman, "Harding Administration."
44 Hoover refuses to pose: "National Affairs," *Crisis*, July 1932.
44 The Parker nomination: Mitchell, *Embattled Democracy*, 128.
45 Franklin's shift on GOP: Wilson, "Chester Franklin and Harry S. Truman."
45 Franklin's praise for Truman: Ibid.
46 "The Knave of Rum and Romanism": "The Brown Derby," *Time*, April 30, 1928.
46 Smith's interest in blacks: Weiss, *Farewell*, 6.

46 Robinson's shouted denial: "Three Whispers," *Time,* September 17, 1928.
46 Hoover ran ahead of FDR among blacks: Weiss, *Farewell,* 29.
46 "The weakest possible candidate": Ibid., 18.
47 Blacks broke with the GOP in smaller numbers: Samuel Lubell, "The Negro and the Democratic Coalition," *Commentary,* August 1964.
47 A notable exception: Grothaus, "Kansas City Blacks."
47 Pendergast's efforts to win blacks: Mitchell, *Embattled Democracy,* 158; Grothaus, "Kansas City Blacks."
47 Pendergast's selection process: Hamby, *Man of the People,* 181–189.
48 "If ever a man deserved public confidence": Grothaus, "Kansas City Blacks."

CHAPTER 4: BACK FROM THE DEAD

49 "To get the Negro vote": Patterson, *Congressional Conservatism,* 98.
50 "Did not want 'niggers' planting gardens": Lash, *Eleanor,* 514.
50 "More things to worry about": Weiss, *Farewell,* 35.
51 "We accepted the pattern": Lash, *Eleanor,* 415.
51 "Has the New Deal Helped?": Weiss, *Farewell,* 208.
51 Accusing Ickes: Ickes, *Secret Diary,* 2:115.
51 Bethune woos the first lady: Weiss, *Farewell,* 138–145.
52 "SASOCPA" lobbies FDR: Ibid., 39.
52 "This is dynamite": Lash, *Eleanor,* 517.
52 The midterm results: Campbell, *Presidential Pulse,* 7.
53 Scene of triumph: Alsop and Catledge, *168 Days,* 22.
53 The framers' dilemmas: Burns, *Deadlock,* 16–23; Fairfield, *Federalist Papers,* 160–161.
53 Madison's strategy: Morris, *Witness,* 96–98, 188–190.
54 Holding companies struggle: Patterson, *Congressional Conservatism,* 52–56.
54 Truman's stand: *Kansas City Star,* April 15, 1935.
55 "I can't afford that risk": White, *Man Called White,* 168–170.
55 A horror and disgrace: Smith, *FDR,* 398.
55 "You know I'm against this bill": Lubell, *Future,* 13. Lubell's anecdote is cited without any qualification in Berman, *Politics,* 10, in Gosnell, *Truman's Crises,* 135, and in Bernstein, *Politics,* 272. Lubell uses this anecdote not to question Truman's sincerity on civil rights but rather to contend that his presidency was defined by "persistent irresolution."
56 "It was going to be impossible": McKenna, *Roosevelt,* 104.
56 FDR's counterattack: Alsop and Catledge, *168 Days,* 32–37.
56 "Fully abreast of its work": *New York Times,* March 23, 1937.
56 The Court pulled the rug: *New York Times,* April 13, 1937; May 25, 1937.
57 "A switch in time saves nine," *New York Times,* June 15, 1937. The New Dealer who authored that quip was Undersecretary of the Interior Abe Fortas, a

future Supreme Court justice who was forced to resign under an ethical cloud in 1969.

57 "The Constitution doesn't need an amendment": Hamby, *Man of the People,* 215.

58 "Like an office boy": Leuchtenburg, *Shadow of FDR,* 4.

58 Truman's financial straits: Steinberg, *Man from Missouri,* 121–125.

58 Truman's hospital stay: Department of the Army, Military Personnel Records of H. S. Truman (1917–1973), HSTL.

58 "He was a boss": Milgram and Milgram, "Man."

58 "Under a cloud": Steinberg, *Man from Missouri,* 125.

59 Truman's eclectic circle: Hamby, *Man of the People,* 208.

59 Blasting the railroad lawyers: *Congressional Record,* 75th Congress, 1st Session, U.S. Senate, June 3, 1937, 5271–5275.

59 Another Bryanite barrage: Ibid., December 20, 1937, 1912–1924; HST to Bess Wallace Truman, December 12, 1937, Ferrell, *Dear Bess,* 409.

59 "Truman attacks reorganization lawyers": *New York Times,* December 21, 1937.

59 Fighting the wage cut: *New York Times,* December 24, 1938.

60 Pendergast's fall: Ferrell, *Truman and Pendergast,* 140–145.

61 Truman's defense of Boss Tom: *Congressional Record,* February 15, 1938, 1962–1964.

61 "He can't lose Harry Truman": *New York Times,* February 17, 1938.

61 Pendergast's guilty plea: Dorsett, *Pendergast,* 134.

61 Lloyd Stark's rise: Hamby, *Man of the People,* 229–230.

62 "Into the Presidential ring": "Democrat's New Face," *Life,* April 24, 1939.

62 "Tell him to go to hell": McCullough, *Truman,* 241.

62 "A dead cock in the pit": *St. Louis Post Dispatch,* January 26, 1940.

62 His friends come through: M. Truman, *Harry S. Truman,* 126.

62 Milligan's candidacy: Ibid.

62 Backing the defense buildup: Hamby, *Man of the People,* 267; HST speech at Caruthersville, Missouri, October 8, 1939, Senatorial and Vice Presidential File, Harry S. Truman Papers, HSTL.

63 Against draft bias: *Congressional Record,* 75th Cong., 2nd Sess. 1940, U.S. Senate, LXXXVI, 10895; MacGregor, *Integration,* 13.

63 The Gaines case: Klarman, *Jim Crow,* 148–150; *Gaines v. Canada,* 305 U.S. 537 (1938); Wilson, "Chester Franklin and Harry S. Truman." Adding a bizarre note to the case, a year after winning his important legal victory, Lloyd Gaines disappeared and is now believed by authorities to have been murdered. *New York Times,* July 12, 2009.

63 Rousting the sharecroppers: M. Truman, *Harry S. Truman,* 129.

64 Franklin's counsel to Truman: Wilson, "Chester Franklin and Harry S. Truman."

64 Glued to their radios: M. Truman, *Harry S. Truman,* 128.

65 A longtime Missouri ally: Wilson, "Chester Franklin and Harry S. Truman," 65; Mitchell, *Embattled Democracy,* 122.

65 The Sedalia speech: *Congressional Record,* 76th Cong., 3rd Sess., 1940 U.S. Senate, LXXXVI, Appendix 4546–4549.
65 A fuller statement: Ibid., Appendix 5367–5369.
66 The tide turns: Hamby, *Man of the People,* 343; McCullough, *Truman,* 250.
67 Crediting Franklin: HST to Franklin, November 28, 1941, Box 131, "Negroes" folder, Senatorial and Vice Presidential File, Harry S. Truman Papers, HSTL.
67 "Through hell three times": Truman, *Memoirs,* 1:162.
67 "I was still Senator": Ibid.

CHAPTER 5: ROAD TO THE TOP

68 Childhood racism: HST to Bess Wallace Truman, August 4, 1939, Ferrell, *Dear Bess,* 417.
69 Inspired by a flood of mail: Ibid., 454.
69 "Make the big man bigger": *Congressional Record,* 77th Cong. 1st Sess., U.S. Senate, February 10, 1941, 83–38.
69 Senate leaders stalled: White, *Man Called White,* 189.
70 Fulton postpones hearings: Telegrams to Walter White from Hugh Fulton, June 28, July 11, 1941, Harry S. Truman folder, 1941, NAACP Papers.
70 Storm over the delay: *Pittsburgh Courier,* July 5, 1941.
70 NAACP answers back: Ibid., July 12, 1941.
70 Harry Vaughn's comments: Roy Wilkins to Ira Lewis, September 10, 1941, Harry S. Truman Folder, 1941, NAACP Papers.
70 Into thin air: HST to E. J. Wallace, December 22, 1941, Senatorial and Vice Presidential File, Harry S. Truman Papers, HSTL.
71 A great success story: Hamby, *Man of the People,* 248ff.
71 FEPC an imperfect weapon: *PM* (newspaper published in New York City from 1940 to 1946), August 6, 1942; White and Marshall, *Detroit Riot,* 15–16; "Along the NAACP Battlefront," *Crisis,* July 1943.
71 Widespread job discrimination: *New York Times,* August 24, 1942.
71 Brawl in Mobile: *New York Times,* June 13, 1943.
72 Violence in Beaumont: *PM,* June 17, 1943.
72 Detroit explodes: Shogan and Craig, *Detroit Race Riot,* 34–66.
72 Biddle's report: Ibid., 112–113.
72 FDR's statement: *New York Times,* July 21, 1943.
72 "Mr. Roosevelt regrets": *Crisis,* August 1943.
73 The president's Jews: Arad, *America,* 6.
74 Bergson's strategy: Wyman and Medoff, *Race,* 30–32.
74 Provincial bigotry: HST to Bess Wallace Truman, December 21, 1939, Ferrell, *Dear Bess,* 436; HST to Bess Wallace Truman, July 7, 1941, ibid., 459.
74 Truman's Jewish friends: Hamby, *Man of the People,* 269.
75 Talking not enough: *Chicago Tribune,* April 15, 1943.
75 "A cruel mockery": *New York Times,* May 4, 1943.
75 Lucas's denunciation: Wyman and Medoff, *Race,* 37.

75 Truman quits: HST to Peter Bergson, May 7, 1943, Recognition of the State of Israel documents, HSTL.
76 Bergson pressed on: Breitman and Kraut, *American Refugee Policy*, 185.
76 "Worse than I've ever seen": Culver and Hyde, *American Dreamer*, 328.
77 "The man who would hurt the least": Flynn, *You're the Boss*, 195–196.
77 "In words of one syllable": HST to Bess Wallace Truman, July 12, 1943, Family, Business, Personal File, Harry S. Truman Papers, HSTL.
77 "Why didn't he tell me": Truman, *Memoirs*, 1:192.
78 Wallace's record against racism: Shannon, "Presidential Politics."
78 "Democrats sell race": *Pittsburgh Courier*, July 29, 1944.
78 Truman responds to criticism: Ibid., August 5, 1944.
79 Committee denies support to Styles: *Los Angeles Times*, September 30, 1944.
79 "If he's ours, we're for him": Ibid., October 17, 1944.
79 Truman explains his stand on Styles: Telegram, HST to Walter White, October 30, 1944, Harry S. Truman folder, 1944, NAACP Papers.
80 "I never have and I never will": *Pittsburgh Courier*, October 21, 1944.
80 Denying links to the Klan: *New York Times*, November 1, 1944.
80 Denying being Jewish: *PM*, October 27, 1944.
80 Impact in Boston: *Boston Herald American*, October 26, 1944.
81 "That takes care of the Klan": Matthew Connelly oral history, HSTL.
81 Last-minute defense: *New York Times*, November 1, 1944.
81 Republicans brag of black support: *Pittsburgh Courier*, November 4, 1944.
81 Black vote in key states: Moon, *Balance of Power*, 18–34.
82 "Keep this quiet": Ferrell, *Harry S. Truman*, 126–127.
82 "The president is dead": Truman, *Memoirs*, 1:6.

CHAPTER 6: THE TURNING POINT

84 "Read the record": PP 1945, No. 4, April 17.
84 "You are the one in trouble": Truman, *Memoirs*, 1:6.
84 "Pray for me": Ibid., 19.
85 FEPC's plight: United States Civil Rights Commission Report 3, Washington, D.C., 1961, 173, cited in Berman, *Politics*, 24.
85 Truman fought back: McCoy and Ruetten, *Quest and Response*, 21.
85 Bottling up the FEPC: *New York Times*, June 6, June 20, 1945.
85 Bilbo's blast: *Christian Science Monitor*, June 30, 1945.
85 Alive but barely: Donovan, *Presidency*, 32.
86 "In name only": *Atlanta World*, July 29, 1945.
86 Truman's twenty-one points: PP 1945, No. 128, September 6.
86 Randolph warns on FEPC: A. Phillip Randolph to Matthew J. Connelly, October 10, 1945, Official File, Harry S. Truman Papers, HSTL.
86 Capital transit fracas: Charles H. Houston to HST, November 25, December 3, 1945; HST to Charles H. Houston, December 7, 1945; both Folder 5, Harry S. Truman, 1945, NAACP Papers.

86 Rosenman's 1938 warning on Jews: Breitman and Kraut, *American Refugee Policy*, 230.
87 "A small handful": PP 1946, No. 2, January 3.
87 Purging Slaughter: Steinberg, *Man from Missouri*, 287–289.
87 Appointments pleasing to blacks: McCoy and Ruetten, *Quest and Response*, 24.
87 Mixed grade: *Pittsburgh Courier*, April 20, 1946.
88 "It was not his fault": *Chicago Defender*, September 15, 1945.
88 "Red summer": Jonathan Yardley, "After WWI, a Burst of Race Riots," *Washington Post*, July 17, 2011.
88 "Moral responsibility": Chicago Commission on Race Relations, *Negro*, 529–530, 605.
89 The Klan strikes: Dudley, "Hate Organizations."
89 "He'll never vote again": Ibid.
89 Released prisoner lynched: *Kansas City Call*, August 2, 1946, cited in McCoy and Ruetten, *Quest and Response*, 43.
89 Rampage in Tennessee and American Federation of Labor complaint: Carey McWilliams, "The Klan: Post-War Model," *Nation*, December 14, 1946.
89 Police mayhem: Egerton, "Days."
90 Yergan's protest: McCoy and Ruetten, *Quest and Response*, 45.
90 Confrontation with Robeson: *New York Times*, September 24, 1946; *Pittsburgh Courier*, September 28, 1946; *Chicago Defender*, September 28, 1946.
91 Truman's other problems: Donovan, *Presidency*, 239–247.
91 "I accept their verdict": PP 1946, No. 250, November 11.
91 Descent in the polls: Gardner, *Truman*, 5.
92 FDR put off action: Philleo Nash oral history, HSTL.
92 White pointed out: White, *Man Called White*, 131.
92 "I have been very alarmed": HST to Tom Clark, September 20, 1946, Official File, Harry S. Truman Papers, HSTL.
92 Chief Shull's trial: *New York Times*, November 7, 1946.
92 Nash's background: Philleo Nash oral history, HSTL.
93 Wilson had cited racial problems: White, *Man Called White*, 132.
93 Franklin Adams's doggerel: Kobler, *Ardent Spirit*, 350.
94 "Democratic institutions under attack": *New York Times*, December 6, 1946.
94 Truman's pep talk: PP 1947, No. 9, January 15.
94 Picket line at the theater: *Atlanta Daily World*, January 24, 1947; *Washington Post*, January 24, 1947.
94 "I wanted to see the show": PP 1947, No. 14, January 23, 1947.
95 "Difficult to accept explanation": *Baltimore Afro-American*, February 1, 1946.
95 DAR controversy: Donovan, *Presidency*, 147.
95 Powell's stormy career: Powell rose to become chairman of the House Labor and Education Committee, a particularly powerful post during the Kennedy and Johnson administrations. However, his freewheeling style and disregard of House regulations led to charges that he had misused House funds and to his expulsion from the House in 1967. Powell claimed that he was only doing what white lawmakers did and got away with. In 1969, he was reelected and ordered reinstated by the U.S. Supreme Court. However, all this took a toll, and in 1970,

he lost his House seat to another Harlem black politician, Charles Rangel. Powell moved to the resort island of Bimini. Though whites and some blacks scorned him as an unscrupulous playboy, NAACP leader Roy Wilkins described him after his death in 1972 as "a perfect example of a man who made the system work for his people." *New York Times,* April 5, 1972, April 28, 1972.

96 Racial epithet: Ayers, *Truman,* 89.

96 Segregation in Washington: *Washington Post,* December 11, 1948; Kluger, *Simple Justice,* 508–509; *Kansas City Star,* January 17, 2009.

97 "Burning core of resistance": *Pittsburgh Courier,* January, 23, 1947.

97 Striking down the Texas primary: *Smith v. Allwright* 321 U.S. 649 (1944); Klarman, *Jim Crow,* 237.

97 Scanning the black vote: David Niles to Matthew J. Connelly, November 12, 1946, political folder, President's Secretary's File, Harry S. Truman Papers, HSTL.

98 Martin punctured the bubble: *Los Angeles Sentinel,* January 9, 1947.

98 Not had time to think: *Atlanta Daily World,* January 17, 1947.

98 White's main point: *Pittsburgh Courier,* January 23, 1947.

CHAPTER 7: MORE THAN A DREAM

99 "Not to exceed one minute": Memorandum to Matthew J. Connelly from David Niles, June 16, 1947, Clark Clifford File, HSTL.

100 White told him: White, *Man Called White,* 348.

100 "I believe what I say": HST to Mary Jane Truman, June 28, 1948, Post-Presidential Papers, Memoirs File, HSTL.

100 Millions heard him: Berman, *Politics,* 62.

100 "More than a dream": PP 1947, No. 130, June 29.

101 "I mean every word": White, *Man Called White,* 348.

101 "The most comprehensive": "The President's Speech," *Crisis,* August 1947.

101 The committee's work: McCoy and Ruetten, *Quest and Response,* 82–83.

101 "An Appeal to the World": *New York Times,* October 24, 1947.

102 Du Bois's response: Dudziak, *Cold War Civil Rights,* 45.

102 Clark felt humiliated: *Washington Post,* October 29, 1947.

102 Essential rights: President's Committee on Civil Rights, *To Secure These Rights,* 20–87.

102 To correct these abuses: Ibid., 139–175.

102 "A guide for action": PP 1947, No. 215, October 29.

102 A special message: PP 1948, No. 20, February 2.

103 Chided the president: *New York Herald Tribune,* February 3,1948.

103 "A great and selfless thing": *Norfolk Journal and Guide,* February 14, 1948.

103 "To wreck the South": Karabell, *Last Campaign,* 47.

103 The compromise plan: Ibid., 144–145.

104 Thurmond's background: Cohodas, *Thurmond,* 121–127.

104 Persistent rumors of affair: *New York Times,* December 15, December 18, 2003; *Washington Post,* December 10, 2003.

104 Praise for Thurmond: *New York Times*, May 18, 1947; Cohodas, *Strom Thurmond*, 110–111.

105 Thurmond's early praise for Truman: Ibid., 123.

105 One of the ritual feasts: Robert Shogan, "1948 Election," *American Heritage*, June 1948.

106 "No," said McGrath: *New York Times*, February 24, 1948.

106 "South not in the bag": Ibid.

106 FDR's triumphs: *Guide to U.S. Elections*, 300–303.

107 McGrath tells the country: *New York Times*, March 9, 1948.

107 Linkage in the *Nation: Nation*, February 14, 1948.

107 FDR's meeting with King Saud: Radosh and Radosh, *Safe Haven*, 26–28; *New York Times*, February 21, 1945.

107 FDR's letter to Saud: Snetsinger, *Truman*, 19.

108 Truman's leanings toward the Zionist cause: Hamby, *Man of the People*, 269–270; Miller, *Plain Speaking*, 214–215; Donovan, *Presidency*, 322.

109 Niles's background: Pika, "Interest Groups"; David Niles Oral History, HSTL.

109 Saudi Arabia let the matter drop: Snetsinger, *Truman*, 19.

110 Yom Kipper statement: PP 1946, No. 227, October 4.

110 Vote for partition: *New York Times*, November 30, 1947.

110 "It doesn't sound like you": Radosh and Radosh, *Safe Haven*, 412.

110 A common understanding: Donovan, *Presidency*, 374.

110 Marshall's stance: Isaacson and Thomas, *Wise Men*, 452–453; *New York Times*, October 17, 1959.

111 Showdown with Marshall: Clifford, *Counsel*, 9–15.

111 Clifford's style: Donovan, *Presidency*, 271.

112 Marshall decides not to quit: Isaacson and Thomas, *Wise Men*, 433.

112 Baptist reaction: *New York Times*, May 20, 1948.

112 "Little he won't do": *Chicago Tribune*, May 19, 1948.

112 Vandenberg's backing: *Los Angeles Times*, May 15, 1948.

113 "I wanted to make it plain": Truman, *Memoirs*, 2:165.

113 "Tears running down his cheeks": Steinberg, *Man from Missouri*, 308.

CHAPTER 8: RUNNING FROM BEHIND

114 Two-week trip: "Riding the Rails," *Newsweek*, June 14, 1948.

114 Touting its importance: PP 1948, No. 114, June 4.

115 "If Negroes feared": *Pittsburgh Courier*, June 12, 1948.

115 "Just one big issue": PP 1948, No. 138, June 17.

115 The "whistle stop" furor: *New York Times*, June 20, 1948.

116 The Clifford memo: Clark Clifford to HST, November 19, 1947, HSTL.

116 Liberal disenchantment: Leuchtenburg, *Shadow*, 14–21.

117 Outright opposition: Ross, *Loneliest Campaign*, 74; *New York Times*, April 13, 1948.

117 Donovan, *Presidency*, 410, "get this straight."
117 TV coverage of the conventions: Karabell, *Last Campaign*, 141–143.
117 The Republican convention: Ibid., 136–150.
119 "My forebears were Confederates": M. Truman, *Harry S. Truman*, 392.
119 Softening the platform: McCoy and Ruetten, *Quest and Response*, 124–125. *Baltimore Afro-American*, July 17, 1948.
120 The floor fight: McCoy and Ruetten, *Quest and Response*, 125–126; *New York Times*, July 15, 1948.
121 Humphrey's speech: Minnesota Historical Society, http://www.mnhs. org.
121 They gave the orders: Ross, *Loneliest Campaign*, 125.
121 Truman's reaction: Truman Diary, July 14, 1948, HSTL; cited in Ferrell, *Off the Record*, 143.
121 The South bolts: *New York Times*, July 15, 1948.
122 Civil rights plank: Ibid.
122 Barkley's speech: Ibid.
122 Truman accepts the nomination: PP 1948, No. 160, July 15.
123 Planning the Dixiecrat convention: Cohodas, *Thurmond*, 113–118.
123 Judge Waring's ruling: Ibid., 172.
124 The scene at Birmingham: Karabell, *Last Campaign*, 167; *Los Angeles Times*, July 18, 1948.
125 "Not enough troops": Cohodas, *Thurmond*, 177.
125 Second thoughts: *New York Times*, July 19, 1948.
125 Southern reluctance to back Thurmond: Cohodas, *Thurmond*, 178–182.
126 "The man nobody wanted": *New York Times*, July 16, 1948.
126 Blacks played a prominent role: MacDougall, *Gideon's Army*, 3:510–514.
126 Progressive Party's civil rights proposals: *New York Times*, July 22 and 25, 1948.
127 Seeing Red: "The Pink Facade," *Time*, August 2, 1948; *Baltimore Sun*, July 25, July 28, 1948.
128 Wallace set the tone: "Third Parties: Iowa Hybrid," *Time*, August 9, 1948.

CHAPTER 9: THE UPSET

129 Black agitation on the draft: Dalfiume, *Desegregation*, 164.
130 Southern rhetoric: Ibid., 167.
130 "Negro less well educated": United States Senate, *Hearings on Universal Military Training*, 995–996, cited in MacGregor, *Integration*, 228–229.
130 "To resist the law": Dalfiume, *Desegregation*, 169.
130 Truman's executive orders 9980 and 9981: Dalfiume, *Desegregation*, 171; *New York Times*, July 27, 1948.
130 "Not out to make social reforms": *Baltimore African American*, August 7, 1948.
131 A flat yes: PP 1948, No. 166, July 29.
131 An eleven-point program: PP 1948, No. 165, July 27.

131 GOP ploy: *New York Times,* July 30, 1948.

132 "I'll be disappointed": HST to Ernest Roberts, August 18, 1948, President's Secretary's File, Harry S. Truman Papers, HSTL.

132 Truman in Texas: *Washington Post,* September 28, 1948.

132 "Send Lyndon Johnson to the Senate": *New York Times,* September 28, 1948.

132 Johnson–Truman alliance of necessity: Caro, *Years,* 2:125, 372.

133 Rosenman squeezed out of trip: *Washington Post,* October 1, 1948.

133 Crump's endorsement: *Chicago Tribune,* October 7, 1948.

133 "A very splendid thing": *Baltimore Sun,* September 28, 1948.

133 Truman's appeals to blacks: *Atlanta World,* October 7, 1948.

133 Dewey's complacency: Smith, *Dewey,* 505.

134 A promise to "press forward": *Baltimore Afro-American,* October 16, 1948.

134 Plumbing the platitudes: *New York Times,* October 22, 1948.

134 Obstacles to third parties: Rosenstone, Behr, and Lazarus, *Third Parties,* 20–25.

135 Thurmond's base states: Karabell, *Last Campaign,* 223.

135 Local Democrats feared: Key, *Southern Politics,* 336–337.

135 "What's the sense of jumping?": Cohodas, *Thurmond,* 188.

135 "Prevent the invasion": *Christian Science Monitor,* October 5, 1948.

136 "The races must be mingled": Cohodas, *Thurmond,* 187.

136 "The issue is nigger": *Louisville Courier Journal,* October 16, 1948.

136 "We need a law for murder": *Christian Science Monitor,* October 6, 1948.

136 "You name the place": Telegram, J. Strom Thurmond to HST, October 11, 1948, Official File, Harry S. Truman Papers, HSTL.

136 He turned down an invitation from Harlem: *New York Times,* October 4, 1948.

136 Wallace's ballot access: MacDougall, *Gideon's Army,* 3:550–552.

137 Spy scare impact: Culver and Hyde, *American Dreamer,* 493.

137 Melee in Durham: *New York Times,* August 31, 1948.

138 More eggs and boos: *Chicago Tribune,* August 31, 1948; *Washington Post,* September 1, 1948.

138 "Highly un-American": *Washington Post,* September 1, 1948.

138 Police step in: *New York Times,* September 5, 1948.

138 "More like an agitator": "Eggs in the Dust," *Time,* September 13, 1948.

139 Redeeming feature: "Wallace in the South," *Nation,* September 11, 1948.

139 Despite talk from the Dewey campaign: *Los Angeles Times,* September 5, 1948.

139 Rayburn had boasted: *New York Times,* September 29, 1948.

139 "An evil old man": *New York Times,* July 27, 1939.

139 "An estimable gentleman": *New York Times,* September 30, 1948.

140 "There are few optimists": Eban Ayers Diary, October 7, 1948, Papers of Eban Ayers, HSTL.

140 Roper quit polling: *New York Times,* September 10, 1948.

140 *Newsweek's* survey: *Newsweek,* October 18, 1948.

140 "It will make me a martyr": Ed McKim oral history, HSTL.

141 Finishing touches: PP 1948, No. 256, October 25; No. 260, October 27; No. 262, October 28.
141 Nash's suggestion: Philleo Nash oral history, HSTL.
142 Harlem talk: PP 1948, No. 265, October 29.
143 "You all go to sleep": Donovan, *Presidency*, 433.
143 Truman's vote: *Guide to U.S. Elections*, 357.
143 Miscalculations of the pollsters: Mosteller et al., *Pre-election Polls*, 290–292. Of the three major surveys, Crossley came closest, predicting Truman would get 45 percent of the vote. Gallup's final forecast for Truman was 44.5 percent, while Roper gave the president 38 percent.
144 "The continuing job": *Los Angeles Sentinel*, October 28, 1948.

CHAPTER 10: FREEDOM TO SERVE

145 Ike calls for black volunteers: Ambrose, *Eisenhower*, 1:370.
145 Smith's objection: MacGregor, *Integration*, 51.
145 "Like a crutch": Ambrose, *Eisenhower*, 1:187.
146 Suppressing the survey: MacGregor, *Integration*, 53–54.
146 Truman's good intentions: *Atlanta World*, December 1, 1948.
146 Call for civil rights action: PP 1949, No. 2, January 5.
146 Lincoln fought hard: Goodwin, *Team of Rivals*.
147 Failure of cloture reform: *New York Times*, March 12, 1949.
147 Criticism of Truman: McCoy and Ruetten, *Quest and Response*, 175.
147 "I sit here all day": Neustadt, *Presidential Power*, 9.
147 "Never yet seen a Congress": Evans and Novak, *Johnson*, 514.
148 Early black experience in uniform: Foner, *Blacks*, vii–ix.
148 Four black regiments: Ibid., 66.
148 Dorrence Brook under fire: *New York Amsterdam News*, June 17, 1925.
149 The Gillem report: Report of Board of General Officers on Utilization of Negro Manpower, November 17, 1945, Desegregating the Armed Forces, HSTL.
149 "No real change of heart": *Pittsburgh Courier*, May 11, 1946.
149 Royal protests: Kenneth Royall to HST, September 10, 1948, President's Secretary's File, Harry S. Truman Papers, HSTL.
150 Royall's background: Polmar and Allen, *World War II*, 709.
150 Makeup of the Fahy committee: *New York Times*, September 19, 1948; David Niles oral history.
150 Fahy and Japanese internment: *Los Angeles Times*, May 25, 2011; *Washington Post*, January 8, 2012.
151 Fahy leaves as solicitor general: Silber, *With All Deliberate Speed*, 147.
151 "I want the job done": Transcript, January 12, 1949, Fahy Committee Meetings Record Group 220, HSTL.
152 "Every step of the way": E. W. Kenworthy oral history, HSTL.
152 "Unfit for combat": Dalfiume, "Fahy Committee."
152 Navy reconciled to change: Ibid.

153 Annapolis's first black graduate: *New York Times*, May 25, 1949.
153 Forrestal's background: Millis, *Forrestal Diaries*, xvi–xxiv.
153 Forrestal's reluctance: MacGregor, *Integration*, 299–305.
153 Forrestal's death: Millis, *Forrestal Diaries*, 550–555.
153 Louis Johnson takes charge: "Master of the Pentagon," *Time*, June 6, 1949.
154 "The president's direct interest": Dalfiume, "Fahy Committee."
154 Johnson's directive: Memorandum from Defense Secretary Louis Johnson to service secretaries, April 6, 1949, Fahy Committee Papers, HSTL.
154 A tough nut to crack: Dalfiume, "Fahy Committee."
155 Just a progress report: *New York Times*, October 7, 1949.
155 Truman sent word: Memorandum to Fahy from Kenworthy, December 9, 1949, Fahy Committee Papers, HSTL.
155 Kenworthy's trap: E. W. Kenworthy oral history, HSTL.
155 Tart editorial: *Washington Post*, November 3 and 4, 1949.
155 "Most amazing upset": "The Air Force Goes Interracial," *Ebony*, September 1949.
156 Compromise on assignments: Memorandum, Charles Fahy to HST, December 14, 1949, Desegregating the Armed Services, HSTL.
156 "I am sure everything will work out": MacGregor, *Integration*, 374.
156 Truman told Fahy: HST to Charles Fahy, July 6, 1950, Fahy Committee Papers, HSTL.
156 Final report: President's Committee on Equality . . . , *Freedom to Serve*, 2.
157 *Time's* rave review: "Ahead of the Country," *Time*, June 5, 1950.
157 Easy to understand: E. W. Kenworthy to Charles Fahy, July 25, 1950, Fahy Committee Papers, HSTL.
157 "American system of values": President's Committee on Equality . . . , *Freedom to Serve*, 67.
157 Korean "Police Action": At a news conference in which he insisted that "we are not at war," Truman was asked if the conflict could be called a police action. He replied, "Yes. That is exactly what it amounts to." The phrase, often used ironically, stuck. PP 1950, No. 179, June 29.
157 Integration at Fort Ord: MacGregor, *Integration*, 435.
158 Impact in Korea: Mershon and Schlossman, *Foxholes*, 218–235.
158 "Possibly the bravest": MacGregor, *Integration*, 434.
158 Disapproval of integration: Nichols, *Breakthrough*, 113.
158 Ridgway's view: Ridgway, *Korean War*, 192–193.
159 Project Clear: Dalfiume, *Desegregation*, 213.
159 Undermined the most powerful argument: MacGregor, *Integration*, 442.
159 Gaining momentum: Nichols, *Breakthrough*, 132–133.
159 It took sustained pressure: Ibid., 128–130; *New York Times*, October 13, 1953.
159 Success in the Air Force: MacGregor, *Integration*, 406.
159 Slower in the Navy: Ibid., 424.
161 Changing the culture of the Marine Corps: *Washington Post*, February 27, 1951.
161 Fahy's satisfaction: E. W. Kenworthy oral history, HSTL.
161 Bringing the day closer: Moskos, "Racial Integration."

CHAPTER 11: FRIENDS OF THE COURT

163 Seeking Clark's guidance: Robert Carr to Tom Clark, May 23, 1947; Tom Clark to Robert Carr, July 10, 1947; both President's Committee on Civil Rights Files, Harry S. Truman Papers, HSTL.

163 Tom Clark's statement: Minutes of President's Committee, April 3, 1947, President's Committee on Civil Rights Files, Harry S. Truman Papers, HSTL.

163 "Thin thread of law": Anderson, "Clutching."

163 Justice department's collapse: Walter White to Truman, June 15, 1946, Official File, Harry S. Truman Papers, HSTL.

164 Conventional wisdom on Clark: "Second Class Government," *New Republic,* August 8, 1949.

164 "Out-Bilbo Bilbo": Kluger, *Simple Justice,* 79.

164 Clark's background: Belknap, *Vinson Court,* 89–91.

164 "We worked well together": Tom Clark oral history, HSTL.

164 No red-letter day: Silber, *With All Deliberate Speed,* 147.

165 Truman would complain: Hamby, *Man of the People,* 429.

165 "Dumbest man": Miller, *Plain Speaking,* 226.

165 Some blind spots: Minutes of President's Committee on Civil Rights, April 3, 1947, HSTL.

165 "A boy named Bellinger": Ibid.

166 As the committee explained: President's Committee on Civil Rights, *To Secure These Rights,* 67–69, 142. The committee did not mention the cases by name but noted that the High Court had agreed to review two challenges to restrictive covenants.

166 Elman's background: Silber, *With All Deliberate Speed,* 19.

167 "We're going in": Ibid., 191.

167 "A bunch of Jewish lawyers": Silber, *With All Deliberate Speed,* 194.

167 The brief wasted no time: Brief for the United States as amicus curiae, *Shelley v. Kramer,* 334 U.S. 1 (1948).

168 NAACP brief: Kluger, *Simple Justice,* 254.

168 Backgrounds of Vinson and Burton: Belknap, *Vinson Court,* 36–41, 77–80.

168 Blacks cheered: *Pittsburgh Courier,* May 8, 1948.

169 Banning religious discrimination also: *New York Times,* May 4, 1948.

169 Perlman "very moved": Silber, *With All Deliberate Speed,* 103.

169 *Plessy v. Ferguson:* 163 U.S. 537 (1896).

169 The *Henderson* case: *Henderson v. The United States* 399 U.S. 816 (1950).

169 "As if you were a pig": Kluger, *Simple Justice,* 277.

169 Clark replaces Murphy: Belknap, *Vinson Court,* 78.

169 McGrath wanted to argue case: Kluger, *Simple Justice,* 277.

170 "Equal rights means the same rights": Brief for the United States, *Henderson v. The United States.*

170 Sweatt's case: Kluger, *Simple Justice,* 261–66, *Sweatt v. Painter,* 210.S.W. 2d442 (1947), 339 U.S. 629, 1950.

171 McLaurin's case: Kluger, *Simple Justice*, 266–269; *McLaurin v. University of Oklahoma State Regents for Higher Education* 339 U.S. 637 (1950).

171 Minton showed little concern for civil liberties: Kluger, *Simple Justice*, 269.

171 Clark made himself an advocate: Associate Justice Tom C. Clark, memorandum, Tom C. Clark Papers, U.S. Supreme Court Case Files, Box A2, Folder 3, Rare Rooks and Special Collections, http://tarlton.law.utexas.edu, Tarlton Law Library, University of Texas.

172 "Let *Plessy* fall": Ibid.

172 If anyone doubted Truman's connection: PP 1952, No. 290, October 11.

173 "The country isn't ready": Silber, *With All Deliberate Speed*, 199.

173 "Kind of a nut": Silber, *With All Deliberate Speed*, 200.

174 Truman gave approval: McCoy and Ruetten, *Quest and Response*, 342, citing an interview with Mrs. James P. McGranery, widow of the former attorney general, October 20, 1967.

174 Frankfurter the New Dealer: Matthew Josephson, "Profiles: The Jurist: I," *New Yorker*, November 30, 1940; Felix Frankfurter, "The Young Men Go to Washington," *Fortune*, January 1936.

174 Considered himself a child prodigy: Hirsch, *Enigma*, 13.

175 He expected deference: Silber, *With All Deliberate Speed*, 75.

175 Justice Frankfurter's advice: Freedman, *Roosevelt and Frankfurter*, 500, 523, 526, 545, 596, 608, 671.

176 An easy way: Brief for the United States as amicus curiae, *Brown, et al. v. Board of Education of Topeka, Kansas, et al.*

177 "The one thing I'm proudest of": Silber, *With All Deliberate Speed*, 202.

177 Not everyone cheered: *New York Times*, December 4 and 14, 1952.

CHAPTER 12: LEGACY

179 "The conscience of America": PP 1952, No. 329, November 14.

179 Truman on sit-ins: *New York Times*, April 18, 19, 1960.

180 Acheson's advice: McCullough, *Truman*, 972–973.

180 Spoke more of integration: McCoy and Ruetten, *Quest and Response*, 329.

180 "Poison to the Negro": *New York Times*, July 23, 1944.

181 Taught the moral code: Hamby, *Man of the People*, 45; Phillips, *Truman Presidency*, 11.

181 "Better in all aspects": PP 1952, No. 169, June 13.

182 Eisenhower was counseled: Lyon, *Portrait*, 468.

182 Race and young Eisenhower: Ambrose, *Eisenhower*, 1:47; Mayer, "Eisenhower and Race."

182 Lamented discrimination: Public Papers of Dwight D. Eisenhower, Nara.gov, No. 6, February 2, 1953.

182 Eisenhower told Morrow: Mayer, "Eisenhower and Race."

183 "Federal law would set back the cause": Eisenhower diary notes on his July 24, 1953, conversation with Byrnes, Whitman file, diary series, Eisenhower Library, cited in Durham, *Moderate*, 61.

183 "Systematic exploitation": *Chicago Tribune,* October 18, 1952.
183 Defending his record: PP 1952, No. 303, October 21.
183 Legal hassle in the capital: Silber, *With All Deliberate Speed,* 206–207.
184 Driving Jim Crow from the capital: *District of Columbia v. John R. Thompson Co.* 346 U.S. 100 (1953).
184 The Court asked all parties: Kluger, *Simple Justice,* 615.
185 Shivers's complaint: Allan Shivers to Dwight David Eisenhower, July 16, 1953, Official File, Box 731, Dwight David Eisenhower Library, Abilene, Kansas, cited by Durham, *Moderate,* 61.
185 Elman did add one touch: Silber, *With All Deliberate Speed,* 212.
185 Rankin supports the 1952 brief: Kluger, *Simple Justice,* 675.
185 "First evidence there is a God": Silber, *With All Deliberate Speed,* 218.
186 One of his biggest mistakes": Ambrose, *Eisenhower,* 1:90; Ewald, *Eisenhower,* 85.
186 "Their sweet little girls": Warren, *Memoirs,* 291.
186 Separate is inherently unequal: *Brown v. Board of Education* 347 U.S. (1954).
186 At Eisenhower's insistence: Mayer, "With Much Deliberation."
186 *Brown II: Brown v. Board of Education* 349 U.S. 294 (1955).
187 He had none to offer: PP 1954, No. 116, May 19.
187 A step-by-step process: Ann Whitman Diary, August 14, 1956, Dwight David Eisenhower Library, Abilene, Kans.
188 Race issue in 1956 campaign: Parmet, *Eisenhower,* 464–467; *New York Times,* October 30, 1956; Burk, *Eisenhower Administration,* 169–173.
188 Black vote for Eisenhower: Bositis, *Blacks,* table 1, p. 9.
188 Eisenhower's gains in South: *Guide to U.S. Elections,* 305–306.
188 "I can't imagine": Public Papers of Dwight D. Eisenhower, 1957, No. 134, July 17.
188 Building crisis in Little Rock: Durham, *Moderate,* 143–150; Burk, *Eisenhower Administration,* 176–180.
189 Letter to Greunther: Ambrose, *Eisenhower,* 2:419.
189 Brownell argued against it: Ibid., 415.
190 Racist mob: *New York Times,* September 24, 1957.
190 Eisenhower intervenes: Durham, *Moderate,* 154–157; *New York Times,* September 25, September 26, 1957.
190 Only to enforce the law: PP Dwight D. Eisenhower, 1957, No. 198, September 24.
190 "Myopic preoccupation": Nichols, *Breakthrough,* 2.
191 "They were a beacon": Author's interview with Harris Wofford, July 2, 2011. In 1960, when Martin Luther King Jr. was being held in a Georgia jail, Wofford was mainly responsible for persuading candidate Kennedy to call Coretta Scott King to offer comfort and support. The call, made just before Election Day, was credited with helping Kennedy gain badly needed black votes. Wofford, *Of Kennedys and Kings,* 17–18.
191 "Committed to non-commitment": Burns, *Kennedy,* 102.
191 "A stroke of the pen": Sorensen, *Kennedy,* 480.
192 Provided the impetus: Ibid., 489.

192 Kennedy demanded action: Public Papers of John F. Kennedy, Nara.gov, No. 237, June 11, 1963.

192 Voted with Southerners: Evans and Novak, *Johnson*, 32.

192 Sam Ealy goes bust: Caro, *Years*, 4:18–19.

192 LBJ's early compassion: Evans and Novak, *Johnson*, 120.

193 Exposure to populism: Caro, *Years*, 1:39.

193 "I knew it was imperative": Ibid., 4:354.

193 "Take a dead man's program": Kearns, *Johnson*, 185.

194 "We've just delivered the South to the GOP": Bill Moyers, "What a Real President Was Like," *Washington Post*, November 13, 1988.

194 "We shall overcome": Public Papers of Lyndon B. Johnson, Nara.gov, No. 107, March 15, 1965.

195 Evidence of polarity: Marc Ambinder, "Race Over," *Atlantic*, January–February 2009.

BIBLIOGRAPHY

ARCHIVAL SOURCES

Harry S. Truman Presidential Library, Independence, Missouri
Harry S. Truman Papers
Library of Congress, Washington, D.C.
National Association for the Advancement of Colored People Records

ARTICLES

"Ahead of the Country." *Time*, June 5, 1950.
"The Air Force Goes Interracial." *Ebony*, September 1949.
"Along the N.A.A.C.P. Battlefront." *Crisis*, July 1943.
Ambinder, Marc. "Race Over." *Atlantic*, January–February 2009.
Anderson, Carol. "Clutching at Civil Rights Straws." In *Harry's Farewell: Interpreting and Teaching the Truman Presidency*, edited by Richard S. Kirkendall. Columbia: University of Missouri Press, 2004.
Appiah, Kwame Anthony. "Battling with Du Bois." *New York Review of Books*, December 22, 2011.
"The Brown Derby." *Time*, April 30, 1928.
Cornwell, Elmer E., Jr. "Bosses, Machines and Ethnic Groups." *Annals of the American Academy of Political and Social Science* 353 (May 1964).
Dabney, Virginus. "Nearer and Nearer the Precipice." *Atlantic Monthly*, January 1943.
Dalfiume, Richard M. "The Fahy Committee and Desegregation of the Armed Forces." *Historian*, November 1968.

"Democrat's New Face." *Life*, April 24, 1939.

Dudley, J. Wayne. "Hate Organizations of the 1940s: The Columbian, Inc." *Phylon* 42, no. 3 (1981).

Egerton, John. "Days of Hope and Horror: Atlanta after World War II." *Georgia Historical Quarterly* 78, no. 2 (1994).

"Eggs in the Dust." *Time*, September 13, 1948.

Frankfurter, Felix. "The Young Men Go to Washington." *Fortune*, January 1936.

Grothaus, Larry. "Kansas City Blacks, Harry Truman and the Pendergast Machine." *Missouri Historical Review* 69 (1974).

Hamby, Alonzo. "Insecurity and Responsibility." In *Leadership in the Modern Presidency*, edited by Fred Greenstein. Cambridge, Mass.: Harvard University Press, 1980.

Josephson, Matthew: "Profiles: The Jurist: I." *New Yorker*, November 30, 1940.

Leuchtenburg, William E. "The Conversion of Harry Truman." *American Heritage* 42, no. 7 (November 1991).

Lubell, Samuel. "The Negro and the Democratic Coalition." *Commentary*, August 1964.

Marshall, Margaret. "Portrait of Truman." *Nation*, April 21, 1945.

"Master of the Pentagon." *Time*, June 6, 1949.

Mayer, Michael S. "Eisenhower and Race." In *Dwight D. Eisenhower*, edited by Joann P. Krieg. Westport, CT: Greenwood Press, 1987.

———. "With Much Deliberation and Some Speed: Eisenhower and the *Brown* Decision." *Journal of Southern History* 52, no. 1 (1986).

McWilliams, Carey. "The Klan: Post-War Model." *Nation*, December 14, 1946.

Milgram, Grace, and Morris Milgram. "The Man from Missouri." *Common Sense* 13 (1944).

Moskos, Charles. "Racial Integration in the Armed Forces." *American Journal of Sociology* 72, no. 2 (September 1966).

Moyers, Bill. "What a Real President Was Like." *Washington Post*, November 13, 1988.

"National Affairs." *Crisis*, July 1932.

Pika, Joseph A. "Interest Groups and the White House under Roosevelt and Truman." *Political Science Quarterly* 102, no. 4 (Winter 1987).

"The Pink Facade." *Time*, August 2, 1948.

Poxpey, C. Spencer. "The Washington–DuBois Controversy and Its Effect on the Negro Problem. *History of Education Journal* 8, no. 4 (Summer 1957).

"The President's Speech." *Crisis*, August 1947.

"Progress Amidst Prejudice." Missouri State Archives. www.sos.mo.gov/archives.

"Riding the Rails." *Newsweek*, June 14, 1948.

"Second Class Government." *New Republic*, August 8, 1949.

Severn, John K., and William Warren Rogers. "Theodore Roosevelt Entertains Booker T. Washington." *Florida Historical Quarterly* 54, no. 3 (1976).

Shannon, J. B. "Presidential Politics in the South." *Journal of Politics* 10, no. 3 (1948).

Sherman, Richard B. "The Harding Administration and the Negro." *Journal of Negro History* 49, no. 3 (July 1964).

Shogan, Robert. "1948 Election." *American Heritage*, June 1948.

"Third Parties: Iowa Hybrid." *Time,* August 9, 1948.
"Three Whispers." *Time,* September 17, 1928.
"Wallace in the South." *Nation,* September 11, 1948.
Weiss, Nancy J. "The Negro and the New Freedom: Fighting Wilsonian Segregation." *Political Science Quarterly* 84, no. 1 (March 1969).
Wilson, Thomas D. "Chester A. Franklin and Harry S. Truman: An African-American Conservative and the Conversion of the Future President." *Missouri Historical Review* 88 (1993).
Yardley, Jonathan. "After WWI, a Burst of Race Riots." *Washington Post,* July 17, 2011.

BOOKS

Alsop, Joseph, and Turner Catledge. *The 168 Days.* Garden City, N.Y.: Doubleday, 1938.
Ambrose, Stephen E. *Eisenhower.* 2 vols. New York: Simon & Schuster, 1983–1984.
Arad, Gulie Ne'eman. *America, Its Jews, and the Rise of Nazism.* Bloomington: Indiana University Press, 2000.
Ayers, Eban. *Truman in the White House: The Diary of Eban Ayers.* Edited by Robert Ferrell. Columbia: University of Missouri Press, 1991.
Belknap, Michael R. *The Vinson Court: Justices, Rulings and Legacy.* Santa Barbara, Calif.: ABC-CLIO, 2004.
Berman, William C. *The Politics of Civil Rights in the Truman Administration.* Columbus, Ohio: State University Press. 1977.
Bernstein, Barton J., ed. *Politics and Policies of the Truman Administration.* Chicago: Quadrangle Books, 1970.
Boller, Paul F., Jr. *Presidential Campaigns.* New York: Oxford, 1984.
Bositis, David. *Blacks and the 2004 Democratic National Convention.* Washington, D.C.: Joint Center for Political and Economic Studies. n.d.
Breitman, Richard, and Alan M. Kraut. *American Refugee Policy and European Jewry, 1933–1945.* Bloomington: Indiana University Press, 1987.
Brendon, Piers. *Ike: His Life and Times.* New York: Harper & Row, 1986.
Burk, Robert Frederick. *The Eisenhower Administration and Civil Rights.* Knoxville: University of Tennessee, 1984.
Burns, James MacGregor. *The Deadlock of Democracy: Four Party Politics in America.* Englewood Cliffs, N.J.: Prentice-Hall, 1963.
———. *John Kennedy: A Political Profile.* New York: Avon, 1961.
Campbell, James E. *The Presidential Pulse of Congressional Elections.* 2nd ed. Lexington: University Press of Kentucky, 1997.
Caro, Robert. *The Years of Lyndon Johnson.* 4 vols. New York: Knopf, 1982–2003.
Chalmers, David M. *Hooded Americanism: The First Century of the Ku Klux Klan, 1865–1965.* Garden City, N.Y.: Doubleday, 1965.
Cherny, Robert W. *A Righteous Cause: The Life of William Jennings Bryan.* Norman: University of Oklahoma Press, 1999.

Chicago Commission on Race Relations. *The Negro in Chicago*. Chicago: University of Chicago Press, 1922.

Clifford, Clark. *Counsel to the President: A Memoir*. New York: Random House, 1991.

Cohodas, Nadine. *Strom Thurmond and the Politics of Southern Change*. New York: Simon & Schuster, 1993.

Culver, John C., and John Hyde. *American Dreamer: A Life of Henry A. Wallace*. New York: Norton, 2000.

Dalfiume, Richard M. *Desegregation of the U.S. Armed Forces: Fighting on Two Fronts, 1939–1953*. Columbia: University of Missouri Press, 1969.

Daniels, Jonathan. *Man of Independence*. Philadelphia: Lippincott, 1950.

Donovan, Robert J. *The Presidency of Harry S. Truman*. Vol. 1, *1945–1948: Conflict and Crisis*. New York: Norton, 1977.

Dorsett, Lyle W. *The Pendergast Machine*. New York: Oxford, 1968.

Dudziak, Mary L. *Cold War Civil Rights: Race and the Image of American Democracy*. Princeton, N.J.: Princeton University Press, 2000.

Durham, James C. *A Moderate among Extremists*. Chicago: Nelson-Hall, 1981.

Evans, Rowland, and Robert Novak. *Lyndon B. Johnson: The Exercise of Power*. New York: New American Library, 1968.

Ewald, William Bragg, Jr. *Eisenhower the President*. New York: Prentice Hall, 1981.

Fairfield, Roy P., ed. *The Federalist Papers*. 2nd ed. Garden City, N.Y.: Doubleday, 1966.

Felman, Michael. *Inside War: The Guerilla Conflict in Missouri during the American Civil War*. New York: Oxford, 1989.

Ferrell, Robert. *Harry S. Truman: A Life*. Columbia: University of Missouri Press, 1994.

———. *Truman and Pendergast*. Columbia: University of Missouri Press, 1999.

Ferrell, Robert, ed. *Dear Bess: The Letters from Harry to Bess Truman*. New York: Norton, 1983.

———. *Off the Record: The Private Papers of Harry S. Truman*. New York: Harper & Row, 1980.

Flynn, Edward J. *You're the Boss*. New York: Viking, 1947.

Foner, Jack. *Blacks and the Military in American History: A New Perspective*. New York: Praeger, 1974.

Foner, Eric, and John Garraty, eds. *The Reader's Companion to American History*. Boston: Houghton Mifflin, 1991.

Freedman, Max. *Roosevelt and Frankfurter: Their Correspondence*. Boston: Little, Brown, 1967.

Gardner, Michael R. *Harry Truman and Civil Rights: Moral Courage and Political Risks*. Carbondale: Southern Illinois University Press, 2002.

Goodwin, Doris Kearns. *Team of Rivals: The Political Genius of Abraham Lincoln*. New York: Simon and Schuster Paperbacks, 2005.

Gosnell, Harold E. *Truman's Crises: A Political Biography of Harry S. Truman*. Westport, Conn.: Greenwood Press, 1980.

Goulden, Joseph. *The Best Years: 1945–1950*. New York: Atheneum, 1976.

Gregory, James N. *The Southern Diaspora: How the Great Migrations of Black and White Southerners Transformed America.* Chapel Hill: University of North Carolina Press, 2005.

Guide to U.S. Elections. 2nd ed. Washington, D.C.: Congressional Quarterly, 1985.

Hamby, Alonzo. *Man of the People: A Life of Harry S. Truman.* New York: Oxford University Press, 1995.

Hillman, William, ed. *Mr. President.* New York: Farrar, Straus & Young, 1952.

Hirsch, H. N. *The Enigma of Felix Frankfurter.* New York: Basic Books, 1981.

Hofstadter, Richard. *The American Political Tradition.* New York: Vintage, 1948.

Ickes, Harold. *The Secret Diary of Harold Ickes.* Vol. 2, *The Inside Struggle.* New York: Simon & Schuster, 1954.

Isaacson, Walter, and Evan Thomas. *The Wise Men: Six Friends and the World They Made.* New York: Simon & Schuster, 1986.

Karabell, Zachary. *The Last Campaign: How Harry Truman Won the 1948 Election.* New York: Knopf, 2000.

Kazin, Michael. *A Godly Hero: The Life of William Jennings Bryan.* New York: Knopf, 2006.

Kearns, Doris. *Lyndon Johnson and the American Dream.* New York: New American Library, 1976.

Key, V. O., Jr. *Southern Politics.* New York: Vintage, 1949.

Klarman, Michael J. *From Jim Crow to Civil Rights: The Supreme Court and the Struggle for Racial Equality.* New York: Oxford, 2004.

Kluger, Richard. *Simple Justice.* New York: Knopf, 1976.

Kobler, John. *Ardent Spirit.* New York: Putnam, 1973.

Lash, Joseph P. *Eleanor and Franklin.* New York: Norton, 1971.

Leuchtenburg, William E. *In the Shadow of FDR.* Ithaca, N.Y.: Cornell University Press, 1983.

Lubell, Samuel. *The Future of American Politics.* New York: Harper & Brothers, 1951.

Lyon, Peter. *Eisenhower: Portrait of the Hero.* Boston: Little, Brown, 1974.

MacDougall, Curtis. *Gideon's Army.* Vol. 3, *The Campaign and the Vote.* New York: Marzani & Munsell, 1965.

MacGregor, Morris, Jr. *Integration of the Armed Forces, 1940–1965.* Washington, D.C.: Center of Military History, United States Army, 1981.

McCoy, Donald R., and Richard T. Ruetten. *Quest and Response: Minority Rights and the Truman Administration.* Lawrence: University Press of Kansas, 1973.

McCullough, David. *Truman.* New York: Simon & Schuster, 1992.

McKenna, Marian C. *Franklin Roosevelt and the Great Constitutional War: The Court-Packing Crisis of 1937.* New York: Fordham University Press, 2002.

Mershon, Sherie, and Steven Schlossman. *Foxholes and Color Lines: Desegregating the U.S. Armed Forces.* Baltimore: Johns Hopkins University Press, 1998.

Miller, Merle. *Plain Speaking.* New York: Greenwich House, 1985.

Millis, Walter, ed. *The Forrestal Diaries.* New York: Viking, 1951.

Mitchell, Franklin D. *Embattled Democracy: Missouri Democratic Politics, 1910–1932.* Columbia: University of Missouri Press, 1968.

Moon, Henry Lee. *Balance of Power: The Negro Vote.* Garden City, N.Y.: Doubleday, 1948.

Morris, Richard B. *Witness at the Creation: Hamilton, Madison, Jay and the Constitution.* New York: Holt, 1985.

Mosteller, Frederick, et al. *The Pre-election Polls of 1948.* New York: Social Science Research Council, 1949.

Murray, Robert K. *Red Scare: A Study in National Hysteria, 1919–1920.* New York: McGraw-Hill, 1964.

———. *The 103rd Ballot.* New York: Harper & Row, 1976.

Myrdall, Gunnar. *An American Dilemma.* Vol. 2, *The Negro Problem and Modern Democracy.* New Brunswick, N.J.: Transaction Publishers, 1996.

Neustadt, Richard E. *Presidential Power: The Politics of Leadership from FDR to Carter.* New York: Wiley, 1980.

Newman, Roger K. *Hugo Black.* New York: Pantheon, 1994.

Nichols, Lee. *Breakthrough on the Color Front.* New York: Random House, 1954.

Parmet, Herbert S. *Eisenhower and the American Crusades.* New York: Macmillan, 1972.

Patterson, James T. *Congressional Conservatism and the New Deal.* Lexington: University of Kentucky Press, 1967.

Phillips, Cabell. *The Truman Presidency: The History of a Triumphant Succession.* New York: Macmillan, 1966.

Polmar, Norman, and Thomas B. Allen. *World War II: America at War, 1941–1945.* New York: Random House, 1991.

President's Committee on Civil Rights. *To Secure These Rights.* New York: Simon & Schuster, 1947.

President's Committee on Equality of Treatment and Opportunity in the Armed Services. *Freedom to Serve: Equality of Treatment and Opportunity in the Armed Services.* Washington, D.C.: U.S. Government Printing Office, 1950.

Radosh, Allis, and Ronald Radosh. *A Safe Haven: Harry S. Truman and the Founding of Israel.* New York: Harper Collins, 2009.

Reddig, William. *Tom's Town: Kansas City and the Pendergast Legend.* Philadelphia: Lippincott, 1947.

Ridgway, Matthew B. *The Korean War.* New York: Doubleday, 1967.

Rosenstone, Steven J., Roy L. Behr, and Edward H. Lazarus. *Third Parties in America: Citizen Response to Major Party Failure.* Princeton, N.J.: Princeton University Press, 1984.

Ross, Irwin. *The Loneliest Campaign: The Truman Victory of 1948.* New York: New American Library, 1968.

Russell, Francis. *The Shadow of Blooming Grove: Warren G. Harding in His Times.* New York: McGraw Hill, 1968.

Shogan, Robert, and Tom Craig. *The Detroit Race Riot: A Study in Violence.* Philadelphia: Chilton, 1964.

Silber, Norman I. *With All Deliberate Speed: The Life of Philip Elman—An Oral History Memoir.* Ann Arbor: University of Michigan Press, 2004.

Smith, Jean Edward. *FDR.* New York: Random House, 2007.

Smith, Richard Norton. *Thomas E. Dewey and His Times.* New York: Simon & Schuster, 1982.

Snetsinger, John. *Truman, the Jewish Vote, and the Creation of Israel.* Stanford, Calif.: Hoover Institution, 1974.

Sorensen, Theodore C. *Kennedy.* New York: Harper & Row, 1965.

Steinberg, Alfred. *The Man from Missouri.* New York: Putnam, 1962.

Truman, Harry S. *Memoirs.* 2 vols. New York: Smithmark, 1955; and New York: Doubleday, 1956.

Truman, Margaret. *Harry S. Truman.* New York: William A. Morrow, 1971.

United States Senate. 80th Congress, 2nd Session. *Hearings on Universal Military Training, March 17–April 3, 1948.* Washington, D.C.: Armed Services Committee, 1948.

Warren, Earl. *The Memoirs of Chief Justice Earl Warren.* New York: Doubleday, 1977.

Weiss, Nancy J. *Farewell to the Party of Lincoln: Black Politics in the Age of FDR.* Princeton, N.J.: Princeton University Press, 1983.

White, Theodore. *The Making of the President, 1960.* New York: Atheneum, 1960.

White, Walter. *A Man Called White.* New York: Viking, 1948.

White, Walter, and Thurgood Marshall. *What Caused the Detroit Riot.* New York: National Association for Colored People, 1943.

Wofford, Harris. *Of Kennedys and Kings: Making Sense of the Sixties.* New York: Farrar, Straus & Giroux, 1980.

Wyman, David S., and Rafael Medoff. *Race against Death.* New York: New Press, 2002.

INDEX